The Poverty of Capitalism

Economic Meltdown and the Struggle for What Comes Next

John Hilary

PlutoPress
www.plutobooks.com

First published 2013 by Pluto Press
345 Archway Road, London N6 5AA

www.plutobooks.com

Distributed in the United States of America exclusively by
Palgrave Macmillan, a division of St. Martin's Press LLC,
175 Fifth Avenue, New York, NY 10010

British Library Cataloguing in Publication Data
A catalogue record for this book is available from the British Library

ISBN   978 0 7453 3331 1   Hardback
ISBN   978 0 7453 3330 4   Paperback
ISBN   978 1 8496 4966 7   PDF eBook
ISBN   978 1 8496 4968 1   Kindle eBook
ISBN   978 1 8496 4967 4   EPUB eBook

Library of Congress Cataloging in Publication Data applied for

10   9   8   7   6   5   4   3   2

Typeset from disk by Stanford DTP Services, Northampton, England
Simultaneously printed digitally by CPI Antony Rowe, Chippenham, UK and
Edwards Bros in the United States of America

The Poverty of Capitalism

Contents

Acknowledgements   vi
Abbreviations   viii

1 Introduction   1
2 Crisis, Continuity and Change   10
3 Corporate Power in Practice   36
4 The CSR Delusion   58
5 Extractives: Dispossession through Devastation   80
6 Garments: Capitalism's False Promise   100
7 Food: The Final Frontier   118
8 Beyond Capitalism   138

Notes   162
Bibliography   199
Index   223

Acknowledgements

This book is a study of poverty, power and injustice in the global political economy of the twenty-first century. It is intended to complement the numerous studies that War on Want has published over the course of its 60-year history into the root causes of poverty around the world, beginning with the original *War on Want: A Plan for World Development* drawn up in 1952. In all these endeavours, the aim has been to look beyond outward symptoms and to identify the underlying social, political and economic forces that deny people the right to decent lives of personal fulfilment, free from the threat of hunger, violence or despair. The current book builds on six decades of active learning not only on the part of War on Want and its many partners, allies and affiliates, but by all who have joined in the struggle for social justice across the world.

On a personal level, this book is the culmination of 25 years' working in the global justice movement, and as such it will be impossible to pay proper tribute to all those who have helped develop my understanding along the way. Firstly, I would like to thank those with whom I have worked over the past ten years at War on Want. From the trustee body, I particularly wish to thank Steve Preston, Sue Branford, Polly Jones, Guillermo Rogel, Gaynelle Samuel, Mark Luetchford and David Hillman for their encouragement, as well as War on Want president Rodney Bickerstaffe for his constant personal support. I also wish to thank all those who have worked on the staff with me for their dedication and commitment, and for proving time and again the power of conviction to bring about change.

From earlier days in the fight against the WTO and other institutions of neoliberal globalisation, I had the privilege of working alongside some of the most inspiring individuals in the movement: Martin Khor, Meena Raman and others from the Third World Network; Walden Bello, Aileen Kwa and all from Focus on the Global South; Naomi Klein, Susan George, Maude Barlow, Tony Clarke and other activists from the Our World Is Not For Sale coalition, as well as many good friends from its European wing, the Seattle to Brussels Network. I have also had the good fortune to work with numerous inspiring individuals in the international labour movement, as well as from many other groups not listed here. I am truly grateful to all.

As for those who have helped with the book itself, I would like to register my gratitude to Roger van Zwanenberg, whose idea it was in the first place, David Shulman, Jonathan Maunder, Melanie Patrick and all the team at Pluto Press. I also wish to thank those who have helped with individual aspects of the book, including Mark Curtis, Peter Fuchs, Kate Ives and Ian Richardson. I would like to express my particular thanks to Andreas Bieler, Puneet Dhaliwal and Doreen Massey for their generosity in reading parts of the text in manuscript, and for their immensely helpful comments. All remaining failures are, of course, mine alone.

The greatest privilege of working in the global justice movement for so many years has been the opportunity to meet people from across the world who have devoted their lives to the struggle for a better future, often in situations of great personal danger. Several of these are partners of War on Want in countries such as Brazil, Sri Lanka, Mozambique, South Africa, Zambia, Palestine, Bangladesh, Colombia or Honduras, to name a few. Hearing the same basic tale of exploitation and dispossession told again and again from so many different contexts brings home the poverty of capitalism in a way that the written word alone could never do: from women factory workers whose health has been broken through endless hours of labour for poverty pay; plantation workers condemned to the stress of perpetual insecurity on casual labour contracts; members of communities that have been evicted at gunpoint so as to make way for the next big capitalist venture on their land. This book is an attempt to reveal this reality to a wider audience, and to argue for a future beyond capitalism. It is dedicated with love to Jan, my soulmate and my inspiration throughout every one of the last 25 years.

John Hilary
June 2013

Abbreviations

AATF	African Agricultural Technology Foundation
ADIA	Abu Dhabi Investment Authority
AGRA	Alliance for a Green Revolution in Africa
ALBA	Bolivarian Alliance for the Americas
ASEAN	Association of South-East Asian Nations
BASD	Business Action for Sustainable Development
BIT	bilateral investment treaty
BRICS	Brazil, Russia, India, China, South Africa
CAFTA	Central America Free Trade Agreement
CBI	Confederation of British Industry
CELAC	Community of Latin American and Caribbean States
CIA	Central Intelligence Agency
CIC	China Investment Corporation
CNOOC	China National Offshore Oil Corporation
CNPC	China National Petroleum Corporation
CSR	corporate social responsibility
DFID	Department for International Development (UK)
EITI	Extractive Industries Transparency Initiative
EPA	Economic Partnership Agreement
ERT	European Round Table of Industrialists
ETI	Ethical Trading Initiative
EU	European Union
FAO	Food and Agriculture Organisation of the United Nations
FDI	foreign direct investment
FLA	Fair Labor Association
FTA	free trade agreement
FTAA	Free Trade Area of the Americas
GATS	General Agreement on Trade in Services
GATT	General Agreement on Tariffs and Trade
GDP	gross domestic product
GIC	Government of Singapore Investment Corporation
GM	genetically modified

IAASTD	International Assessment of Agricultural Knowledge, Science and Technology for Development
ICA	International Cooperative Alliance
ICC	International Chamber of Commerce
ICMM	International Council on Mining and Metals
ICSID	International Centre for Settlement of Investment Disputes
IFAD	International Fund for Agricultural Development
IMF	International Monetary Fund
IOE	International Organisation of Employers
ILO	International Labour Organisation
ITT	International Telephone and Telegraph
JOAC	Joint Operational Access Concept
JO-IN	Joint Initiative for Corporate Accountability and Workers' Rights
KNOC	Korea National Oil Corporation
KRRS	Karnataka State Farmers' Association (India)
M&As	mergers and acquisitions
MAI	Multilateral Agreement on Investment
MAS	Movement for Socialism (Bolivia)
MDGs	Millennium Development Goals
MFA	Multi-Fibre Arrangement
MNC	multinational corporation
MST	Landless Rural Workers' Movement (Brazil)
NAFTA	North American Free Trade Agreement
NGO	non-governmental organisation
OAS	Organisation of American States
OECD	Organisation for Economic Cooperation and Development
ONGC	Oil and Natural Gas Corporation (India)
PDR	People's Democratic Republic
PPP	purchasing power parity
QIA	Qatar Investment Authority
SPP	Sundanese Peasants Union (West Java)
TABD	TransAtlantic Business Dialogue
TAFTA	Trans-Atlantic Free Trade Agreement
TNC	transnational corporation
TPP	Trans-Pacific Partnership

TRIMs	Trade-Related Investment Measures
TRIPs	Trade-Related Aspects of Intellectual Property Rights
UNAC	National Union of Peasant Farmers (Mozambique)
UNASUR	Union of South American Nations
UNCED	United Nations Conference on Environment and Development
UNCITRAL	United Nations Commission on International Trade Law
UNCTAD	United Nations Conference on Trade and Development
UNDP	United Nations Development Programme
UNEP	United Nations Environment Programme
UNICEF	United Nations Children's Fund
UNRISD	United Nations Research Institute for Social Development
USCIB	United States Council for International Business
WBCSD	World Business Council for Sustainable Development
WEF	World Economic Forum
WHO	World Health Organisation
WRAP	Worldwide Responsible Accredited Production
WSSD	World Summit on Sustainable Development
WTO	World Trade Organisation
WWF	World Wide Fund for Nature
€	euros
$	US dollars, unless stated otherwise

1

Introduction

Of the many consequences of the global economic meltdown that swept the world from 2008 onwards, perhaps the most important for the long term was that it exposed to public attention the true nature of the capitalist world system in the modern age. The immediate trigger for the Great Recession may have been a liquidity crisis brought on by mass panic at the bursting of the US housing bubble, once it was realised that no one could predict to what extent the world's banking system was contaminated with toxic debt. Yet it soon became clear that there was something rotten in the state of the global economy far beyond the greed and grasping of a few creative financiers. Most obviously, the crisis served to reveal the economic, social and ecological imbalances that had developed over the previous three decades of neoliberal globalisation, a period during which states had granted unprecedented powers to capital while steadily undermining the sovereign rights of their own peoples. The neoliberal programme of privatisation, liberalisation and deregulation had aimed at nothing less than a second 'great transformation' to rival the free market fundamentalism of the nineteenth century, directing state intervention away from social redistribution towards an unambiguous role as enforcer of the enduring freedoms of capital.[1] Any suggestion that these freedoms would be to the greater benefit of society was finally laid to rest in 2008, as unimaginable sums of public money were commandeered to rescue the system from itself. Yet in addition to exploding once again the myth of the self-regulating market, the global economic meltdown also stimulated recognition of a more profound truth: that independently of the excesses of neoliberalism, the massive accumulation of capital at the core of the system offers only crisis and poverty to hundreds of millions of people across the world.

To many people, particularly those living outside the core economies of the capitalist world system, this was not news. The experience of colonialism had taught the peoples of the global South that the accumulation of capital in the metropolitan centres of empire required the violent suppression and immiseration of the colonised, to the extent that it negated the possibility of their historical development.[2] Nor was this experience confined to some dim and distant past, as the 'new imperialism' exercised through international financial institutions such as the World Bank and International Monetary Fund (IMF) had continued to condemn the same peoples to exploitation throughout the decades following their liberation from colonial rule.[3] The result of this systematic dispossession has been mass poverty on a global scale. In August 2008, one month before the collapse of investment bank Lehman Brothers sent financial markets into freefall, the World Bank acknowledged that it had previously overstated the numbers lifted out of poverty in the previous three decades of neoliberal globalisation, and that a staggering 1.4 billion people were still living below the extreme poverty line (the equivalent of what it means to be poor in the world's very poorest countries, such as Mali, Ethiopia or Chad). A total of 2.6 billion people – over half the entire population of the global South – were calculated to be living below the $2 a day poverty line, following the extensive structural adjustment programmes undertaken at the behest of the World Bank and IMF in order to 'integrate' their national economies into the capitalist world system.[4] Before the global economic meltdown, in other words, the majority world was already in crisis.

At the same time as this social reality was brought home to new audiences, capitalism's drive for growth at all costs was also shown to be the root cause of the ecological crisis facing the planet.[5] The finite limits of natural ecosystems are unable to support the infinite process of expansion that capital must engineer in order to prosper, and the consequences of that conflict are apparent in every new media report detailing the latest evidence of irreversible climate change, biodiversity loss or resource depletion. Nowhere is this crisis more obvious than in the additional pressure on the world's natural resource base generated by the rise of today's emerging economies, whose 'outward turn' into the global economy has further intensified a rush for land, oil, minerals and other strategic resources that was already driving stocks towards exhaustion. Increasingly, in international conferences as well as local articulations of protest, the connection between capitalist expansion and its ecological consequences is made explicit, with system change recognised as the last and only means of avoiding ecological disaster. While this book focuses primarily on the human poverty of globalised capitalism, the connection between the social and ecological should be understood as an unspoken reality throughout.

As the economies of Europe and North America slid into recession, resulting in dramatic contractions of world trade and investment, the deeper imbalances of the system became a mainstream topic of discussion. Leaders from the core capitalist economies that had brought the world to the brink of disaster issued statements acknowledging that business could no longer continue as usual. France's president Nicolas Sarkozy famously announced in January 2009 that the crisis signalled the return of the state and the end of public impotence in the face of the market, and called for a renewed 'moralisation' of capitalism. As London prepared to host the G20 summit three months later, UK prime minister Gordon Brown declared that the old Washington consensus of liberalisation, privatisation and deregulation was dead, and that the world now needed 'shared global rules founded on shared global values'. Barack Obama spoke of the 'massive failure of responsibility' that had led to the crisis, and of the need for comprehensive regulatory reform to prevent its recurrence. Yet it soon became clear that the call for a more ethical form of capitalism represented a determination among the core economic powers to restore the system as it had been before the crash, only strengthened this time by virtue of being cleansed of the taint of bankers' greed. Incorrectly portrayed in the Anglo-Saxon world as a return to traditional French *dirigisme*, Sarkozy's speech to the 'New World, New Capitalism' conference had been recognised in France as an explicit call to defend the system against its detractors, and to reposition the state as the active partner of capital in place of a finance sector that had failed.[6]

Thus it was that the G20 used its 2009 London summit to announce a $1 trillion stimulus package for the global economy, in addition to the even greater sums of public money injected into national economies to bail out the banks and restart the circulation of capital that had frozen in the wake of Lehman Brothers' collapse. Thus also, once it had calculated that its interventions had done enough to restore private lending, the G20 used its 2010 summit in Toronto to announce an abrupt end to stimulus and the beginning of 'fiscal consolidation' in those countries deemed to have run up unsustainable public debts. This in turn signalled the launch of a capitalist counteroffensive in the austerity programmes to be visited on the peoples of Europe and North America – the latest application of neoliberal 'shock doctrine' to further the radical programme of social and economic reengineering that was initiated at the end of the 1970s.[7] The long-term consequences of these structural adjustments – already so familiar to countries of the global South – are only now beginning to reveal themselves, as the threat of 'perma-austerity' and simultaneous recession across many of the core capitalist economies causes even friendly commentators to raise the alarm.[8]

Lest there should be any doubt that the global economic system was to be restored in its neoliberal form, the G20 announced that, despite their manifest failures, the same institutions of capitalist rule would return to police the system as before. The IMF was brought back from the dead by the G20, despite the fact that its catastrophic mishandling of previous crises had destroyed its credibility and consigned it to a marginal role in world affairs. Similarly, despite its persistent failure to conclude the Doha Round of multilateral trade negotiations launched in 2001, the G20 confirmed the World Trade Organisation (WTO) as its chosen instrument of discipline to prevent any possible restrictions on capitalist expansion in the wake of the crisis. The return of these two institutions represented a clear statement of intent on the part of the world's leading economies, and an intensification rather than a revision of the model of corporate globalisation that had developed with such negative consequences over the previous 30 years. Importantly, too, this strategic direction was agreed not by the G8 grouping of old colonial powers but by the G20, which includes among its members several states that had previously mounted vocal opposition to such imperialist manoeuvres.

The power granted to transnational corporations (TNCs) to continue operating in the global economy with ever increasing freedom reaffirmed the political elite's choice of capital as lead agent in the process of historical development. Earlier it had been understood that the private profit-making interests of TNCs operating in the global economy were incompatible with broader public policy goals; yet such an understanding had gradually been eroded by a dominant narrative which portrayed transnational capital not just as part of the solution, but at the heart of any solution. According to this orthodoxy, which not even a full-scale crisis of capitalism was enough to unseat, the expansion of TNCs into every corner of the global economy is the best (if not the only) way to ensure progress towards humanity's development goals.

This book seeks to challenge the notion that transnational capital is a benign force in the service of humanity, and to set against that orthodoxy the evidence of its actual operations around the world. The international focus of the book is deliberate and necessary, as the most extreme injustices of the system are manifest in its relations with the peoples of the majority world, forced to survive their integration into the global economy in situations of incomparable stress and insecurity. The continuing impoverishment of the peoples of the global South, incorporated into the bottom of global value chains so as to generate ever greater profits for those at the top, is a lasting reminder that the programme of corporate globalisation was developed not for public benefit but to further the interests of the few. Years of low inflation and cheap credit allowed the champions of neoliberalism to conceal this reality from people in the rich world, and to sustain the central myth of globalisation as a 'win-win' or positive sum equation. This book seeks to restore the experience of the peoples of the majority world to a debate from which they are invariably excluded.[9]

By the same token, this book also seeks to articulate alternatives of hope to replace the barren wasteland of any future under the current system. These alternatives exist not only in the everyday resistance of social movements to the threat of capitalist expansion, but in the existing operations of those movements and cooperative ventures that are already constructing their own paths out of capitalism. The fact that such alternatives are so often hidden from public view is a result of the power exercised by transnational capital over the economic development discourse, often with the active connivance of 'respectable' non-governmental organisations. This book is an attempt to challenge that closed system and to show that there are genuine alternatives to the monoculture of corporate globalisation.

This book is not a work of theory; it has the more modest ambition of seeking to reveal to a wider audience how the expansion of global capitalism continues to bring riches to the few and poverty to the many. I have, however, benefited enormously from the theoretical writings of others in developing my own understanding, and it will quickly become obvious how much this book owes to insights from many traditions that illuminate the workings of the global political economy. The book is also not a polemic in the same sense as the two famous works whose titles it inevitably evokes: Marx's critique of Proudhon in *The Poverty of Philosophy* or E.P. Thompson's of Althusser in *The Poverty of Theory*. It is, however, intended to refute those who contend that the future of global development lies with increasing the power of TNCs to roam the earth in search of ever greater profits, with or without the convenient fiction of corporate social responsibility and other public relations tools.

The book is structured as follows. Chapter 2 explores how the global economic meltdown experienced across the world from 2008 onwards is a consequence of more profound dynamics of change in the global political economy, including the emergence of new powers from the semiperiphery of the capitalist world system to challenge those at its core. Despite the truly historic development this represents, such an emergence is in no way the common experience of most countries from the global South: inequality between and within countries is now running at record levels, so that polarisation between rich and poor remains the defining characteristic of corporate globalisation in the twenty-first century. While the rise of the BRICS (Brazil, Russia, India, China, South Africa) has introduced new forces into the global political economy, it has strengthened the dominance of capitalism as their governments seek to promote the interests of their own 'national champions' around the world. This rise of new imperialisms in turn raises broader questions as to whether the North-South framing of the global political economy that has dominated since the publication of the Brandt Report in 1980 is still fit for purpose. With business representatives from the global South now joining forces with their Northern counterparts in the elite forums of the transnational capitalist class, it may be necessary to reframe the battle lines of globalisation in contemporary rather than historical terms.

Chapter 3 shows how the interests of TNCs not only differ from public policy goals in theory, but are now in conflict with the democratic pursuit of those goals in practice. The neoliberal programme embodied in globalisation was explicitly developed by the core capitalist states as a mechanism for the expansion of corporate power, first through the Uruguay Round of world trade talks that led to the founding of the WTO in 1995, and then by means of the bilateral free trade agreements and investment treaties that have proliferated since. In particular, the elevation of transnational capital to a *de facto* legal status equivalent to that of sovereign states has granted corporations the power to challenge government actions directly before international arbitration tribunals, and to claim compensation where their profits might be limited by local or national interventions. The threat posed to democracy by this new development has generated its own backlash, with the first states now beginning to acknowledge that the balance of forces under globalisation may indeed have swung too far in capital's favour.

Chapter 4 examines one of transnational capital's most insidious mechanisms for expanding into new markets: the strategy of corporate social responsibility (CSR). Originally developed as a means to deflect public criticism and see off the threat of external regulation, CSR has developed into an offensive initiative through which to expand the reach of TNCs into new areas of the global economy, and to roll back the frontiers of the state. The chapter looks at the changing significance of the United Nations as a forum in which to contest the rise of transnational capital, and the controversial role it has played in legitimising corporate power. The new corporate mantra of 'responsible competitiveness' now seeks to transcend the old contradictions between public and private that were implicit in CSR programmes; if there is no tension between the corporate pursuit of profit and the broader goals of society, then capital can indeed be entrusted with the lead role in delivering public goods.

The next three chapters each examine one sector in which the expansion of capital has led to intensifications of poverty and conflict. Each of the three sectors exemplifies different forms of corporate activity, as well as different forms of resistance that have been mounted in order to contest the power of capital, both locally and internationally. The extractive industries, examined in Chapter 5, have traditionally represented the most violent form of accumulation by dispossession, depriving local communities of their natural resource wealth and generating the most brutal human rights violations in the suppression of protests against their continuing operations. With the boom in world prices for oil, gas and minerals showing no signs of abating, the profits made by the extractive industries have repeatedly broken records, leaving no doubt as to the importance of securing access to the strategic natural resources of foreign countries at all costs. Corporate complicity in abuses up to and including crimes against humanity has been exposed in legal challenges seeking to obtain redress for human rights violations and ecological disasters, yet the power of the sector remains unassailable. Instead, the response from the extractive industries has consisted of a welter of CSR initiatives, plus financial settlements of legal cases whenever companies look likely to be adjudged liable by the courts.

The garments sector, profiled in Chapter 6, represents a different form of corporate expansion: the model of 'networked capitalism' that has come to characterise so many sectors of the outsourced global economy. Dominant power over the value chain allows Western brands and retailers to force down factory prices, playing suppliers off against each other in their insatiable demand for lower costs and higher profits. Local trade union action to combat such exploitation remains the most important form of resistance, backed up by worldwide solidarity campaigns to challenge the companies that ultimately control the value chain. Yet such strategies can only ever be partly successful when buyers are able to switch to new suppliers as soon as the terms of their existing contracts no longer offer them sufficient profit, or exposure of their practices becomes too embarrassing. New forms of coordinated cross-border action, such as the campaign for an Asia Floor Wage profiled towards the end of the chapter, seek to combat the structural challenge posed by a system that again guarantees capital unassailable power.

Chapter 7 examines the global food regime, which combines the worst aspects of networked capitalism with the most violent forms of dispossession known from the extractive industries. New attempts to expand corporate control over farming in Africa, in particular, have seen a resurgence of the model of industrial agriculture developed in the Green Revolution, whereby farmers are forced into increasing dependence upon the most powerful seed and agrochemical companies for their livelihoods, or see their land turned over to plantation agriculture in brutal acts of appropriation. The existential threat posed by such corporate domination to peasant farmers and rural communities alike has generated mass resistance; more than this, however, it has inspired the development of an international movement for the positive alternative of food sovereignty, embodied in small-scale peasant farming based on principles that are both socially progressive and ecologically sound. The food sovereignty movement lays down a challenge that goes to the very heart of the corporate food regime, and thus provides a rich example for other alternatives to the capitalist system as a whole.

Chapter 8 addresses these broader alternatives as they present themselves in practice and in theory. It looks in particular at the alternative paths of historical development under construction in three Latin American countries that have recently embarked on democratic transitions away from capitalism: Bolivia, Ecuador and Venezuela. The transformations already achieved in each of these three countries are based on a number of common initiatives, including the construction of new national constitutions and the renegotiation of contracts with TNCs operating in key sectors, reasserting sovereignty over each country's natural resource base and securing a more equitable distribution of the revenues resulting from its extraction. The foundational basis of these and other alternative models can be encapsulated in three principles around which to build towards a more equitable and sustainable future: popular sovereignty, common ownership and social production – principles already in evidence in myriad different operations undertaken on a cooperative basis, large and small, across the world. The positive experience of so many such initiatives proves that another world is truly possible, and offers hope to all those seeking to move beyond the poverty of capitalism towards a better future.

2

Crisis, Continuity and Change

I n August 2011, despite a last-minute deal that saved the US government from defaulting on its $14.3 trillion debt by allowing President Obama to raise the debt ceiling by a further $2.1 trillion, credit rating agency Standard & Poor's downgraded the country's triple-A status for the first time in 70 years. While commentators around the world scrambled to interpret the event, China's official state news agency Xinhua editorialised as follows:[1]

> The days when the debt-ridden Uncle Sam could leisurely squander unlimited overseas borrowing appeared to be numbered as its triple A-credit rating was slashed by Standard & Poor's (S&P) for the first time on Friday. Though the US Treasury promptly challenged the unprecedented downgrade, many outside the United States believe the credit rating cut is an overdue bill that America has to pay for its own debt addiction and the short-sighted political wrangling in Washington ... The US government has to come to terms with the painful fact that the good old days when it could just borrow its way out of messes of its own making are finally gone.

This very public scolding of the US government was, in one respect, a measure of China's concern at its own exposure to US debt: China's holdings of US Treasury securities amounted to a colossal $1.14 trillion at the time of the downgrade, a position that had long troubled Chinese government officials. Yet the official reaction was even more significant in revealing Beijing's irritation at the USA's inability to fulfil its obligations as, supposedly, the ultimate guarantor of global economic stability. As its number one creditor, China was calling on Washington to put its house in order or risk undermining global economic recovery – yet by the beginning of 2013, US government borrowing had already reached its new debt ceiling of $16.4 trillion, and the country faced the prospect of plunging over the so-called 'fiscal cliff'. This time Xinhua made its feelings even clearer: 'As the world's sole superpower, US domestic failures to reach deals on critical issues have implications for the whole world.'[2]

The first two decades of the twenty-first century have been marked by epochal changes in global economic power and governance. In what is a truly historic development, a number of countries from the semiperiphery of the capitalist world system – China foremost among them – have emerged to challenge those at its core.[3] Those at the core, by contrast, are struggling to come to terms with structural economic crisis and the prospect of their own long-term decline. The old colonial powers of Europe face an especially bleak future, in view of their ageing populations, dwindling natural resources and uncompetitive production base. Internal conflicts over pension reform, social welfare and the role of the state are only the most obvious paroxysms of adjustment to a new historical reality. For the first time in 500 years, global power is being transferred from Europeans and their North American descendants towards those whom they have exploited with impunity for so long.

Beneath these momentous changes, however, many other aspects of the global political economy remain stubbornly the same. Despite political challenges at the centre, the capitalist world system is still characterised by increasing polarisation within and between nation states, with levels of inequality now at unprecedented historical levels. Likewise, and not coincidentally, the power structures and institutions which underpin the system and guarantee its continuity have emerged from the crisis unscathed, and in some cases strengthened. The emerging economies that have successfully challenged the supremacy of the old colonial powers have pointedly refrained from challenging the system itself, preferring to promote the interests of their own corporations as they expand outwards into the global economy, and establishing themselves as new imperialist forces to rival the old. Capital has thus retained its power to roam the world in search of ever higher profits, while local communities and working people are as exposed as ever to poverty and dispossession. While much has changed, in other words, too much has remained the same.

Epochal Changes

The global economic meltdown of 2008 onwards can be most fully understood as a seismic upheaval in the tectonic plates of world history, as the American twentieth century gives way to a multipolar order defined by the emergence of new powers.[4] This deeper significance emerged most clearly as the crisis laid bare the structural imbalances that have developed within the capitalist world economy over the past four decades. Most notably, the relocation of production from global North to South through which capital had temporarily resolved its earlier crisis of overaccumulation had led to a dramatic widening of the trade balance between surplus and deficit economies (three times greater in 2008 than it had been in 1990; see Figure 2.1), and thereby also of the balance between creditor and debtor states.[5] This offshoring of industrial production led to an increased dependence on the financial sector and the 'hollowing out' of mature capitalist economies: while manufacturing accounted for 50 per cent of all domestic US profits during the 1960s, by 2005 it accounted for less than 15 per cent of such profits; conversely, financial profits accounted for 15 per cent of US domestic profits in the 1960s, but 40 per cent by the eve of the 2007 crash.[6] At the same time, wage repression brought with it unprecedented levels of inequality, and a crisis of overproduction that necessitated, in its turn, a creative expansion of new forms of credit – in particular, US subprime mortgages – and a resulting explosion in household debt that could never be repaid.

The USA remains the largest economic and military force on the planet. Yet Washington's ability to project its power across the globe has foundered in the face of six decades of popular resistance in Asia, Latin America and the Middle East, just as the USA's military supremacy also continues to decline relative to other sovereign forces, particularly those of China.[7] In the sphere of non-military domination, the structural crisis facing the US economy has fatally compromised its ability to discipline other states, even if it retains unrivalled power in the institutions of global economic governance. The heightened importance of finance capitalism in the USA since the 1970s can itself

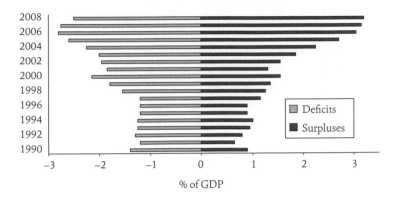

Figure 2.1 Global current account balance, 1990–2008

Source: UNCTAD, *The Global Economic Crisis: Systemic Failures and Multilateral Remedies*, New York and Geneva: United Nations Conference on Trade and Development, 2009, p. 6.

be seen as a harbinger of hegemonic restructuring at the world systems level: according to the compelling schema in Giovanni Arrighi's *Long Twentieth Century*, increasing financialisation represents a 'sign of autumn' for the declining US empire just as it did for the Genoese, Dutch and British empires before it, and presages the eventual loss of its superpower status.[8] It is far from clear that China wishes to assume the mantle of global hegemony from the USA rather than taking its place in a new multipolar global settlement, as its official statements have long maintained it would prefer to do. The first official report published by the governments of the BRICS states – Brazil, Russia, India, China and (since 2010) South Africa speaks of their being catapulted into a joint leadership role in a new world order undergoing a process of rebalancing towards the emerging economies, as a result of playing a 'pivotal role' in the global economic recovery.[9] Certainly, the eclipse of the G8 by the G20 as the *de facto* forum for global economic governance from 2008 onwards was no more than a formal acknowledgement of the importance of the emerging economies on the world stage, as well as a recognition of the impotence of the core capitalist powers in the face of the crisis they had created.

The economic trends underlying these momentous changes are visible in the global figures for foreign direct investment (FDI) flows across the world. For the first time, 2010 saw 'developing'

and 'transition' economies overtake the countries of the industrialised North to receive more than half of all world FDI inflows (see
Figure 2.2). Even more significantly in the longer term, outward FDI
from developing and transition economies reached record levels,
accounting for almost 30 per cent of world FDI outflows. As detailed
below, state-owned enterprises from emerging economies have been
particularly active investors, as the BRICS led the way in acquiring
natural resources and strategic assets in foreign markets, while
sovereign wealth funds have maintained (even if more cautiously)
the high level of foreign investment activity that began in 2005.[10] This
strategy by emerging economies represents a major development from
the 1970s, when sovereign wealth from the oil price boom was largely
invested in US government securities or deposited in private banks,
and it reflects the countries' growing ambitions. China is predicted
to overtake the USA as the world's largest economy by 2020, with
India pushing Japan into fourth place as Brazil, Russia and Germany
compete for the fifth, sixth and seventh spots.[11]

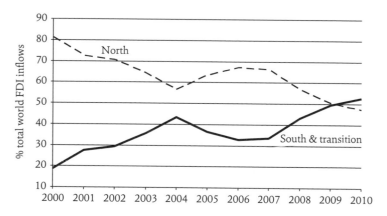

Figure 2.2 Distribution of FDI inflows, 2000–10

Source: United Nations Conference on Trade and Development online statistical
database, UNCTADstat.

Yet the trajectories of these awakening giants and other emerging
economies are in no way representative of the global South as a
whole. The aggregate FDI figures for developing and transition
economies cited above conceal profound differences between national
experiences. While overall FDI to developing economies was substan-

tially greater than in 2009, foreign investment into sub-Saharan Africa declined for a further year in 2010, as it did also to least developed countries, small island developing states and South Asia; the share of world FDI going to sub-Saharan Africa now stands at just 3 per cent. Even these figures are misleading, however. The vast majority of FDI into sub-Saharan Africa is directed towards the highly problematic extractive sector, especially oil, and only to a handful of countries. Of the total $38 billion in FDI to sub-Saharan Africa in 2010, a full 70 per cent was taken by Angola, Nigeria, Democratic Republic of Congo, Congo, Ghana, South Africa and Zambia, while the remaining 42 sub-Saharan countries received just over $11 billion between them – less than 1 per cent of the global total. Similarly, of the substantial $48 billion in FDI flows to the Caribbean in 2010, over $43 billion – fully 90 per cent – went into the twin tax havens of the Cayman Islands and British Virgin Islands for purposes of 'round-tripping' and other tax minimisation schemes. The rest was shared out, unevenly, between the remaining 19 Caribbean states.[12]

The same polarisation can be seen in trade. While the countries of the global South have seen their aggregate share of world trade increase from 27 per cent in 1980 to 40 per cent today, much of this is due to the performance of individual countries such as China, which is now far and away the world's leading exporter of merchandise, with $1.58 trillion in exports in 2010 compared to its nearest rivals the USA ($1.28 trillion) and Germany ($1.27 trillion).[13] The countries of sub Saharan Africa, by contrast, have seen their share of world merchandise trade decline from an already meagre 3.48 per cent in 1980 to just 1.96 per cent of the total in 2010 – much of this still dependent on the export of primary commodities.[14]

Nor is there any truth in the claim that this increased marginalisation results from such countries' failure to liberalise their economies so as to facilitate their integration into the global economy. On the contrary, as a result of the trade liberalisations imposed upon the continent through the structural adjustment programmes of the World Bank and International Monetary Fund (IMF), Africa is now more open to agricultural trade than any other region in the world, according to the World Bank's own trade restrictiveness index, and more open to manufacturing trade than South Asia, Latin America or the Middle East. Globalisation's failure to improve the development prospects of the world's poorest nations is confirmed by UN findings that those least developed countries which liberalised their trade regimes most during the 1990s, as they were required to do under World Bank and IMF conditionality, also experienced the most dramatic increases in poverty.[15] The 'fallacy of composition', whereby plausible economic strategies become self-defeating if adopted by several different actors at once, has been shown to apply not only to export-oriented agriculture – as known from decades past – but also to trade in labour-intensive manufactured goods.[16]

Many of the foremost cheerleaders for globalisation have been forced to reconsider their interventions in light of this evidence. In his much vaunted book *The Bottom Billion*, former World Bank research director Paul Collier has recanted his previous faith that the world's poorest countries could rely on international markets to trade their way out of poverty: 'Don't count on trade to help the bottom billion. Based on present trends, it seems more likely to lock yet more of the bottom-billion countries into the natural resource trap than to save them through export diversification.'[17] The IMF itself, in an internal evaluation of its past involvement in trade policy issues, has now admitted that its 'aggressive' use of conditionality on trade liberalisation 'exceeded a reasonable definition of macro-critical, went beyond staff's technical competence, and fell prey to political interference from large shareholders of the IMF'. Such confessions will be cold comfort to the millions whose lives were destroyed as a result of IMF and World Bank intervention.[18]

While a handful of countries may be thriving, therefore, the majority of poorer nations find themselves more marginalised than ever, as their 'integration' into the global economy continues to be characterised – as it was in the colonial era – by the dispossession of their natural resources and the exploitation of their labour. In calculations of global inequality, consequently, inequality between countries is now an even greater component than inequality within them – a reversal of the position at the time of the Industrial Revolution.[19] The Panglossian myth that globalisation was a benign force that would benefit all nations – a 'rising tide to lift all boats' – was abandoned years ago by even its most ardent champions. The theory that the capitalist world economy is predicated upon uneven geographical development, on the other hand, and in particular the impoverishment of those on the periphery, is fully borne out by the dynamics of the past 40 years. The era of corporate globalisation has been characterised not by convergence but by polarisation between winners and losers at the level of the nation state.[20]

Rising Inequalities

If polarisation between states has been one defining characteristic of globalisation, polarisation within countries has been widely recognised as another. Many have remarked on this increased inequality, and many too have recognised its causal role in the current crisis.[21] However, the widening gap between rich and poor must be addressed not simply as a statistical phenomenon to be measured by a rise in the Gini or Theil indices, but as a sign of class polarisation.[22] Studies of the functional distribution of income between capital and labour have shown how comprehensively the working class has been excluded from the benefits of growth in the era of corporate globalisation. Far from keeping pace with growth, in three quarters of all countries for which data were available the share of national income going to wages declined between 1985 and 2006. The most precipitous fall occurred in Latin America and the Caribbean, where the share of income going to wages decreased by 13 percentage points in just ten years, while dramatic declines were also experienced in Asia (10 per cent), the industrialised North (9 per cent) and sub-Saharan Africa.[23] As the proportion of national income returning to labour has fallen, the share going to capital has risen; indeed, so marked has this trend been in the countries of the Organisation for Economic Cooperation and Development (OECD) during the current period that it has been characterised as having 'no precedent over the past 45 years'.[24] In the USA, this profit share reached a record high in 2006 and has continued to rise since, while labour's share has sunk to an all-time low.[25] Wage levels for full-time male earners in the USA are well known to have stagnated in real terms over the past 40 years, even while per capita gross domestic product (GDP) has more than doubled – leading to the 'great divergence' in US income levels.[26] Yet when increases in unemployment are taken into account in addition to inflation, the median wage for all working-age men in the USA actually declined by 28 per cent between 1969 and 2009.[27] By the year 2007, the eve of the

Great Recession, income inequality had surpassed the previous high water mark of 1928, the eve of the Great Depression.[28]

The UK has experienced similar trends, as the wage share of national income has declined by around 5 percentage points from its average during the early 1970s, and by 10 points from its 1975 peak.[29] The impact of this decline on lower-paid workers has been particularly severe, underlining the added importance of taking wage distribution into account when making such calculations in countries with a broad divergence in pay between ordinary workers and top executives (whose remuneration packages are also included in calculations of overall wage share). While those in the bottom half of the UK earnings distribution experienced a considerable loss in wage share between 1977 and 2010, those in the top 10 per cent saw an increase in their share – and a very handsome increase in the case of the executives who make up the top 1 per cent of UK earners.[30] The UK is now a more unequal society than it has been at any time in the past 40 years.[31]

Nor has the increase in inequality within richer countries been confined to the Anglo-Saxon economies. The eurozone experienced an average 10-point decline between 1980 and 2000 in the share of national income going to wages – one of the largest such decreases in the OECD and 'a clear sign of redistribution from labour to capital', according to the UN's research project on the impact of policy regimes on poverty and inequality.[32] In the case of Mexico, the share of national income going to wages has fallen dramatically from what was already an extremely low level in comparison to other OECD economies, from an average of 38.5 per cent in 1980–85 to just 29.9 per cent in 2004–07. The collapse in the real terms value of wages was so pronounced that by 2000 the average wage for blue-collar workers in Mexico was worth half its 1981 value, while the minimum wage was worth just one fifth of its 1976 value.[33] In the emerging economies of India and China, similar increases in inequality have taken place against the backdrop of hundreds of millions living in absolute poverty. The sharp rise in inequality in India can be attributed to the introduction of liberalisation reforms from 1991 onwards, where the combination of rapid growth in the services sector, jobless growth in the industrial sector and prolonged distress in agriculture has led to a situation where India has more people living in poverty than any other nation, while still boasting the fastest rising number of millionaires.[34] In the case of

China, the wage share of GDP fell from 53 per cent to 41.4 per cent in the years between 1998 and 2005, and inequality levels have risen so dramatically that they now rival those seen in the USA.[35] Indeed, the country's spectacular growth over the past 30 years may actually have been dependent upon the decline in labour's share of national income, more recent increases in wage levels notwithstanding.[36]

The overall effect of this twin process of polarisation between and within countries is that the affluent have seen their wealth expand many times over, while most other people have continued to experience impoverishment. By the year 2000, the richest 1 per cent in the world already owned 40 per cent of its assets, while the bottom half of the world's population between them owned barely 1 per cent of global wealth; the Gini coefficient for wealth inequality in the world as a whole was calculated at 0.89 – equivalent to the Gini value that would be registered for a population of 100 where the richest person is given $900 and the remaining 99 people each receive $1 only. By 2012, the richest 1 per cent in the world had seen their share of global assets increase still further, so that it now accounts for 46 per cent of the total. There were an estimated 13.7 million US dollar millionaires in the world in 2000, and 553 billionaires; by 2012 there were 29 million millionaires and 1,226 billionaires.[37] Whether at the national or international level, globalisation has succeeded in enriching a new class of oligarchs at the expense of the majority of humankind.[38]

New Kids on the Block

The rise of this new class reflects, in part, the dramatic development of capitalist enterprise in the emerging economies. The largest corporations from the global South are now vying for size with established giants such as General Electric, Shell and ExxonMobil. China ranks third behind the USA and Japan in national representation on the Forbes list of the world's 2,000 largest companies, with four Chinese banks and three non-financial corporations (PetroChina, Sinopec and China Mobile) now listed in the top 50.[39] While the largest corporations of the global South may not yet rival their counterparts from the North in terms of their transnationality (that is: foreign assets, sales and employees), it is notable that eleven of the world's 50 largest companies in 2012 came from China, South Korea and

Brazil. Moreover, as the findings below demonstrate, there has been a dramatic outward expansion of capital from the emerging economies in the past ten years which is threatening to shift the balance of power away from the core.[40]

The sovereign wealth funds of the Gulf states, Singapore and China led the way in the period from 2005 onwards, investing tens of billions of dollars in a spending spree which peaked in 2009 but continues to this day. In particular, the financial crash of 2007 offered these funds an opportunity to buy into the ailing banking sectors of the USA and Europe – investments which some came to repent at their leisure later. The Government of Singapore Investment Corporation (GIC) spent more than $16 billion on minority shares in UBS and Citigroup, while Singapore's smaller Temasek Holdings invested over $6 billion in Barclays and Merrill Lynch. The Abu Dhabi Investment Authority (ADIA) also invested heavily in Citigroup, while the China Investment Corporation (CIC), established in 2007, bought a 10 per cent stake in Morgan Stanley for $5 billion.

State-owned companies in the extractive industries have also expanded into all regions of the world in order to satisfy their economies' growing appetite for natural resources. PetroChina's parent company China National Petroleum Corporation (CNPC) now has significant oil and gas production operations in Algeria, Azerbaijan, Burma, Canada, Chad, Ecuador, Equatorial Guinea, Indonesia, Iran, Iraq, Kazakhstan, Libya, Mauritania, Mongolia, Niger, Nigeria, Oman, Peru, Russia, Sudan, Syria, Thailand, Tunisia, Turkmenistan, Uzbekistan and Venezuela, while its counterparts from Brazil (Petrobras), India (Oil and Natural Gas Corporation – ONGC), South Korea (Korea National Oil Corporation – KNOC) and Malaysia (Petronas) have similarly widespread portfolios. Most recently, the national companies' expansion has increasingly been achieved through mergers and acquisitions (M&As) as well as new contracts and greenfield investment: China's oil companies spent around $25 billion on overseas acquisitions in 2010, accounting for a fifth of all such activity in the oil and gas sector worldwide.[41] In the first ever hostile takeover by a state-owned oil company, KNOC acquired Britain's Dana Petroleum in 2010, giving the Korean corporation access to Dana's assets in the North Sea, Egypt and West Africa; the move came just a year after KNOC had bought up Canada's Harvest

Energy for just under $4 billion. China's largest oil refiner Sinopec outbid KNOC in 2009 to acquire Addax Petroleum and its operations in Nigeria, Gabon, Cameroon and Iraqi Kurdistan for $7.2 billion, and also bought the two Canadian companies Tanganyika Oil and Daylight Energy for $2 billion each, in 2008 and 2011 respectively. China National Offshore Oil Corporation (CNOOC), China's largest offshore oil and gas producer, concluded its $2 billion acquisition of distressed energy company OPTI Canada in summer 2011, giving it a 35 per cent stake in the Long Lake tar sands project in Alberta. That deal was subsequently eclipsed by CNOOC's $15 billion takeover of the Canadian company operating the Long Lake project, Nexen, in February 2013.

Mining companies are also making significant acquisitions. In 2011, Brazilian transnational Vale – the world's largest miner of iron ore – announced its intention to invest close to $10 billion in foreign operations over four years, the majority of it designed to expand the company's presence in Africa; the announcement came only a year after Vale's $3.8 billion acquisition of the Brazilian phosphate mines of US agribusiness giant Bunge, the company's largest investment since its $19 billion takeover of Canadian nickel mining company Inco in 2006. In 2010, India's Adani Enterprises bought the Galilee coal block in Queensland, Australia, from Linc Energy for $2.7 billion, adding to the company's pre-existing arrangements for importing coal from Indonesia and China. As a result of its substantial mineral resources, Australia is also a particularly important investment market for Chinese corporations: in 2009, Yanzhou Coal Mining made a successful takeover bid of $2.8 billion for Australian coal producer Felix Resources, while China Minmetals Corporation acquired OZ Minerals for $1.4 billion. As a result of these and many other deals over the past few years, Australia holds more Chinese FDI stock than any other country.[42]

Other sectors have also witnessed major takeovers by corporations from the semiperiphery of the world system. Chinese computer manufacturer Lenovo bought IBM's personal computer business for $1.8 billion in 2005, enabling it to move ahead of Dell as the world's second largest PC manufacturer (behind Hewlett Packard) by the end of 2011. The acquisition by Indian telecomms giant Bharti Airtel of the Zain Group's African assets for just under $11 billion in 2010

Table 2.1 Selected cross-border M&As, 2007–11

Value ($bn)	Acquisition	Owner	Home country	Acquiring company	Home country	Sector	Shares acquired (%)
2011							
6.3	OAO Polyus Gold	Polyus	Russia	KazakhGold	Kazakhstan	Metals & mining	73
5.0	CEPSA	CEPSA	Spain	IPIC*	Abu Dhabi	Oil & gas	49
3.6	ING Mexico	ING	Netherlands	Sura	Colombia	Insurance	100
3.3	GDF Suez	GDF Suez	France	CIC*	China	Oil & gas	30
3.1	Peregrino (Brazil)	Statoil	Norway	Sinochem	China	Oil & gas	40
2.1	Daylight Energy	Daylight Energy	Canada	Sinopec	China	Oil & gas	100
2.0	OPTI Canada	OPTI	Canada	CNOOC	China	Oil & gas	100
2010							
10.7	Zain Africa	Zain	Kuwait	Bharti Airtel	India	Telecomms	100
9.1	EDF Energy (UK)	EDF	France	Cheung Kong	China (HK)	Energy	100
7.1	Repsol Brasil	Repsol	Spain	Sinopec	China	Oil & gas	40
4.8	PetroCarobobo	PDVSA	Venezuela	consortium	India, Spain, Malaysia	Oil & gas	40
3.8	Bunge BPI	Bunge	USA	Vale	Brazil	Metals & mining	100
3.1	Bridas	Bridas	Argentina	CNOOC	China	Oil & gas	50
2.7	Linc Energy	Linc	Australia	Adani Group	India	Metals & mining	100
2.6	Dana Petroleum	Dana	UK	KNOC	Korea	Oil & gas	100
2.5	BSG Guinea	BSG	Switzerland	Vale	Brazil	Metals & mining	51
2.4	Parkway Holdings	Parkway	Singapore	Khazanah*	Malaysia	Healthcare	70
2.2	Hyundai Oilbank	IPIC*	Abu Dhabi	Hyundai	Korea	Oil & gas	70
2.2	Harrods	Harrods	UK	QIA*	Qatar	Retail	100
2009							
9.6	Volkswagen	Porsche	Germany	QIA*	Qatar	Automobiles	15
7.2	Addax Petroleum	Addax	Switzerland	Sinopec	China	Oil & gas	100
4.4	CEPSA	CEPSA	Spain	IPIC*	Abu Dhabi	Oil & gas	38
3.9	Harvest Energy	Harvest Energy	Canada	KNOC	Korea	Oil & gas	100
3.9	Chartered	Chartered	Singapore	ATIC*	Abu Dhabi	Semiconductors	100
2.9	AMD	AMD	USA	ATIC*	Abu Dhabi	Semiconductors	66

	Acquired company		Nation	Acquiring company	Nation	Industry	%
2.8	Felix Resources	Felix	Australia	Yanzhou Coal	China	Metals & mining	100
2.6	MangistauMunaiGaz	Setdco	Indonesia	CNPC, KMG	China, Kazakhstan	Oil & gas	100
2.5	Dunedin Holdings	George Weston	Canada	Grupo Bimbo	Mexico	Food	100
2.2	ASARCO	ASARCO	USA	Grupo Mexico	Mexico	Metals & mining	100
2008							
14.3	Rio Tinto	Rio Tinto	UK/Australia	Chinalco	China	Metals & mining	9
5.6	Standard Bank	Standard Bank	South Africa	ICBC	China	Banking	20
4.4	Merrill Lynch	Merrill Lynch	USA	Temasek*	Singapore	Banking	9
4.1	Lafarge	Lafarge	France	NNS Holding	Egypt	Cement	11
4.0	PrimeWest Energy	PrimeWest	Canada	TAQA*	Abu Dhabi	Oil & gas	100
3.4	Nasdaq OMX	Nasdaq	USA	Borse Dubai	Dubai	Financial services	20
2.0	Tanganyika Oil	Tanganyika	Canada	Sinopec	China	Oil & gas	100
2007							
14.2	Rinker Group	Rinker	Australia	Cemex	Mexico	Cement	100
11.8	Corus Steel	Corus	UK	Tata Steel	India	Metals & mining	100
11.6	GE Plastics	GE	USA	SABIC*	Saudi Arabia	Plastics	100
9.7	UBS	UBS	Switzerland	GIC*	Singapore	Banking	9
7.5	Alinta	Alinta	Australia	Singapore Power	Singapore	Energy	100
7.5	Citigroup	Citigroup	USA	ADIA*	Abu Dhabi	Banking	5
6.9	Citigroup	Citigroup	USA	GIC*	Singapore	Banking	9
5.8	Novelis	Novelis	USA	Hindalco	India	Metals & mining	100
5.0	Morgan Stanley	Morgan Stanley	USA	CIC*	China	Banking	10
4.9	Bobcat	Ingersoll-Rand	USA	Doosan Group	Korea	Construction	100
4.1	Chaparral Steel	Chaparral	USA	Gerdau	Brazil	Metals & mining	100
3.7	Solectron Corp	Solectron	USA	Flextronics	Singapore	Electronics	100
3.0	Blackstone	Blackstone	USA	CIC*	China	Banking	10
2.0	Barclays	Barclays	UK	Temasek*	Singapore	Banking	2

* Denotes sovereign wealth fund.

Sources: Drawn from UNCTAD figures on cross-border M&A deals, supplemented by other reports for full details of ultimate acquiring company and number of shares acquired; www.unctad.org.

positioned the Indian company to challenge South Africa's MTN Group and Vodafone for the continent's 180 million mobile phone customers. The Qatar Investment Authority (QIA), established in 2005, paid close to $10 billion in 2009 for a 10 per cent stake in German car manufacturer Porsche plus a 15 per cent stake in Volkswagen, while the following year China's Zhejiang Geely took over full ownership of Volvo from Ford for a relatively modest $1.5 billion. In 2007, Borse Dubai agreed to pay $3.4 billion for a 20 per cent share in the new company formed out of Nasdaq's takeover of Nordic stock exchange group OMX AB, as well as acquiring Nasdaq's 28 per cent stake in the London Stock Exchange. Qatar has also invested in the European exchanges through the QIA, as well as acquiring a 25 per cent stake in British supermarket chain Sainsbury's in 2007 and buying the London department store Harrods outright for over $2 billion in 2010.

This new expansion by investors from emerging economies is still in its infancy when compared to the historical transnationalisation of capital from the global North. As noted above, outward FDI from developing and transition economies has risen over recent years to account for 30 per cent of world FDI flows; yet the proportion of overall FDI stock originating from the global South remains at just 15 per cent of the world total, while that from the North still represents over 80 per cent. Only one company from the South features in the top 50 list of non-financial transnational corporations (TNCs) as ranked by foreign assets – and that company is the Hong Kong-based conglomerate Hutchison Whampoa, originally a colonial trading house before being taken over by Hong Kong billionaire Li Ka-shing.[43] Even China's much discussed 'going out' policy has been selective in its implementation, and its national champions are still clustered in a limited number of industries.[44]

Yet even if it is still a relatively new phenomenon, emerging economies' quest to acquire strategic assets and natural resources in foreign territories is already challenging the balance of power in the global economy, and in some instances meeting with stern political resistance. Most notably, opposition from Congress has blocked a number of high profile investments by state-owned foreign companies within the USA.[45] CNOOC's $18.5 billion bid for US oil giant Unocal in 2005 met with such opposition from Congress that the Chinese company eventually withdrew its offer, while in the following year

Dubai Ports World, which had just acquired British shipping firm P&O for $6.8 billion, was blocked by Congress from taking over that company's existing US ports operations on grounds of national security – grounds which had not been considered relevant when the foreign operator had been British. China Minmetals met with similar resistance over its abortive bid for Canadian mining company Noranda in 2004, just as Petronas was blocked from taking over Canada's Progress Energy in 2012, while political opposition persuaded China's state-owned chemicals group Sinochem to abandon its attempt to take over the Saskatchewan-based fertiliser giant PotashCorp in 2010. Chinalco's $19.5 billion bid to increase its stake in Anglo-Australian mining company Rio Tinto was frustrated in 2009 after Australian political parties took out 'No' adverts in national newspapers to protest against increasing Chinese control of the country's national resources.[46] Nor is it just control over tangible assets that has sparked such political reaction: two of China's leading technology companies, Huawei and ZTE, were branded a 'security threat' in a 2012 investigation by the US House of Representatives intelligence committee, which recommended that both should be excluded from future US business deals. Australia had already moved against Huawei earlier in the same year when it banned the company from participating in the country's national broadband network.[47]

The 'outward turn' of investors from emerging economies raises important considerations for any analysis of the global political economy. To begin with, it is increasingly misleading to divide the world into capital-exporting and capital-importing states, if those terms are taken to distinguish between countries of the global North and South, respectively.[48] While the distinction may have been useful in marking historical tensions between different actors at a time when Northern governments represented the interests of transnational capital and Southern governments were primarily on the defensive, that era has now been superseded. The increasing transnationalisation of capital from emerging economies means that those governments are also looking to secure favourable terms of access for their own investors around the world, even while they are still important hosts to inward investment in their own territories. Categorising countries into capital-exporting and capital-importing states according to the relative weight of their outward or inward investment therefore risks oversimplifying their political positioning.

This in turn raises fundamental questions as to the continuing relevance of the North-South framework, both for analysis and for action. Ever since the Brandt Report was published in 1980, the distinction between countries of the North and those of the South has been widely employed as the salient cleavage in the global political economy – not only because the countries of the South faced a 'common predicament ... of being dependent on the North, and unequal with it', but also because many shared the experience of having suffered under colonial rule.[49] Now, however, as emerging economies begin to build their own global empires, there is a need to reassess both the North-South framework and the assumptions that go with it. If certain countries from the global South are themselves pursuing capital accumulation in unequal relations with other countries of the South, either through their dominant position in value chains or through accumulation by dispossession, then any 'common predicament' that may once have unified those countries ceases to exist.[50]

World systems analysis reveals itself here as more dynamic and sensitive than the static North-South framing of the Brandt Report, in particular through its conceptualisation of the semiperiphery as a zone between core and periphery of the capitalist world economy.[51] Not only does the concept allow for the possibility of graduation from the periphery over time, but it also highlights current differences between countries of the South according to their status in the world economy. Indeed, a defining characteristic of semiperipheral states is that they accumulate capital through their appropriation of surplus from the periphery, even as they also cede capital by the same token to the countries of the core. In this respect, the BRICS and other emerging economies are now exemplifying their nature as exploiters of the periphery far more than at the time the Brandt Report was written (when a number of them were still classed as peripheral states themselves), and their political positioning in global governance forums reflects the same.

Maintaining the Status Quo

Nowhere has this new dynamic been more obvious than in the positions taken at the G20 by the BRICS and other emerging economy governments in response to the global economic crisis of 2008 onwards. Despite the historical change represented by the G20's assumption of the G8's mantle as the primary forum for global economic governance, there has been no challenge forthcoming from that body to the dominant model of corporate globalisation. While calling for specific modifications such as a new international reserve currency to replace the US dollar, the leaders of the emerging economies have shown themselves to be fully acquiescent in perpetuating the system which caused the crisis. Any suggestion that government representatives from the global South might seize the opportunity to call for more radical change in the global economic order, in line with their previous criticism of the G8's mismanagement of world affairs, has foundered on the rocks of self-interest.[52]

Most importantly, the member states of the G20 have chosen to resurrect the failed institutions of twentieth-century globalisation – and in particular, the IMF – to police the new world order. At its 2009 London summit, the G20 pledged $500 billion in extra financing for the IMF in order to re-establish its power as principal source of credit and, thereby, enforcer of austerity programmes in the countries of Europe as well as elsewhere in the world. This massive injection of finance was repeated in April 2012, when G20 finance ministers committed an additional $430 billion to the IMF for use in meeting the crisis in European and other states. Brazil, Russia, India and China all pledged financial support to the initiative, as did Indonesia, Malaysia, Thailand, Singapore, Saudi Arabia and South Korea.[53]

This represents a dramatic reversal of fortunes for the IMF, as the institution's future had been thrown into serious doubt following its catastrophic mismanagement of the East Asian financial crisis of 1997–98. Not only had the IMF exacerbated the worst effects of that crisis by demanding draconian stabilisation programmes to protect foreign investors at the expense of the populations of countries such as Indonesia, Thailand and South Korea, but its policy of encouraging the elimination of capital controls was widely held to have been responsible for causing the crisis in the first place. Just as with the internal evaluation of its trade policy interventions mentioned above, the IMF subsequently admitted that it had failed to highlight the considerable risks involved in capital account liberalisation in all the years that it had acted as 'cheerleader' for the policy.[54] As one former

IMF employee put it in 2006, the East Asian financial crisis ensured that the IMF 'lost its legitimacy and never recovered it'.[55] By 2007, major debtors Brazil, Argentina and Indonesia had all terminated their loan arrangements with the IMF ahead of schedule, paying off their debts early in order to free themselves from the institution's damaging political and economic control.

Having brought the IMF back from the dead, the G20 made a parallel attempt to revive the Doha Round of multilateral trade negotiations at the World Trade Organisation (WTO). As described in the next chapter, the creation of the WTO on 1 January 1995 had represented the institutional high water mark of globalisation, and its Director-General at the time, Renato Ruggiero, was not held to be exaggerating when he claimed: 'We are no longer writing the rules of interaction among separate national economies. We are writing the constitution of a single global economy.'[56] The Doha Round, launched in 2001 under the shadow of the US-led invasion of Afghanistan, had sought to affirm the WTO as the premier forum for further deepening the neoliberal programme of globalisation, but the negotiations collapsed repeatedly over the subsequent decade as countries of the global South banded together to resist the predatory agenda of the EU and USA. The demise of the Doha Round dealt a huge blow to the credibility of the WTO, and the G20 at its 2011 Cannes summit was forced to issue a call for 'fresh, credible approaches' to see if anything could be salvaged from the wreck.[57]

At the same time, the G20 signalled its continuing support for the WTO in its role as enforcer of the global trading regime, issuing a call for enhancement of the dispute settlement mechanism that acts as the world court for international trade-related cases. This strengthening of the dispute settlement mechanism underlines the WTO's ultimate function as an institution of discipline and control for the benefit of capital – indeed, only in this framing, rather than through the more familiar prism of North-South international relations, can the true significance of the WTO, World Bank and IMF in the global political economy be appreciated.[58] In contrast to the rounds of trade negotiations held under the auspices of the WTO and its predecessor the General Agreement on Tariffs and Trade (GATT), the WTO's dispute settlement mechanism is the legal body responsible for maintaining compliance with the rules of global commerce, and as such it is the only institution with the power to authorise sanctions on those countries that are deemed to have restricted access to their economies or otherwise harmed the interests of capital. While only member states can bring cases to the WTO for adjudication, it is unfailingly on behalf of corporate interests that they do so. With multilateral negotiations stalled, the primary function of the WTO is therefore to discipline member states to the benefit of corporations seeking to expand their market access around the world.

Similarly, just as the World Bank and IMF have long imposed their structural adjustment programmes on client states in the global South, those same policy packages have since 2008 been forced on the populations of Europe as a condition of the multi-billion dollar bailouts of their economies. The IMF had already acknowledged its failure to honour the commitments made at the beginning of the millennium to reduce structural conditionality in its lending, and its recent record confirms the institution's continuing bias towards financial interests in times of crisis.[59] As the UK experienced when it was forced to accept stringent conditions in return for its $3.9 billion IMF loan in 1976, the function of the institutions of global governance is to discipline all those on whom they have the power to impose their will, irrespective of whether they be from North or South. The ongoing programme of reforms to World Bank and IMF governance systems, with its cosmetic reallocation of voting rights to emerging economies, will do nothing to change the institutions' essential function as agencies of control.[60]

Transnational Capitalist Elites

The G20's decision to resurrect the failed institutions of twentieth cen tury globalisation in the interests of transnational capital represents the greatest structural continuity between the new world order and the old. It is also testament to the resilience of a transnational capitalist class that seeks to direct the governance of global economic affairs from behind the throne. This elite grouping exercises its power through both strategic and proximate interventions, and the inner circle of its transnational policy community comprises no more than a few hundred individuals at any one time. As with other changes that have come about in the global economic order, however, membership of the transnational capitalist elite may now be about to expand.

The transnational capitalist class exercises its power through a number of institutions that intersect with one another in a complex web of interrelations.[61] Most well known, perhaps, are the invitation-only forums at which corporate and government elites establish consensus at the highest level on the direction of future world development, such as the annual Bilderberg conferences or the closed meetings of the Trilateral Commission and World Economic Forum. Equally important is the privileged access granted to corporate bodies such as the TransAtlantic Business Dialogue (TABD), the US Business Roundtable and the European Round Table of Industrialists (ERT). Alongside these are numerous bilateral groupings organised on similar lines; for the UK alone, these include the British-German Königswinter conference established in 1950; the Franco-British Colloque, which alternates annually between Britain and France; the British-Spanish Tertulias, established in 1986; and the British-Italian Pontignano conference, now held each year in Rome. These invitation-only forums differ from the corporate lobby groups which will feature in following chapters, as they allow corporate and political elites to develop positions of overarching consensus behind closed doors, free from any concerns of attribution or accountability. By careful management of access to the forums, the transnational capitalist class controls not only the dominant discourse that pertains in international debates on the global political economy, but also – by virtue of their control over succession planning and appointments – the direction of the institutions that wield hard power in the global economic order.

The governance structures of the major invitation-only forums are drawn almost exclusively from the Triad of North America, Europe and Japan. Unsurprisingly for an institution that defines itself as a European-American forum, Bilderberg is entirely dominated by participants from the West. The group's steering committee, which prepares the agenda and selects the participants for each year's conference, consists of three dozen members exclusively from North America and Europe (including Turkey). Invitees to its conferences are hand-picked mostly from the corporate and government elites of the Triad countries, and number between 120 and 130 each year. Two Chinese participants (China's Vice-Minister of Foreign Affairs and former ambassador to the UK, Fu Ying, and Huang Yiping of Beijing University) were included in the 2011 and 2012 Bilderberg conferences, but stewardship of the conferences remains squarely in the hands of the traditional elite.[62]

The Trilateral Commission was founded in 1973 as a sister organisation to Bilderberg by David Rockefeller and Zbigniew Brzezinski, with the aim of including participants from Japan in a similar forum. The Commission was therefore structured exclusively towards the countries of the Triad, although the Japan Group has been expanded into a Pacific Asian Group and the North American Group now includes members from Mexico. The leadership of the Trilateral Commission remains in European, North American and East Asian hands, through three chairmen drawn one from each region and an executive committee of around 50 individuals from the interface of their corporate and political elites.

The TABD is a small, invitation-only forum composed of chief executives from around 40 leading US and European companies, whose mission is to work towards a free market in trade and investment on both sides of the Atlantic. The TABD's significance comes through its role as the official corporate adviser to the Transatlantic Economic Council, the intergovernmental body established between the EU and USA in 2007 with an identical mandate of seeking economic integration through the deregulation of their respective markets and further liberalisation of trade.[63] In much the same way, the ERT brings together around 45 chief executives and chairpersons of European companies with the stated aim of eliminating any obstacles that prevent business from securing the full benefits of the single European market. The ERT was founded after the model of the US Business Roundtable, which was established in 1972 with the explicit aim of ensuring that the business sector should play a more active role in the formation of public policy.[64] All three bodies played a key role in pressing for the launch of negotiations towards the new TransAtlantic Trade and Investment Partnership between the EU and USA announced in February 2013 (see next chapter).[65]

The World Economic Forum (WEF) differs from the above groupings in that it seeks to engage a broader geographical constituency than just the Triad countries. The Forum's annual meetings at Davos in January bring business and political leaders together behind closed doors in order, in its own words, 'to shape the global agenda at the start of each year'.[66] The Forum then holds regional and national conferences throughout the year which seek to spread the 'spirit of Davos' across the world: in 2012, for instance, the Forum followed up its January meeting with regional conferences on Latin America (in Mexico, April), Africa (Ethiopia, May), East Asia (Thailand, May/June) and Europe and the Middle East (Turkey, June) before holding its annual New Champions meeting – the so-called 'summer Davos' – in China in September, and a special India Economic Summit in November. Under the 'intellectual stewardship' of its International Business Council, composed of chief executives from leading global corporations, the Forum thus sees its mission as one of spreading the capitalist gospel to all corners of the earth.

One of the most important functions of the transnational capitalist forums is to undertake succession planning for key power brokering roles at the global level. As only existing members are allowed to recommend newcomers to the invitation-only forums listed above, their meetings act as important opportunities for the transnational capitalist class to vet potential newcomers and groom the next generation of global power holders. Accounts of the presentation of Margaret Thatcher to the Bilderberg conference in 1975 have become legendary, as have similar reports of the initiations of Bill Clinton and Tony Blair in 1991 and 1993 respectively. Christine Lagarde was a regular attendee at Bilderberg conferences and a member of the WEF's Foundation Board before being appointed as IMF Managing Director in June 2011, while Robert Zoellick, appointed as Managing Director of the World Bank in 2007 from his position as Managing Director at Goldman Sachs, was a former member of the Trilateral Commission and another regular Bilderberg attendee. Similarly, the appointment of Mario Monti as Italian prime minister in November 2011 ensured that the post was back in 'safe hands' after the premiership of Silvio Berlusconi: as well as having served formerly as a European Commissioner and international adviser to Goldman Sachs, at the time of his appointment Monti was not only on the Bilderberg steering committee but also European chairman of the Trilateral Commission.

The development of a transnational capitalist class has in no way eliminated the significance of national states or governments, as is sometimes claimed. Rather, the workings of these elite forums show how highly the corporate world rates the importance of national government representatives, who remain key invitees. As argued by Ralph Miliband 30 years ago, the relationship between the state and the dominant class in advanced capitalist societies is one of partnership, with the exact terms of the partnership in constant flux and with occasional conflict over individual decisions, but broad agreement on overall direction.[67] National governments remain critically important to the transnational capitalist class as the powers reaffirming the direction of global governance in international forums, just as nation states are also of prime importance as fields of resistance to those seeking to contest corporate power. Often, of course, the dividing line between corporate and political representatives is blurred to the point of non-existence, as the 'revolving door' between business, government and other public institutions ensures that key officials are fully embedded with the capitalist elite. Grandees of the transnational capitalist class move between the public and private realms with apparently no conflict of interest: Peter Sutherland, for example, chairman of Goldman Sachs and former chairman of BP, was the European Commissioner for competition and thereafter Director General of GATT in its transition to becoming the WTO; he is also an Honorary Chairman of the Trilateral Commission (whose European Group he chaired from 2001 to 2010), while sitting on both the steering committee of Bilderberg and the WEF's Foundation Board.

Nor does the existence of these forums signify that competition between national capitalist interests has come to an end. On the contrary, one of the most important functions identified by participants for the forums' existence is that they enable national business and political leaders to transcend such rivalries in favour of systemic unity, thereby forestalling more serious outbreaks of internecine capitalist warfare that could threaten the whole. The forums act as a safety valve to ensure that the system is safeguarded for the benefit of capital, at the same time as individual corporations are able to compete with one another for supremacy in any particular market. With the rise of a new generation of competitors from the emerging economies, however, any equilibrium that the transnational elites have been able to fashion between competing national interests and the greater capitalist good is potentially at risk. Major state-owned enterprises, in particular, may well have national strategies that cannot be so easily aligned with the interests of TNCs from the core capitalist states, and such tensions could yet explode into full-scale inter-imperialist antagonism, as classical theory would predict.[68]

In this respect, the B20 Business Summit that now takes place as part of the annual G20 leaders' summit has introduced itself as a new means for the transnational capitalist elite to manage national antagonisms, as it expands the reach of the class outwards to incorporate business representatives from beyond the countries of the G8. The B20 was initially established to influence the G20's 2010 summit in Seoul, and includes business organisations and individual companies from South Africa, China, India, Indonesia, Brazil, Mexico, Saudi Arabia, South Korea, Turkey and Argentina, as well as from the core capitalist states. By the time of the G20's 2011 summit in Cannes, the B20 had prepared a 260-page report which carried the imprimatur not only of the French business federation MEDEF, which was hosting the summit, but also of the International Chamber of Commerce (ICC) and the WEF, which were both instrumental in setting up the working groups that fed in to the report.[69] The publication was an attempt to rearticulate familiar demands for expanded markets, capital account deregulation and liberalised investment regimes as a truly global business agenda backed by capitalist forces from the core and semiperiphery alike. Certainly, the early engagement by the ICC and WEF indicates their intention to use the B20 as a vehicle for the globalisation of capitalist interests in the future.

New Imperialisms

This growing engagement of business lobby groups and companies from the emerging economies introduces a new phase in the development of the global political economy. Instead of the traditional division between the capital-exporting countries of the North and the capital-importing countries of the South, the increasing accumulation of capital in the semiperiphery has generated a new wave of imperialism from the emerging economies themselves. This is by no means a new phenomenon at the regional level; subimperialisms such as those of Brazil, South Africa and India have been well documented since the 1970s.[70] Yet the outward expansion of the BRICs and other emerging economies now represents a challenge at the level of the world system itself, where previously most talk of 'empire' has tended to focus on the old colonial powers.

Such an observation is not to join with Western critics of these new imperial expansions – especially of China in Africa – who claim that they somehow lack some mythical civilising mandate of the older colonial interventions; in addition to the racist overtones of much of this commentary, it is based on a studied delusion as to the true character of the West's imperial nature, present as well as past.[71] The contention here is that the new imperialisms of the emerging economies represent the same inherent dynamic of capitalist expansion as those of the established powers, albeit with different characteristics.[72] As subsequent chapters will show, capital from countries of the global South can pose just as grave a threat to labour, local communities and the environment as capital originating from the North – and the positioning of their state representatives in international forums can be equally self-interested. As noted by one Chinese participant at the World Social Forum held in Nairobi in 2007, 'Do not expect capital to act any differently just because it has a Chinese face.'

The opening two decades of the twenty-first century have seen the capitalist world system shaken to its roots by ongoing and unresolved crisis, and the shock has been the catalyst for a formal shift in the distribution of power at the highest levels of global economic governance. Yet the system has survived the shock, and the emerging economies that have now taken their place in the new dispensation have affirmed their support for those same institutions that have driven forward the neoliberal programme for the supremacy of capital over the past four decades.[73] That programme has condemned the peoples of the majority world to mass poverty, and now threatens to do the same to those living in the core capitalist economies as they slide towards permanent austerity and social disintegration. The power granted to capital comes at a price, and as the next chapter demonstrates, that price is democracy itself.

3

Corporate Power in Practice

At 2.46 pm on Friday 11 March 2011, a rare and complex double earthquake measuring 9.0 on the Richter scale struck the eastern coast of Japan. The tsunami unleashed by the quake destroyed over a million buildings, inundated 560 square kilometres and caused the deaths of almost 20,000 people. It also triggered a 'catastrophic, unprecedented emergency scenario' at the Fukushima Daiichi nuclear power plant, leading to the meltdown of three of its reactors, a series of major explosions and the release of large quantities of radioactive material into the surrounding environment. The disaster was given the highest rating 7 on the International Nuclear Event Scale – only the second such event in human history, together with the Chernobyl disaster of 1986.[1]

Two months after the Fukushima disaster, the German government announced that as a result of the risks involved it would not be extending the life of the country's nuclear power plants beyond the year 2022. Hundreds of thousands of people had taken to the streets in anti-nuclear protests across Germany in the weeks following Fukushima, reflecting the deep popular opposition to nuclear power that has existed within German society for decades, and the legislation to phase out the country's nuclear programme was passed through parliament with an overwhelming majority. The German announcement coincided with the Swiss government's decision to phase out its own nuclear power plants, and was followed soon after by an Italian referendum in which 94 per cent of voters rejected the possibility of restarting a nuclear power programme in Italy. In a special edition reviewing the global situation one year on from the Fukushima disaster, *The Economist* confirmed that no private company could take on the huge cost of building new plants without government backing, and ruefully dubbed nuclear power 'the dream that failed'.[2]

Shortly after Germany's newly revised Atomic Energy Act had passed into law, the Swedish energy company Vattenfall, which had operated two of Germany's oldest nuclear power plants, gave notice of its intention to sue the German government as a result of the decision not to extend their operating life. According to Vattenfall, the reduced book value of the two plants required the company to register an impairment loss in its 2011 accounts of just under €1.2 billion, including provisions for dismantling the plants, and as a foreign investor it claimed the right to pursue the German government for 'compensation' under the terms of the multilateral Energy Charter Treaty, which Germany had ratified in 1997. That treaty was ostensibly designed to protect foreign investors in the energy sector from political risks such as discrimination and expropriation, in keeping with many other bilateral and multilateral treaties introduced during the 1990s. Yet by opening up the possibility for foreign companies to sue host country governments when changes in public policy are not to their commercial advantage, the treaty had handed investors unprecedented power to challenge the authority of sovereign states and their democratic structures. Despite the fact that neither of Vattenfall's two plants were operational at the time of the phase-out decision, having been out of service since 2007, the company demanded €3.7 billion in compensation from the German state.[3]

Vattenfall's suit against the German government was formally registered in May 2012 at the World Bank's International Centre for Settlement of Investment Disputes (ICSID) (for more on which, see below). The company had reason to be confident in making the claim, in that it had already been successful in a prior claim brought against the German government under the terms of the same Energy Charter Treaty three years earlier. That case had centred on the city of Hamburg's environmental regulations for the River Elbe, where Vattenfall had been granted a permit to construct its new Moorburg coal-fired power plant on condition that it meet the water quality standards required of industry along the river. Vattenfall argued that those requirements made their investment 'unviable' and sued the German government (as host state under the Energy Charter Treaty) for €1.4 billion plus costs and interest. The case was settled between the two parties in early 2011, and although the details of the settlement were kept secret, insiders remarked that Vattenfall could consider the outcome a 'complete success'. The company was granted a new permit to continue its construction of the Moorburg power plant, duly revised in its favour to include less demanding environmental conditions.[4]

The twin Vattenfall cases illustrate how corporate power has expanded to the point that public policy in even the strongest states can now be held hostage by commercial interests, and how transnational capital has been elevated to a legal status equivalent to that of the sovereign state. Capital has assumed this position in the global political economy as a direct result of four decades of pro-corporate engineering at the global level, under the auspices of multilateral institutions such as the World Bank, the International Monetary Fund (IMF) and the World Trade Organisation (WTO); through regional customs unions and financial institutions; and through the bilateral free trade agreements and investment treaties that have proliferated in recent years. This chapter charts the rise of corporate power into the second decade of the twenty-first century, and focuses on the direct challenges to democracy and public policy now being mounted by capital on the back of such power.

Neoliberal Expansion

The current ascendancy of corporate power over sovereign states can be traced back to the 1980s, as the crisis of the previous decade led not to the New International Economic Order called for by many in the global South, but to a period of intense capitalist expansion. In country after country, government elites redesigned social and economic systems in order to create new market opportunities for capital, often taking advantage of natural disasters or political traumas to drive through the most extreme measures.[5] At the international level, a new generation of trade agreements negotiated in multilateral, regional and bilateral forums secured the foundations of a globalisation that prioritised the interests of transnational corporations (TNCs) over the needs of labour, society or the environment. In particular, transnational capital benefited from the increasing inclusion of investment rights within these negotiations, giving ever greater powers to corporate actors seeking to expand into new markets or territories at the expense of national sovereignty or public policy goals.

The Uruguay Round of world trade talks, held under the auspices of the General Agreement on Tariffs and Trade (GATT), marked a watershed in the development of the globalisation programme. Previous rounds of negotiations held under GATT had focused on the reduction of border tariffs and non-tariff barriers relating to trade in industrial goods, and the earliest rounds had involved negotiation among a small minority of countries only, predominantly from the global North. Launched in 1986 and concluded in 1994, the Uruguay Round involved 123 countries, thereby expanding coverage of the international trade regime to a substantial majority of nation states. Even more significantly, the Uruguay Round succeeded in expanding the GATT negotiating agenda to encompass entire economic sectors such as services and agriculture that had previously been excluded from the negotiations, as well as securing multilateral agreements on trade-related aspects of intellectual property rights (TRIPs), trade-related investment measures (TRIMs) and a host of issue areas that had previously been addressed on a plurilateral basis only (where countries can opt in voluntarily). This dramatic expansion ensured that the WTO, which the Uruguay Round brought into being at the beginning of 1995 as successor organisation to GATT, could now reach 'behind the border' into areas of social and economic life which had previously been untouched by the rules of globalisation, with potentially limitless consequences for the public sphere.

This important step towards 'completion' of the world market was understood even during the Uruguay Round negotiations as being wholly to the benefit of transnational capital, which saw its power to access and control new markets increase exponentially as a result of the agreements signed at the end of the round.[6] This is hardly surprising in light of those agreements' origins. The Uruguay Round's Agreement on Agriculture, for example, was initially drafted by Dan Amstutz, former Vice-President of Cargill, the USA's largest private company and still today one of the big three transnational grain traders.[7] The TRIPs Agreement was first negotiated between US, European and Japanese companies from the pharmaceutical, publishing and software industries before being handed over to governmental officials to complete.[8] And according to David Hartridge, former director of the

WTO Services Division, 'Without the enormous pressure generated by the American financial services sector, particularly companies like American Express and Citicorp, there would have been no services agreement and therefore perhaps no Uruguay Round and no WTO.'[9] The General Agreement on Trade in Services (GATS) and the TRIMs Agreement, which was also included in the Uruguay Round at the behest of US capital, saw notable transfers of power towards foreign investors in the services and goods sectors, respectively. GATS seeks to effect the permanent opening of services markets through successive rounds of negotiations in which WTO member states commit individual service sectors of their economies to liberalisation, thereby restricting their governments' ability to control foreign investments in those sectors but significantly expanding TNCs' pre- and post-establishment rights.[10] The TRIMs Agreement, by contrast, introduced a straight prohibition on governments' use of investment measures such as local content requirements, which had been widely used to stimulate local economies by requiring TNCs to source a given proportion of their inputs from domestic suppliers; and trade balancing or foreign exchange balancing requirements, which sought to ensure that the activities of foreign investors would not expose the host economy to current account crises.[11] In both cases, the effect of the new WTO agreements was to restrict host countries' ability to use foreign investment positively for their own national development purposes, while corporate investors gained increased freedom to profit from their operations without having to contribute to the host economy.

In addition to being established as the forum for future rounds of trade liberalisation negotiations, the WTO was also mandated to police the agreements established in the Uruguay Round. To this end, the WTO's dispute settlement mechanism was granted more power of enforcement than GATT had enjoyed, in that its rulings were to be binding on member states and backed up with the power to authorise sanctions in cases of non-compliance; as a result of this unique authority, WTO dispute rulings boast an extremely high rate of compliance for an international governance body, at around 95 per cent.[12] The pre-eminence of capitalist interests over public policy objectives was reaffirmed early in WTO jurisprudence as a direct inheritance from GATT dispute settlement cases, despite the increasing threat to national sovereignty that this posed. Indeed, it was primarily the recognition of this threat to valued social and environmental policies that brought 100,000 demonstrators onto the streets of Seattle in 1999 to protest at the WTO's third ministerial conference and prevent, at least temporarily, the launch of a new round of trade negotiations.

Despite these increased powers to discipline the global market in favour of transnational capital, additional areas of national economies were subsequently identified that had not yet been opened up sufficiently to foreign penetration. In particular, the government procurement contracts of national and subnational authorities represented a vast untapped market, while the investment regimes of those states which still sought to link FDI with national development remained a cause of frustration to TNCs in comparison with the powers granted to them under the global trade regime. To this end, the European Union (EU) and other leading capitalist states pressed successfully for the four new issues of investment, government procurement, competition policy and trade facilitation to be included on the agenda of the WTO's first ministerial conference, held in Singapore in 1996. Working groups were established by the conference to explore these new issues (known thereafter as the 'Singapore issues') and their relationship to the trade regime, without prejudice as to whether the WTO's agenda should be expanded to include negotiations on them in addition to all the other new issue areas that had just been taken on by the WTO.

This programme to expand the WTO's negotiating agenda was given added urgency when attempts to introduce a Multilateral Agreement on Investment (MAI) at the Organisation for Economic Cooperation and Development (OECD) ended in failure. The MAI was designed to prioritise the interests of transnational capital over host countries by liberalising investment regimes beyond the level of existing bilateral treaties and providing foreign investors with unprecedented rights to, *inter alia*, establishment, full equity ownership, national treatment (that is: at least equal treatment with domestic investors) and repatriation of profits, as well as investor-state dispute settlement. As was noted at the time, and is discussed in more detail below, this last power would have been wholly without precedent at the multilateral level, as it promised to raise private economic actors to *de facto* international legal status alongside sovereign states, enabling them to challenge public policy interventions in host economies.[13] Moreover, the agreement

41

was intended to apply not only to foreign direct investment but also to foreign portfolio investment, conventionally understood to mean an equity stake of less than 10 per cent in a particular company – an expansion of coverage which threatened to expose host economies still further to the dangers associated with foreign capital flows. Negotiations were launched in 1995 with the intention of first securing agreement on the MAI among OECD member states and later opening up the agreement for accession to non-OECD countries as well. However, as the result of a concerted international campaign to defeat the MAI on the part of civil society, as well as growing divisions between OECD member governments themselves, the negotiations were abandoned in 1998.

By means of intense bullying and brinkmanship in the shadow of the US-led invasion of Afghanistan, a new round of international trade negotiations was launched at the WTO's ministerial conference held in Doha in November 2001.[14] Despite widespread opposition from Southern governments, the EU managed to engineer the inclusion of the four Singapore issues in the Doha Round's work programme at the eleventh hour – a coup widely credited to the personal persistence of EU Trade Commissioner Pascal Lamy, who would four years later be appointed Director-General of the WTO itself. Only a last-minute intervention by India's ministerial team ensured that any final decision to initiate negotiations on those issues would still require explicit consensus from all WTO members at a later date. By way of a public relations exercise, the Doha Round was dubbed the 'Doha Development Agenda' – a vain attempt to silence criticism from Southern governments, incensed that their concerns had again been ignored in the formulation of the WTO's work programme, just as they had been at the Seattle ministerial conference two years earlier.

Ironically, it was the determination of the EU and its allies to force the Singapore issues onto the WTO's negotiating agenda that led to the first major collapse of the Doha Round, at its 2003 ministerial conference in Cancún; this in turn sowed the seed for the round's suspension in 2006 and its ultimate stagnation. Following the launch of the Doha Round, civil society groups from around the world had formed a close alliance with Southern country negotiators at the WTO to prevent the introduction of the Singapore issues onto the negotiating agenda, linking up political mobilisations at the national level with technical lobbying in Geneva around the negotiations themselves to create a powerful movement of international opposition. Southern countries had also formed their own negotiating blocs at the WTO to contest the worst excesses of the North's agenda, and the fight over the Singapore issues provided these groupings with their first common cause. In a signal victory for the alter-globalisation movement, plans to launch WTO negotiations on investment, government procurement and competition policy were formally abandoned in July 2004, leaving trade facilitation as the only Singapore issue remaining on the round's negotiating agenda. The EU was particularly humiliated by the defeat.[15]

The Bilateral Turn

At the same time as attempting to advance the interests of capital through multilateral forums such as the OECD and WTO, many governments have actively promoted those same interests through bilateral and regional channels as well.[16] While sharing the same fundamental orientation towards the interests of TNCs at the expense of labour, society and the environment, free trade agreements (FTAs) negotiated in bilateral or regional forums are typically even more ambitious than those negotiated multilaterally – hence their common categorisation as 'WTO plus'. The first bilateral FTAs were negotiated during the 1980s, but it was not until talks started towards the North American Free Trade Agreement (NAFTA) between Canada, Mexico and the USA that global public attention was alerted to the structural threat such FTAs pose. Coming into effect at the beginning of 1994, NAFTA became infamous not only for the massive loss of jobs and bargaining power by workers across all three countries, but also for the new threat posed by foreign investors winning the right to challenge signatory states directly in investment disputes, as described in detail below. The profoundly negative experience of NAFTA caused such a regional backlash that the USA's subsequent attempt to create a Free Trade Area of the Americas (FTAA) across the western hemisphere was thwarted by a coordinated campaign of mass popular opposition, combined with government resistance from Brazil, Argentina and Venezuela.[17] Despite this setback, the USA did succeed in concluding an FTA with Central America (CAFTA, eventually lengthened to

CAFTA-DR when the Dominican Republic was also included), and recently embarked upon construction of a Trans-Pacific Partnership (TPP) that will form a 'super-FTA' between the Americas and Asia, covering a full range of issues related to trade and investment, and beyond. The first round of TPP negotiations took place in 2010 between Australia, Brunei Darussalam, Chile, New Zealand, Peru, Singapore, Vietnam and the USA; Malaysia joined the talks later in the same year, followed by Canada and Mexico in 2012, with Japan, Thailand and the Philippines all waiting in the wings. Envisaged as an open agreement that future states will be able to join at will, the TPP aims to create a free trade area that will eventually encompass the entire Asia-Pacific region. The fact that the negotiations have taken place in secret, with the public learning about developments only through leaked documents and other fragments of information, underlines the severity of the threat posed by the TPP initiative to democracy and livelihoods alike.[18]

Stung by its repeated humiliation at the WTO and concerned at the prospect of falling behind the USA and Japan in the race to conclude FTAs with major trading partners, the EU launched its own programme for bilateral and inter-regional expansion by means of the aggressive 'Global Europe' trade strategy introduced in 2006. Drawn up by EU Trade Commissioner Peter Mandelson in close collaboration with European business representatives, the strategy opened up a new front in the neoliberal assault on labour and society both within and outside Europe, demanding greater powers for European capital to penetrate new markets in government procurement and services sectors and to gain unrestricted access to the natural resources needed by European corporations, in particular its high-tech industries. Within Europe, the strategy aimed at a dramatic deregulation of national economies so as to bring European social and environmental standards into 'harmony' with those of other trading partners, notably the lower standards of the USA.[19] Following the adoption of Global Europe as the official trade strategy of all EU member states, the EU embarked on negotiations towards FTAs with South Korea, India, Canada, Ukraine, Central America, Peru and Colombia (following the collapse of negotiations towards a full EU-Andean agreement), as well as with individual member states of the Association of South-East Asian Nations (ASEAN), following the collapse of negotiations towards a full EU-ASEAN FTA. Negotiations towards the highly controversial Economic Partnership Agreements (EPAs) with African, Caribbean and Pacific island states continued, as before, to make uneven progress. In addition, with confirmation in 2010 that the Global Europe strategy would remain the basis of EU trade policy for the coming period, the EU announced new negotiations towards FTAs with a further range of countries including the Mercosur bloc (Argentina, Brazil, Paraguay, Uruguay and Venezuela); Egypt, Jordan, Morocco and Tunisia; Georgia, Armenia and Moldova; and Japan. Another major threat has come with the revival of plans to negotiate a Transatlantic Trade and Investment Partnership between the EU and USA, as revealed to the world by President Barack Obama in his 2013 State of the Union address. Previously advocated by the TransAtlantic Business Dialogue and other corporate lobbyists in the 1990s, the rationale for an FTA between two trading partners which already present minimal tariffs to each other's exports has been made explicit by those promoting the idea again in the current context: business on both sides of the Atlantic wishes to see the removal of all non-tariff 'barriers' posed by those social and environmental standards that restrict the accumulation of capital, thereby allowing trans-Atlantic trade and investment to continue in future free of any reference to broader societal goals.[20]

With less fanfare than traditionally accompanies the negotiation of bilateral and regional trade agreements, the past 30 years have witnessed the proliferation of a vast number of bilateral investment treaties (BITs) between countries, which have created an international investment environment in which the balance of power has swung dramatically and unmistakably towards capital. The first ever BIT (between Pakistan and Germany) was concluded in 1959, but it was during the 1990s and 2000s that their numbers increased most dramatically, as countries from the global South increasingly signed such treaties with one another as well as with countries of the North (see Figure 3.1). By mid 2012, there were 2,843 BITs in force worldwide, covering over two thirds of global foreign direct investment (FDI) stock, plus a further 333 other international investment agreements.[21]

From the 1980s onwards, reforms of national investment regimes had already tended towards deregulation, with the vast majority of policy changes serving to liberalise the regulatory systems of host states in favour of foreign investors. For many countries of the global

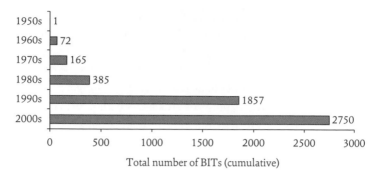

Figure 3.1 Cumulative growth in number of BITs, 1959–2009

Sources: UNCTAD, *Bilateral Investment Treaties 1959–1999*, New York and Geneva: United Nations Conference on Trade and Development, 2000; UNCTAD, *World Investment Report*, New York and Geneva: United Nations Conference on Trade and Development, various years.

South, this relaxation of rules linking foreign investment to national development programmes was a requirement of continued financial support from the IMF and World Bank. As a result, in the ten years from 1991 to 2000, fully 95 per cent of all changes made to investment regimes around the world were deregulatory, relaxing restrictions on foreign investors.[22] BITs introduced a further shift in power relations between transnational capital and host states, and swiftly established themselves as the vehicle for the most far-reaching provisions in favour of foreign investors. In particular, BITs have granted foreign investors the right to bring direct claims against host states in international arbitration forums for losses suffered in their jurisdictions, irrespective of whether any contractual relationship exists between the state and the foreign investor in question. This provision for investor-state dispute settlement runs contrary to the established norms of the international system, which have traditionally upheld the principle that states are the juridical representatives of their people when it comes to the international arena, and that states alone have the power to bring claims against other states on behalf of their investors, as is the case with dispute settlement in bodies such as the WTO. As recounted above, the OECD's attempt to secure access to investor-state dispute settlement for TNCs at the multilateral level failed with the defeat of the MAI in 1998. Since the 1980s, however, it has become standard practice for bilateral treaties to enshrine the right of foreign investors to bring claims against host states for damages, effectively establishing investor-state dispute settlement as 'the backbone of an emergent international system of investor protection' which provides TNCs with a general right to international arbitration even when they have no contractual relationship with the host state.[23]

In bestowing this right on foreign investors, BITs commonly identify the forum (or forums) in which international arbitration is to take place, as well as the procedural rules to be followed. The only international dispute settlement system specifically designed to deal with investor-state disputes is the World Bank's ICSID, but others such as the International Chamber of Commerce's (ICC's) Court of Arbitration and the United Nations Commission on International Trade Law (UNCITRAL) offer alternative forums for investor-state dispute settlement. The Permanent Court of Arbitration in The Hague, originally established in 1899 to facilitate dispute resolution between nations, has developed its own rules for arbitration between states and non-state actors, and has become increasingly involved in investor-state cases over recent years.[24]

The new-found power of TNCs to bring states before international arbitration tribunals has brought with it many additional dangers. To begin with, BITs commonly grant foreign investors the choice between bringing claims first before national courts or going directly to international arbitration – an innovation which breaches the customary rule that local remedies must be exhausted before foreign investors can have recourse to international forums. Secondly, investors can disguise or switch their home country so as to take advantage of these powers, as in the infamous case of the failed water privatisation in Cochabamba, Bolivia, where Bechtel subsidiary Aguas del Tunari was able to take advantage of the Netherlands-Bolivia BIT by virtue of having inserted Dutch holding companies into its ownership structure – a ploy which 'makes a mockery of investment arbitration', according to one expert.[25] Domestic companies have also reinvented themselves as 'foreign' investors in order to challenge their own government in international arbitration: despite the dissenting opinion of its presiding arbitrator, an ICSID tribunal in 2004 granted the 'Lithuanian' company Tokios Tokelès permission to bring a claim against Ukraine under the Lithuania-Ukraine BIT even though it had been shown that the company was 99 per cent owned by Ukrainians (see also the AbitibiBowater case, below).[26] Thirdly, there are serious questions as to the independence and accountability of the private tribunals established to rule on international investment cases, as the arbitrators – who are appointed on a case-by-case basis rather than having public authority as tenured judges – stand to increase their chances of being asked to arbitrate again in future cases, or of being hired to represent the corporations themselves, if they rule in favour of capital. There is a small clique of just 15 'super arbitrators' who have adjudicated over half of all the cases known to have been heard to date, and who represent 'not just the mafia' of international arbitration, according to one of their peers, 'but a small, inner mafia'.[27] Some treaties, such as the aforementioned Netherlands-Bolivia BIT or Netherlands-Czech Republic BIT, provide for the arbitrators to be appointed directly by business lobby groups such as the ICC or Stockholm Chamber of Commerce – an inbuilt bias towards capital that has been dubbed 'an affront to judicial independence'.[28] As a result, tribunals have often treated the system of international arbitration more as a means of securing the rights of investors than as a mechanism for adjudicating between the competing claims of two equal parties.[29]

The emergence of a system of investor protection by means of bilateral treaty rights represents a fundamental challenge to national sovereignty and democracy, as it threatens to constrain the public policy choices available to government authorities at all levels of the state. As the examples below demonstrate, the threat of legal challenge – and the substantial penalties to which states can be exposed when they are ruled to have breached their treaty obligations – can undermine policies that have been chosen for genuine social, economic and environmental reasons, as well as having the 'chilling' effect of turning public bodies away from future policy choices which could potentially impact on private sector investors in years to come. Where almost any national or local government intervention that affects the investment context can be interpreted as denying an investor 'fair and equitable treatment' under international law, the interests of transnational capital are effectively granted precedence over the social, economic and environmental policies of the host state. The fact that many of the arbitration cases to date have been conducted in secret further exacerbates the challenge to democracy posed by elevating capital to a status equivalent to that of a sovereign state.[30]

NAFTA Chapter 11

One of the earliest contexts in which the threat of investor-state dispute settlement came to public attention was that of NAFTA, mentioned above, which entered into force between Canada, Mexico and the USA in January 1994. Under Chapter 11 of NAFTA, any company or individual that 'seeks to make, is making or has made an investment' in one of the other member countries can bring a claim against the host state for losses suffered as a result of an alleged breach of NAFTA provisions. Not only does this open up the possibility of claims to prospective as well as actual investors, but 'investment' is broadly defined in NAFTA to encompass almost any form of capital interest. NAFTA Chapter 11 claims are heard by a private tribunal of three arbitrators: one chosen by the investor, one chosen by the defending state and the third chosen jointly by the first two. The investor may choose to file the claim for arbitration under either ICSID or UNCITRAL rules.

The first investor-state case under Chapter 11 of NAFTA was brought by the US fuel additive company Ethyl Corporation against Canada in 1997.[31] In April of that year, the Canadian government had introduced a ban on imports and interprovincial trade of the fuel additive MMT on public health and environmental grounds, not the least of which was the risk associated with inhaling particles of manganese, a known neurotoxin. Ethyl's Canadian subsidiary, which was the sole supplier of MMT in Canada, had already served notice of its intent to submit the Chapter 11 claim in September 1996, as the bill to ban imports of MMT was still going through the Canadian parliament. The company claimed compensation not only for the loss of profits caused by the ban, but also for the 'expropriation of intellectual property' caused by damage to Ethyl's commercial reputation worldwide, and an arbitration panel was constituted under UNCITRAL rules to hear the case. The Canadian government mounted a procedural defence by pointing out, among other arguments, that Ethyl had not waited six months from the passing of the legislation before filing its claim, as it was required to do under NAFTA Chapter 11 rules. Despite this, the tribunal ruled in favour of Ethyl that the case should be allowed to go ahead. Rather than defend the case, the Canadian government moved to settle the claim by paying out $13 million to Ethyl. More significantly still, the government rescinded the ban on MMT and issued a statement apologising to Ethyl, declaring that the state had no evidence of MMT's toxicity.

While the Ethyl case showed how investor-state challenges could undermine the national public policies of host countries even without going through the full arbitration process, the first NAFTA Chapter 11 case filed against Mexico showed how local practices were also vulnerable to challenge, and resulted in an even larger financial gain for the investor. The municipal authorities of Guadalcázar in the Mexican state of San Luis Potosi had denied the US landfill management company Metalclad a permit to operate a site for hazardous waste disposal in their municipality, but the company had proceeded with construction of the site regardless, in spite of substantial local protest at the environmental threat posed by its operations. When it eventually found itself unable to commence operation of the site, Metalclad served notice in December 1996 that it intended to submit a claim under NAFTA Chapter 11. In September 1997, the governor of the state of San Luis Potosi declared the site to be part of a special ecological zone for the preservation of biodiversity, including several rare species of cacti.

Metalclad filed its claim against the government of Mexico for the actions of the Guadalcázar municipal and San Luis Potosi state authorities, claiming damages for expropriation and also for the Mexican government's failure to provide Metalclad with 'fair and equitable treatment' in accordance with international law. On both counts, the ICSID arbitration tribunal found in favour of Metalclad, although the original award of $16.7 million was later reduced to $15.6 million. In particular, the ICSID tribunal ruled that the measures taken by the municipal and state authorities were 'tantamount to expropriation' under NAFTA Chapter 11, even though no seizure of property or nationalisation had taken place. This ruling concurred with the submission that had been made to the tribunal by the US government that NAFTA Chapter 11 must be understood to cover both direct and indirect expropriation alike.

In three more recent Chapter 11 awards, Mexico was required to pay even larger damages to Corn Products International ($58.4 million), ADM and Tate & Lyle ($33.5 million) and Cargill ($77.3 million) relating to the imposition of an excise tax on soft drinks sweetened with high fructose corn syrup, which was ruled to be discriminatory in favour of Mexican cane sugar producers and thus in breach of NAFTA provisions on national treatment. In a highly controversial and even more costly case, Canada paid $122 million to pulp and paper manufacturer AbitibiBowater to settle its claim over the provincial government of Newfoundland's reappropriation of water and timber rights from a mill which the company had already closed. The provincial government had been justified under Canadian law in reclaiming the water and timber rights, but AbitibiBowater used the investor-state provisions of NAFTA Chapter 11 to bypass the national courts and take advantage of pro-business international arbitration instead. As Canadian parliamentarians noted in their subsequent inquiry, there was double irony in the fact that AbitibiBowater is actually a Canadian company headquartered in Montréal, which only had recourse to NAFTA Chapter 11 by virtue of also being registered in the USA.[32]

BIT Arbitations

While NAFTA may have first raised public awareness of the threats posed by investor-state dispute settlement, there have been numerous other cases in the past two decades that have underlined how widespread those threats have become. No country has been more adversely affected by such cases than Argentina, which has been targeted by numerous European and US corporations for losses sustained as a result of the country's decision to unpeg the peso from the US dollar in January 2002 – an emergency measure introduced to counter the financial crisis that had brought Argentina to the point of total economic collapse. While the subsequent depreciation of the peso and renegotiation of Argentina's national debt led to economic recovery, foreign investors that had succeeded in negotiating privatisation contracts pegged to the dollar in the 1990s found themselves unable to secure profits at the same levels as before. In dozens of separate claims brought under a number of different BITs, TNCs sought billions of dollars in compensation from Argentina before ICSID and UNCITRAL tribunals alike.[33]

One of the first claims against Argentina to complete the arbitration process concerned the Michigan-based CMS Gas Transmission Company, which from 1995 had secured almost 30 per cent equity in one of the two new gas transportation companies that had been created out of the privatisation of Argentina's national gas company three years earlier. In a case brought under the terms of the US-Argentina BIT, CMS claimed compensation for losses sustained as a result of the measures taken by the Argentinian government as the country slid deeper into crisis, including a suspension of gas tariff increases and the aforementioned abandoning of the dollar peg in January 2002. The ICSID tribunal constituted to hear the case awarded CMS damages of $133 million in May 2005. The ad hoc ICSID committee which later heard Argentina's appeal for annulment of the earlier judgment acknowledged that the original award had 'contained manifest errors of law', but deemed itself unable to reverse the decision.

In a similar case brought under the terms of the UK-Argentina BIT, the British energy company National Grid claimed that it too had suffered damages as a result of Argentina's abandoning the dollar peg in 2002. The UNCITRAL panel established to hear the case dismissed Argentina's defence that it was exempt from its liabilities under the BIT because its actions had been taken in response to a 'state of necessity'; the panel cited an IMF report into Argentina's handling of the crisis as evidence that the government had itself contributed to the state of necessity, which rendered the defence inadmissible. National Grid was awarded $53 million in damages in November 2008, and Argentina's successive appeals against the award were turned down by the District of Columbia, the US Court of Appeals and, in December 2011, by the US Supreme Court.

Nor have the cases against Argentina been restricted to those connected with its financial and economic crisis; several are related to problems caused by the country's earlier privatisation of public services during the 1990s. One of the most infamous cases was generated by the 30-year water concession for Tucumán province, granted in 1995 to the Argentinian subsidiary of French transnational Compagnie Générale des Eaux (later renamed Vivendi). The privatisation had led to a doubling of water tariffs almost overnight, but the company failed to maintain the level of investment required under the concession, and the quality of the service deteriorated. When the water in Tucumán 'turned brown', eight out of ten households in the province stopped paying their bills altogether. The concession was terminated by the Tucumán provincial authorities in September 1997, on the grounds that the company had defaulted on the contract by virtue of its poor performance. Already in December 1996, Compagnie Générale des Eaux had filed a claim against Argentina under the terms of the Argentina-France BIT, alleging that its investment had not been granted fair and equitable treatment and had been expropriated. In November 2000, the ICSID tribunal ruled in favour of Argentina, dismissing the company's claims. Yet within six months the company (by now Vivendi) applied for an annulment, and its eventual success cleared the way for a fresh claim. In August 2007, a new ICSID tribunal reversed the original decision by ruling against Argentina, and awarded Vivendi $105 million in damages.

In 2001, the Texas-based company Azurix brought a similar claim against Argentina relating to the company's 30-year concession to provide sewerage and drinking water in Buenos Aires province, beginning in July 1999. The concession had run into difficulties almost immediately, with numerous public complaints over supply contamination and low water pressure, and accusations by the provincial government that Azurix was failing to honour its investment commitments. For its part, Azurix abandoned the concession after just two years on the grounds that it was not commercially viable, and filed a claim under the US-Argentina BIT. The ICSID tribunal found against Argentina in 2006 for failing to accord Azurix's investment fair and equitable treatment or full protection and security, and awarded the company $165 million in damages. Argentina failed in its attempt to have the award annulled, and by the end of 2011 interest had increased its value to $235 million.[34]

The problems inherent in the privatisation of water services have meant that they are a regular cause for arbitration cases.[35] However, the absurdity of TNCs failing to provide the necessary standard of service and then claiming millions of dollars in damages when their contracts are cancelled has not gone unnoticed. In July 2008, an ICSID tribunal rejected the claim brought against the Tanzanian government by UK engineering company Biwater and its German partner Gauff over their failed privatisation of water and sewerage supplies in the Tanzanian capital Dar es Salaam. The privatisation, which was heavily backed by aid money from the UK government's Department for International Development, had been an acknowledged disaster, and an UNCITRAL panel had already awarded the Tanzanian government damages in an arbitration to resolve the two parties' contractual differences. In the case of the failed privatisation of water in Cochabamba, Bolivia, US engineering giant Bechtel was forced to abandon its ICSID claim altogether at the beginning of 2006 in the face of public outrage. According to Bolivia's lead negotiator Eduardo Valdivia, the CEO of Bechtel had personally intervened to stop the case in light of the adverse publicity being generated for the company by the international campaign against it.[36]

The Backlash Begins

The annulment of a number of high profile ICSID awards in recent years has further undermined the legitimacy of the investment treaty arbitration system. In June 2010, an ICSID review panel overturned an earlier award of $128 million against Argentina in favour of the California-based company Sempra Energy, on the grounds that the original ICSID tribunal had failed to deal properly with Argentina's 'necessity' defence in taking the emergency measures it did in the financial crisis of 2001. An earlier $106 million award to the bankrupt US energy giant Enron was annulled by an ICSID review panel in July 2010 on similar grounds. Nor is it just ICSID tribunal decisions that have been overturned: in January 2012 the US Court of Appeals found in favour of Argentina when it annulled the $185 million in damages awarded to BG Group (formerly British Gas) by an UNCITRAL tribunal in December 2007 – an award which had remained confidential until Argentina brought the appeal. Brought under the terms of the UK-Argentina BIT, the original claim had again centred on losses sustained as a result of the emergency measures taken by Argentina at the time of its financial crisis in 2001. Interestingly, in light of the concerns highlighted earlier in this chapter, the US Court of Appeals overturned the award on the procedural grounds that BG Group had failed to exhaust local remedies before resorting to international arbitration, as it was required to do under the terms of the UK-Argentina BIT.

Inconsistency in the decisions of arbitration tribunals had already brought the legitimacy of the system into question prior to these cases, even in the eyes of individuals well disposed to the international arbitration of investment disputes.[37] A public statement issued in

August 2010 by over 50 law professors and other academics called for a thorough review of the international investment regime itself and the replacement of investment treaty arbitration by alternative mechanisms, including the strengthening of domestic justice systems so that they can again become the primary locus for the regulation of investor-state relations.[38] In June 2012, UNCTAD launched an alternative Investment Policy Framework for Sustainable Development, which highlighted the threat of 'undue interference with legitimate domestic policies' posed by investor-state dispute settlement measures, and recommended that countries should consider abolishing investor-state dispute settlement provisions in favour of alternative mechanisms.[39]

Several individual countries have also begun to register their disaffection with the investment arbitration system. In 2007, Bolivia became the first country to withdraw from ICSID, followed by Ecuador in 2009 and Venezuela in 2012; by the beginning of 2013, Argentina had also indicated its intention to leave.[40] In April 2011, the Australian government announced that it would no longer include provisions for investor-state dispute settlement in future bilateral or regional trade agreements; one motivating factor behind the decision may have been the UNCITRAL claim brought against the state by US tobacco company Philip Morris, under the terms of the Australia-Hong Kong BIT, for losses 'potentially amounting to billions of dollars' as a result of Australia's decision to require all tobacco products to be sold in plain packaging from December 2012 onwards.[41] Under threat of challenges by companies such as Vodafone (UK), Telenor (Norway) and Sistema (Russia), India has also reportedly been trying to remove investor-state dispute settlement provisions from existing and future treaties alike.[42]

A number of other governments have embarked on reviews of their existing BITs, including the Czech Republic and Argentina. In July 2009, South Africa embarked on a review of all BITs it had entered into since 1994. The position paper drafted by the government's Department of Trade and Industry to launch the review argued that the introduction of investor-state dispute settlement had not been to the benefit of the host state:[43]

Investors have become aware of the attractive *status quo* under the global investment regime – literally hundreds of long-ignored investment treaties offer investors access to an investor-state dispute settlement mechanism, allowing them to take their disputes directly to international arbitration – leapfrogging domestic legal systems (and thus, any safeguards designed to protect important public goods). Some investors are using bilateral investment treaties to challenge treatment of foreign investments in various sensitive areas, including water and sewerage provision, oil and gas exploitation and mining concessions. Major law firms are using BITs as the tool of choice for challenging host state regulation of public services.

The South African government accepted most of the review's recommendations, including its concerns over investor-state dispute settlement, and concluded that all the country's BITs should be revisited 'with a view to termination' or possible renegotiation on the basis of a new model to be developed in future years.[44]

The growing rejection of investor-state dispute settlement is consonant with states' increasing confidence in re-establishing control over foreign investors by means of new regulations. In 2000, fully 98 per cent of all investment policy measures introduced at the national level served to liberalise the investment regime in host countries, while just 2 per cent introduced new regulations or restrictions on foreign investors. In 2010, while the balance still favoured liberalisation, 32 per cent of the investment policy measures introduced new regulations on inward investment – the culmination of a trend of rebalancing seen throughout the first decade of the 2000s. This rebalancing in favour of regulation was most apparent in the extractive industries, where 93 per cent of the national regulatory changes introduced in 2010 placed new restrictions on foreign investors, including the introduction of performance requirements and new tax regimes, and the renegotiation of contracts.[45] This resurgence in natural resource sovereignty extends also to the agricultural sector, where 62 per cent of regulatory changes introduced during 2010 were restrictive, and 38 per cent liberalising. For its part, business has responded by calling on the G20 to create an international framework agreement on investment that would guarantee transnational capital open access and protection in its cross-border activities, including the permanent right to investor-state dispute settlement. Despite the fact that previous attempts to introduce an investment agreement to the WTO's agenda resulted in the collapse of the Doha Round, the B20 business lobby still identifies the WTO as its preferred forum for international rules and standards on investment.[46]

The past 40 years of neoliberal globalisation have seen a massive transfer of power to transnational capital, the consequences of which are now being played out in varying scenarios across the world. It is only in the most recent years, and particularly in the context of the economic crisis, that the full scale of this transformation of the global political economy has been appreciated, and it is only now that the system is being subjected to reconsideration in national policy contexts. There have, however, been previous attempts to hold corporations accountable for the negative impacts of their activities, at both the national and international levels, and business organisations have fought hard against any such restrictions on their power. The next chapter explores how capital has used the banner of corporate social responsibility to defend the freedoms it has won over the past 40 years of neoliberal globalisation, and to roll back still further the frontiers of the state.

4

The CSR Delusion

During the first week of May each year, several hundred corporate executives from around the world gather in London for the annual Responsible Business Summit. According to its organisers, the summit offers participants a chance to discuss the latest developments in corporate responsibility and sustainability, and to build career-enhancing relationships with acknowledged leaders in the field.[1] Responsible Business Summits of recent years have brought together high ranking executives from companies such as Coca-Cola, McDonald's, BAE Systems, Lockheed Martin, British American Tobacco, Shell, BP, RBS, Barclays, Tesco, Nestlé, Rio Tinto, Pfizer and GlaxoSmithKline. The casual observer, mindful of the scandals that have engulfed such companies, could be forgiven for wondering what the guest list at an Irresponsible Business Summit would look like.

It is easy to ridicule the Looking Glass world of 'responsible' business, and the claims that companies concoct in their desire to gloss over their most unethical practices with a veneer of responsibility. From its earliest days, the public relations industry has promised to deliver business the magic of 'reputation management' through the judicious use of advertising, sponsorship and philanthropic giving – with a view not only to building legitimacy and neutralising opposition in society at large, but also to establishing brand loyalty and overcoming employee demoralisation within companies themselves. As the communications revolution has made it increasingly simple to source details of corporate malfeasance from all corners of the world, and to publish those details just as widely, the threat of reputational risk has loomed ever larger in corporate eyes. The inaugural issue of the magazine *Ethical Corporation* – published by the company which runs the annual Responsible Business Summit and subtitled 'the business case for corporate responsibility' – featured on its cover a photograph of masked protesters wreathed in tear gas at the 2001 anti-G8 protests in Genoa, and the question: 'Would you like this to happen outside your HQ?'[2]

Yet there is a more serious purpose to the promotion of transnational corporations (TNCs) as responsible global citizens sharing a common agenda with other societal groups. As corporate power has grown exponentially over the past four decades, a number of attempts have been made to address the imbalance between capital and society, at national and international levels alike. Business has successfully fought off these attempts to restrict its power, and corporate social responsibility (CSR) has been its weapon of choice. In the process, CSR has not only grown into an industry in its own right but has increasingly come to define the terms of the relationship between TNCs and other societal groups, and eventually to redefine the relationship between capital and the state itself. As this chapter will demonstrate, for all its claims to be channelling the power of business in pursuit of humanity's common goals, CSR has successfully undermined the very cause it purports to serve.[3]

The single most important characteristic of all CSR initiatives is that they are voluntary undertakings on the part of the companies concerned; indeed, CSR is commonly defined by reference to its voluntary nature.[4] By way of an example, the European Commission's 2006 policy document on making the EU a 'pole of excellence' on CSR opens with the statement: 'Corporate social responsibility (CSR) is a concept whereby companies integrate social and environmental concerns in their business operations and in their interaction with their stakeholders on a voluntary basis.'[5] It is also standard practice to distinguish between the voluntarism of CSR, on the one hand, and binding, non-voluntary regulation that seeks to hold corporations to account for their activities, on the other. For most critical commentators, the essence of CSR lies in the continuing power of capital to set the terms of its own behaviour rather than succumb to external control. From our current vantage point, moreover, the historical development of CSR can be seen as a strategic response on the part of capital to the threat of external regulation. As this chapter demonstrates, CSR has developed over the past 40 years as the chosen mechanism to forestall any efforts at binding regulation of TNCs. It is incorrect, therefore, to portray CSR as a weaker variant of corporate accountability, lacking the coercive power of external regulation but essentially to be welcomed as working towards the same ends. Instead, CSR exists in direct opposition to the aims of corporate accountability, reinforcing corporate power against those who would bring it back into balance with other elements in society. As such, CSR plays an integral part in sustaining the programme of neoliberal globalisation itself.[6]

Yet CSR is more than just a defensive strategy to neutralise the threat of external regulation and to safeguard the gains won by capital in the process of corporate globalisation. As shown in its most recent historical development, CSR is itself a mechanism for expanding the reach of capital and appropriating key roles of the state as lead economic agent and adjudicator of power relations. Through CSR, capital has been able to rebrand itself first as a partner in the struggle for sustainable development and then as the principal provider of public goods, entailing the structural transformation of the economy and the privatisation of the public sphere to the detriment of democracy and accountability. CSR in its latest formulation has thus become an offensive strategy through which to roll back the frontiers of the state. Nor should it be assumed that national governments have been unwilling victims in this process. A defining characteristic of globalisation in the modern era has been state complicity in augmenting the power of capital, which has included assiduous government promotion of CSR as the alternative to binding regulation by national or international authorities. This in turn has become an indicator of the bad faith of governments towards their own peoples. As this chapter shows, not only has the state abdicated its responsibility for constraining corporate power; it has freely conferred its blessing upon capital as heir apparent of its own key functions.

The UN Code

The first concerted attempt to address the rising power of transnational capital in the modern era came with the initiative to draft a UN Code of Conduct on Transnational Corporations in the 1970s. This was a period when countries of the global South were seeking to redress centuries of colonial exploitation and post-colonial dependency by means of a New International Economic Order, the programme for which was formulated at the summit of the Non-Aligned Movement in September 1973 and adopted by the UN General Assembly in May 1974. The countries of the industrialised North, by contrast, faced turmoil both nationally and internationally as levels of profitability declined, the post-war social contract unravelled and rising oil prices brought to an abrupt end the so-called Golden Age of capitalism.[7]

The immediate impetus for a Code came as a raft of new corporate scandals demonstrated the urgent need for action to curb the power of transnational capital.[8] Hearings before the US Senate's Subcommittee on Multinational Corporations (known as the Church Committee after its chairperson, Senator Frank Church) had lifted the veil on the nefarious activities of US companies overseas, while investigations of the US Securities and Exchange Commission had exposed bribery and corruption in the foreign operations of over 400 corporations, including household names such as Exxon, Gulf Oil, Lockheed and Northrop.[9] Chief among these corporate scandals was the active involvement of US companies in the CIA's covert actions to prevent the election of Salvador Allende to the presidency of Chile and, once he had been elected, to overthrow him. Details of corporate complicity in the CIA campaign came out in the Church Committee's 1973 hearings, the conclusions of which were published following Allende's death in the CIA-backed coup that led to the brutal 17-year dictatorship of General Pinochet.[10] International opinion was inflamed by revelations that US companies such as International Telephone and Telegraph (ITT) had funded political and media campaigns against Allende over a ten year period, coordinating their actions with the CIA in much the same way as executives of the United Fruit Company (now Chiquita) had done in the US-backed coup which ousted Guatemala's democratically elected president Jacobo Arbenz 20 years earlier.[11] Indeed, it was shortly after Allende's speech to the UN condemning ITT's actions that he was killed.

In 1974, the UN Economic and Social Council approved the establishment of an intergovernmental Commission on Transnational Corporations composed of 48 experts from all continents, which was to serve as the central forum within the UN system for dealing with issues related to TNCs. A research and information centre was also established to assist the Commission, which came into operation the following year as the UN Centre on Transnational Corporations. Both bodies were entrusted with the elaboration of a code of conduct for

TNCs as a high priority on their respective agendas, in light of the recent revelations of corporate malpractice across the world.

Battle lines were drawn from the outset over the legal status of any code that might come out of the UN negotiations. Given that the vast majority of TNCs were based in the industrialised North, Organisation for Economic Cooperation and Development (OECD) governments represented the views of capital in the debate. From the very first session of the Commission, held in New York in March 1975, European and US representatives sought to downgrade any future code to a set of voluntary guidelines, rather than the binding instrument demanded by governments of the global South. In so doing, they represented the views of the corporate executives who had already spoken out against any binding code during the preliminary hearings held in New York and Geneva during 1973, including the president of the International Chamber of Commerce (ICC), Renato Lombardi, and representatives of companies such as Fiat, Pfizer, Siemens, Rio Tinto, Unilever, IBM, Exxon and the Royal Dutch Petroleum Company (now Shell).[12]

Similarly, as the debate progressed over the coming years, the two sides sought to include radically different elements in the Code. Representatives from the global South argued for positive provisions whereby foreign companies might contribute to development in host countries, such as local equity partnerships, technology transfer, training and employment of nationals at all levels of management, assistance with balance of payments problems, and respect for human rights and fundamental freedoms. Equally, the Code should restrict illicit activities by TNCs such as transfer pricing, tax avoidance, corrupt or anti-competitive business practices, and any interference in the internal affairs of the host country. Representatives from the North, on the other hand, argued for provisions in the Code which would provide greater powers and access for foreign companies in the markets of host countries, including 'national treatment' to place them on an equal footing with domestic firms, plus freedom from restrictions on the repatriation of capital. On the central issue of nationalisation or expropriation of the assets of TNCs, these governments argued that host countries should be required to cede sovereignty over their right to determine the compensation due to foreign firms.

This clash of interests divided participants well into the 1980s. The special session of the UN Commission convened in June 1984 with the aim of finalising work on the Code was unable to bridge differences on a wide range of issues, including the right of states to sovereignty over their natural resources (to which OECD governments objected), the contribution to be made by TNCs to the host country's balance of payments (to which OECD governments also objected), and the principle of national treatment (which OECD governments demanded for their companies overseas). The special session was reconvened in June 1985 and still hoped to make a breakthrough on key issues, but was unable to reconcile what were by now entrenched positions on a large number of points.[13] Despite the increasingly conciliatory language in which the Code was redrafted, the countries of the North eventually withdrew support for it altogether. The initiative was finally laid to rest at the UN General Assembly in September 1992 with the conclusion that no consensus was possible on the Code and that a 'fresh approach' was required to the issue of foreign investment. The UN Centre on Transnational Corporations was abolished – offered up as a 'sacrificial lamb' to appease US antagonism, according to its official historians.[14] The Commission on Transnational Corporations was submerged under the UN Trade and Development Board.

The Rise of Voluntarism

From the outset, capital's strategic response to the threat of binding rules was to promote voluntary codes of conduct as the alternative to regulation. The ICC had already adopted its own Guidelines for International Investment in 1972, with voluntary recommendations directed towards TNCs as well as host governments. However, it was the OECD that took the lead role in establishing voluntarism as the norm when it set up its own Committee on International Investment and Multinational Enterprises in January 1975, drawing up a set of voluntary guidelines that would undermine and eventually neutralise the draft UN Code.

The OECD Guidelines for Multinational Enterprises were first adopted in 1976 and have since been revised and updated several times, most recently in 2011.[15] While they have been cited as the most efficient example of government-endorsed 'soft law' on TNCs, it is commonly recognised that they have done little to influence corporate behaviour, and nothing to curb corporate power.[16] They have, however, been immensely successful in establishing the principle of voluntarism as the dominant model at the international level, spawning numerous codes of conduct for specific sectors as well as an industry of market-based incentives and inducements to cajole TNCs into being more responsible global citizens.[17] In this normative exercise, the OECD Guidelines were supported by other international treaties and codes of conduct that operate on a non-binding basis. In 1977, the member states of the International Labour Organisation (ILO) adopted its Tripartite Declaration of Principles concerning Multinational Enterprises and Social Policy, based on previously existing ILO conventions and recommendations on issues such as job creation, non-discrimination, training, safety regulation, freedom of association, collective bargaining and dispute settlement mechanisms. In 1981, the World Health Assembly adopted the International Code of Marketing of Breast-Milk Substitutes, designed to restrict the activities of TNCs promoting baby milk formula and other substitutes to breastfeeding, particularly in the countries of the global South.[18] Important though these developments were in their own fields, the absence of any international enforcement mechanisms to substantiate them ensured the dominance of the voluntarist paradigm over attempts to hold capital accountable for its activities around the world.

Voluntarism's high water mark came with the UN Conference on Environment and Development (UNCED) – more commonly known as the Earth Summit – held in Rio de Janeiro in June 1992. Just as any last hopes of a binding UN Code were being extinguished, the Earth Summit affirmed the principle of voluntary self-regulation as the dominant model in place of corporate accountability. The Agenda 21 programme of action adopted at the summit was conspicuously silent on the threats posed by TNCs to environmental and developmental sustainability, instead waxing lyrical on the 'crucial role' played by business and industry in social and economic development. In a wholesale abdication of responsibility, Agenda 21 suggested only that TNCs 'should be encouraged' to establish their own corporate policies on sustainable development. On the central issue of corporate accountability, the programme of action stated:

> Business and industry, including transnational corporations,
> should ensure responsible and ethical management of products and

processes from the point of view of health, safety and environmental aspects. Towards this end, business and industry should increase self-regulation, guided by appropriate codes, charters and initiatives integrated into all elements of business planning and decision-making, and fostering openness and dialogue with employees and the public.

UN agencies, by contrast, were downgraded to a supporting role providing 'mechanisms for business and industry inputs, policy and strategy formulation processes, to ensure that environmental aspects are strengthened in foreign investment'.[19]

The Agenda 21 programme of action also committed governments, TNCs and civil society to establishing 'partnerships' in the common pursuit of sustainable development, initiating a model that would be brought to fruition at the World Summit on Sustainable Development (WSSD) in Johannesburg ten years later. To promote the involvement of a broad spectrum of stakeholders, section III of the programme of action listed the 'major groups' who would have to be involved in decision making on an equal footing, including business. Leaving aside the obvious political issues concerning which social groupings might be included in stakeholder engagement (and the concomitant exclusion of grassroots social movements and local communities),[20] the central dynamic of Agenda 21 was that people's rights would thereafter be downgraded from being inalienable entitlements to becoming dependent on negotiation with other actors, and conditional upon their stake (or lack of it) in the activities of a corporation.[21]

Corporate pressure played a critical role in steering the Earth Summit away from accountability and towards voluntary mechanisms. Lobby groups such as the ICC (which had launched its own voluntary Business Charter for Sustainable Development in 1991) and the Business Council for Sustainable Development were granted unparalleled access to the innermost core of the UNCED process – indeed, the Business Council for Sustainable Development had been set up by Swiss billionaire Stephan Schmidheiny at the request of the UNCED chairperson, Canadian businessman Maurice Strong, for the express purpose of influencing the Earth Summit's outcomes.[22] With assistance from public relations consultancy Burston-Marsteller, the Business Council for Sustainable Development was able to position itself as the key player directing the Summit's outcomes, and Schmidheiny was appointed as Strong's only special adviser. It is unsurprising, under such circumstances, that the Agenda 21 programme of action closely mirrored the recommendations for self-regulation set out in the Business Council for Sustainable Development book *Changing Course* that was launched by Schmidheiny just prior to the start of the Earth Summit.[23]

The years following the Earth Summit saw an explosion of voluntary initiatives at the international level, including the Caux Round Table Principles for Business (1994); Sustainable Forestry Initiative (1994); ISO 14001 standard (1996); ICC Rules of Conduct to Combat Extortion and Bribery (1996); Global Reporting Initiative (1997); Ethical Trading Initiative (1998); Fair Labor Association (1999); Global Mining Initiative (1999); Global Sullivan Principles (1999); SA8000 certification (1999); SIGMA Project (1999); AA1000 Framework Standard (1999); Worldwide Responsible Accredited Production (2000); Voluntary Principles on Security and Human Rights (2000); International Council on Mining and Metals (2001); Global Corporate Citizenship (2002); Extractive Industries Transparency Initiative (2002); International Council of Toy Industries Code (2002); Kimberley Process (2002); Equator Principles (2003); Business Social Compliance Initiative (2003); Electronic Industry Code of Conduct (2004) and many more. Alongside these, a host of national and regional codes were also instituted, and large numbers of individual industry and company codes.[24] Yet the extent of any genuine change arising out of these initiatives was thrown into question by a number of influential UN studies. Peter Utting of the UN Research Institute for Social Development (UNRISD) characterised any shift in corporate behaviour following the Earth Summit as a 'minimalist' response involving 'imagery, public relations and relatively minor adjustments in management systems and practices, as opposed to significant changes in the social and environmental impact of a company's activities'. Utting concluded that there was 'a considerable mismatch between rhetoric and reality' when it came to the business community's claims to have changed direction as a result of voluntary codes of conduct, and warned non-governmental organisations (NGOs) against colluding in any false claims as to the success of sustainable development partnerships between business and civil society.[25] Other UNRISD studies concluded that the main incentive for TNCs to introduce voluntary codes had been 'the protection of brand value' rather than any genuine commitment to change, and that the companies in question could justifiably be accused of 'bad faith'.[26]

A Global Compact

Despite mounting evidence of the ineffectiveness of voluntarism in achieving any meaningful change, the paradigm's dominance was assured by means of two UN initiatives championed by UN Secretary-General Kofi Annan at the beginning of the new millennium: the Global Compact, launched in 2000, and the WSSD held in Johannesburg in 2002. Annan had trailed the Global Compact in his speech to business leaders at the World Economic Forum in 1999, in which he denounced attempts by what he termed 'various interest groups' to preserve standards in the fields of human rights, labour and environmental protection by means of 'restrictions' on trade and investment. Instead of any such regulatory approach, the notoriously pro-corporate Annan called on representatives of the transnational business community to join him in a crusade to defend the 'open global market' against its detractors by voluntarily adopting certain standards in their own activities worldwide.[27] Under the direction of Professor John Ruggie, whom Annan had appointed UN Assistant Secretary-General for Strategic Planning, and Georg Kell, who was to become Executive Director of the Global Compact, these standards were subsequently developed into the Ten Principles to which all companies seeking to join the Compact are required to commit themselves.[28]

The Global Compact was widely derided from the start for its absence of meaningful content and enforcement mechanisms, even in comparison with other voluntary initiatives.[29] While the OECD, for example, had established a network of national contact points through which complaints could be brought relating to violations of their Guidelines, the Global Compact had no mechanism for redress or censure. Members were simply required to send a letter to the UN Secretary-General affirming their commitment to the Ten Principles, to pay an annual membership fee and to submit a regular 'communication on progress' reaffirming the company's continuing support for the Ten Principles and outlining steps taken towards them. Even the internal review conducted by the UN's Joint Inspection Unit in 2010 slated the Compact in the strongest terms for its 'lack of effective screening and monitoring of engagement of participants', noting that the risk of allowing companies to use the UN brand without conforming to its principles was 'unmitigated'.[30] Such lenient membership requirements, combined with the obvious legitimacy gains of being able to associate one's brand with the UN, have made the Global Compact into the world's largest CSR initiative, boasting over 6,000 corporate signatories from more than 135 countries. The principal architects of the Compact have responded to criticism of its regulatory weakness by arguing that it had never sought to be a substitute for government action, but that it should be understood as a 'social learning network' or 'value-based platform designed to promote institutional learning'.[31] Yet the Global Compact is regularly cited by business and governments alike as an example of why binding regulation is unnecessary, thus ensuring that it continues to play a normative role in the rejection of corporate accountability as an alternative model.

Not only did the Global Compact commit the UN and its member agencies to the voluntarist paradigm. It also took forward the concept of 'partnership' between civil society and business that had been introduced at the Earth Summit in 1992. In particular, Annan offered the assistance of the United Nations in helping the world's most notorious corporate wrongdoers to establish dialogue with their critics as a means to neutralising the threat posed by civil society to their reputations. This contribution to corporate brand management was enhanced through the participation of several prominent international NGOs such as Amnesty International, Human Rights Watch, Oxfam, Save the Children and the WWF as civil society partners in the Global Compact, adding legitimacy both to the corporate participants and to the initiative itself.[32]

The WSSD in 2002 gave concrete expression to this concept of partnership, as the UN called on business to come forward with proposals for voluntary initiatives to address the most pressing challenges facing the world in the twenty-first century. These partnerships were afforded the status of 'Type 2' summit outcomes, to distinguish them from inter-governmental commitments negotiated between states, which were dubbed 'Type 1' outcomes for the purposes of the WSSD. Over 200 Type 2 partnerships were launched at the summit with great fanfare, and many more have been initiated since.[33] For those of us who were present, the WSSD had the surreal appearance of a trade fair in which corporations competed for advertising space rather than any attempt to address the serious problems of sustainable development – indeed, the annual follow-up sessions of the Commission on Sustainable Development in New York have actually introduced a Partnerships Fair as part of their official programme each year.

As with the Earth Summit ten years before, the business community had prepared for the WSSD by establishing a dedicated lobby group to see off any efforts to constrain corporate power. Business Action for Sustainable Development (BASD) was created especially for the summit as a joint initiative of the ICC and the World Business Council for Sustainable Development, and chaired by Sir Mark Moody-Stuart, formerly Managing Director of Shell and a member of the UN Secretary-General's Advisory Council for the Global Compact since 2001. BASD enjoyed unparalleled access to the innermost workings of the summit, and ensured that any reference to corporate accountability was restricted to just one fleeting mention in the WSSD Plan of Implementation, which went nowhere. In contrast to condemnation from all civil society organisations (and a number of governments), BASD welcomed the summit's final Plan of Implementation as 'a framework for entrepreneurial opportunities, long-term planning and partnership possibilities'.[34]

UN agencies were themselves encouraged to enter into partnerships with business both before and after the WSSD, and many did so. The United Nations Children's Fund (UNICEF) was one of the most enthusiastic advocates of the approach, establishing over 1,000 partnerships with a range of companies and bringing in a total of $142 million from the corporate sector as a result.[35] Indeed, the uncritical zeal with which UNICEF embraced the concept of partnership soon threatened to undermine its own credibility: there was outrage from public health professionals when UNICEF rebranded its annual celebration of child rights as 'McDonald's World Children's Day' to mark its partnership with the fast food multinational.[36] Other UN agencies such as the World Health Organisation (WHO), UN Development Programme (UNDP), UN Environment Programme (UNEP) and UN Commission on Sustainable Development also entered into hundreds of business partnerships. Yet while these alliances may have raised extra funds for the agencies concerned, it is far from clear that they were of net benefit to the cause of sustainable development. One major study published jointly by the South Centre and UNRISD concluded not only that UN partnerships with business 'cannot make a significant contribution to development' but that 'they may actually be counterproductive', inasmuch as they legitimise the interests of TNCs in the global economy without requiring any change in behaviour or introducing complementary measures to restrict corporate power.[37] Despite this reality check, the language of partnership came to characterise international discourse on the role of business in the pursuit of sustainable development, with subsequent ventures reinforcing it as the dominant paradigm. Indeed, an entire industry soon sprang up to service the concept of partnership in its own right, as the Partnering Initiative set up by the International Business Leaders Forum in turn established a training programme and accreditation scheme for 'partnership brokers', a Partnering Toolbook to share best practice between them, and an international Partnership Brokers Association to champion their cause.

While partnerships with business may offer little to advance public policy objectives, they provide TNCs with unique opportunities to penetrate markets that would otherwise be closed to them. New market access through public-private partnerships is more important to capital in the long term than any legitimacy offered by collaboration with UN agencies or NGOs, as it allows for the structural transformation of whole economies in favour of the private sector. This privatisation of the public sphere is perhaps the greatest single achievement of the CSR industry in the twenty-first century. Not only has the reputation of transnational capital been detoxified in respect of the threat it was once seen to pose to human rights and sustainable development; it is now portrayed as having taken over from the state as lead provider of public goods. In this way, as detailed at the end of this chapter, CSR has played its own role in deepening corporate globalisation in the modern era.

The UN Norms

While the Global Compact and other such initiatives set the seal on an era of 'rampant voluntarism',[38] a raft of high profile corporate scandals during the 1990s – including Shell's operations in the Niger Delta, BP in Colombia, and the court case of the Union Carbide disaster in Bhopal – ensured that the call for regulation of TNCs was also gathering new momentum. A working group was formed in 1998 under the UN Sub-Commission on the Promotion and Protection of Human Rights – a group of independent human rights experts set up to inform the work of the intergovernmental UN Commission on Human Rights – to examine the activities of TNCs and to develop a set of instruments relating to the human rights responsibilities of business. In August 2003, the Sub-Commission unanimously adopted its final Norms on the Responsibilities of Transnational Corporations and Other Business Enterprises with Regard to Human Rights, and submitted them to the UN Commission on Human Rights for consideration and adoption in their turn.[39]

The Norms adopted by the Sub-Commission represented the first concerted attempt since the demise of the draft UN Code to redress the imbalance of power between transnational capital and other economic forces.[40] While the Norms contained none of the positive conditions included in the earlier draft Code to ensure that foreign investment would contribute to the development of the host economy, they did commit TNCs and other business enterprises to respect for national sovereignty. More particularly, the focus of the Norms was on corporate respect for human rights, including workers' rights – not only in the activities of the companies themselves but also within their sphere of influence. This last point was important in establishing accountability for human rights violations throughout the supply chains that typically serve businesses in the global economy, as well as seeking to pierce the 'corporate veil' behind which parent companies are able to disavow liability for the human rights abuses of their subsidiaries.[41]

Business groups reacted swiftly to the threat posed by the UN Norms to their impunity. Already in January 2001, the ICC had written to Mary Robinson, UN High Commissioner for Human Rights, voicing its concern over the Norms. The International Organisation of Employers (IOE) had called for the drafting of the Norms to be abandoned on the grounds that they conflicted with the voluntary approach exemplified by the Global Compact, and the United States Council for International Business (USCIB) weighed in with similar criticism.[42] In the lead-up to the April 2004 session at which the UN

Commission on Human Rights would first consider the Norms, the ICC joined forces with the IOE to submit a number of stronger statements attacking the UN Sub-Commission as a body, condemning the Norms it had adopted and calling on the Commission to reject them unequivocally. The joint statement submitted by the ICC and IOE in March 2004 claimed that the Norms 'will undermine the rights and legitimate interests of private businesses, and, as a consequence, will impede the realization of every society's right to development', and called on the Commission to make a public statement clarifying that the Norms could not be referred to as 'UN Norms' and that they had no legal authority.[43] The Multinationals Group of the ICC's UK section sent Commission members a legal opinion damning the Norms as 'extremely unsatisfactory from a legal viewpoint', while the Confederation of British Industry (CBI) attacked the Norms as 'ill-judged and unnecessary'.[44] The USCIB reassured its members that it was working with the US Department of State on a strategy to 'deal with' the Norms at the Commission's April 2004 meeting.[45]

The April 2004 meeting of the UN Commission did indeed deal with the Norms, declaring that they had not been requested by the Commission, that they had no legal standing, and that the Sub-Commission should not engage in any monitoring function in respect of the Norms, as it had planned to do. This decision, which was adopted at the request of the UK government on behalf of twelve other countries, faithfully acceded to each of the demands that had been put forward by the ICC and IOE. Instead of adopting the Norms as the Sub-Commission had recommended, the Commission asked the Office of the UN High Commissioner for Human Rights to compile a new report on existing standards relating to the human rights responsibilities of business, based on consultation with 'all relevant stakeholders'.[46] That process of consultation brought a renewed effort from industry lobby groups to kill off the Norms. In addition to fresh submissions from the ICC, IOE, USCIB and CBI, new criticism came in from the Federation of German Industry, Confederation of German Employers' Associations and a number of individual companies, which contrasted the Norms unfavourably with the many voluntary initiatives which they had introduced over the years. Several government submissions similarly backed the voluntary approach, with the USA and Australia openly opposing any moves to take the Norms further. On the other side, a number of civil society groups submitted their own responses to the consultation in an attempt to save the Norms.[47]

The 2005 session of the UN Commission on Human Rights debated the report, with the US and Australian governments again representing the position of the corporate lobby groups in opposition to any binding accountability of business at the international level. The Commission duly adopted a resolution requesting UN Secretary-General Kofi Annan to appoint a Special Representative for business and human rights with the aim of compiling a further report. Yet the resolution conspicuously failed to mention the Norms, and when Professor John Ruggie was appointed as the Special Representative in July 2005, they would swiftly be consigned to history. In his first interim report, published in February 2006, Ruggie declared that the Norms had become 'a distraction rather than a basis for moving the Special Representative's mandate forward'. Speaking at a CSR forum later that same year, Ruggie declared that the initiative to produce the Norms had created 'a train wreck' on the grounds that 'much of the business community was vehemently opposed to it', and he pronounced the Norms 'dead'.[48] This implication that corporate acquiescence would be a necessary precondition for the success of any future initiative raised serious concerns as to whether Ruggie would bring sufficient rigour or independence to the position of Special Representative, a question already raised in relation to his lead role in the development of the notoriously weak Global Compact, described above.[49]

The UN Framework and Guiding Principles

Ruggie's own work as Special Representative of the UN Secretary-General was divided into three phases. The first of these, lasting two years from his appointment in 2005, was in effect a fact-finding mission, establishing patterns of corporate complicity in human rights abuses and mapping the existing legal and other frameworks for addressing such abuses. While Ruggie maintained an uncritical faith in the beneficial potential of markets, the evidence presented to him of the power imbalance in favour of capital was undeniable. In the 2007 report in which he presented the findings of this first phase to the UN Human Rights Council, Ruggie pointed to the 'fundamental institutional misalignment' between capital and society that had been created as a consequence of the international community's reliance on voluntary CSR initiatives, and the 'permissive environment' resulting from this misalignment that allowed corporations to commit crimes or other blameworthy acts with impunity.[50]

The second phase of Ruggie's mandate was to make recommendations to the Human Rights Council based on his findings. In his 2008 report, Ruggie recommended adoption of a framework which would differentiate between the state's established duty to *protect* human rights and the recognised duty of business to *respect* human rights – the latter already referenced in voluntary instruments such as the OECD Guidelines for Multinational Enterprises and the Global Compact. The third principle underlying Ruggie's recommendation concerned the need for adequate redress mechanisms (both judicial and non-judicial) to allow *remedy* in cases of corporate human rights abuse. This three-part 'Protect, Respect and Remedy' framework was formally welcomed by the UN Human Rights Council at its June 2008 session, and Ruggie's mandate was extended by a further three years so that he could elaborate further on how the framework might be operationalised.[51]

This third phase of Ruggie's work was arguably the most critical, since it was expected to provide the concrete recommendations on how to instantiate what was now called the UN 'Protect, Respect and Remedy' Framework. Yet the Guiding Principles that constituted the substance of Ruggie's final report in 2011 did not, by his own admission, create any obligations on business to respect human rights.[52] To begin with, the section on corporate responsibility was cast entirely in the language of 'best endeavour' rather than obligation, whereby business enterprises 'should' respect human rights (rather than the binding terminology of 'shall' or 'must'). This non-binding language had been a central demand of the business lobbies in their joint response to Ruggie's earlier draft guidelines, which had been circulated for consultation in November 2010.[53] On the key issue of whether the corporate responsibility to respect human rights would also encompass a company's relationships with suppliers and other parties, the draft guidelines circulated in November 2010 had affirmed that the responsibility 'applies across a business enterprise's activities and through its relationships with third parties associated with those activities'. Yet the final version of the guidelines was watered down –

again, on the express demand of the business lobby – so that companies would be required only to 'seek to prevent or mitigate adverse human rights impacts that are directly linked to their operations, products or services by their business operations'. This marked a further step backwards.

Most significantly, given that they were supposed to provide for concrete implementation of the UN 'Protect, Respect and Remedy' Framework, the Guiding Principles suggested no mechanism of enforcement that would have taken forward that task. Endorsing the Guiding Principles in June 2011, the UN Human Rights Council did no more than establish a working group of five experts, assisted by an annual consultative forum, to promote and disseminate the Guiding Principles and to share best practice on their implementation. Business groups expressed their satisfaction that there had been no attempt to create new obligations on them or to assign legal liability to corporations for human rights abuses.[54] Human rights organisations denounced the failure to do so as an opportunity squandered, given the significant labour that had been expended by all parties during the six years of Ruggie's mandate.[55]

Responsible Competitiveness

In its earliest formulations, CSR offered companies an opportunity to manage reputational risk while fighting off the threat of external regulation, deflecting calls for corporate accountability so that any change would be restricted to marginal modifications rather than genuine shifts in the balance of power. CSR subsequently developed to a stage where TNCs felt able to present themselves as honest partners with government and civil society in the quest for sustainable development: no longer part of the problem but part of the solution. In its final apotheosis, CSR has allowed capital to take over the role of lead agent with primary responsibility for the delivery of public goods and development goals, thereby gaining access to formerly closed markets, resources and powers. At the same time, the pursuit of CSR has been reconceptualised within the corporate world as an integral part of a company's competitiveness rather than an extraneous activity, ostensibly reconciling what had previously been assumed to be contradictory imperatives of capital accumulation and social responsibility. This double shift in the division of labour between the public and private sectors represents the last development of CSR, and its most decisive contribution to the neoliberal capitalist programme to date.[56]

The clearest example of capital's expansion into fields previously considered to be unsuitable for private sector involvement has come in the mass privatisation of state-owned enterprises and public services over the past 30 years. In the core countries of the capitalist world system, this process was the result of the sharp neoliberal turn of the 1980s onwards, beginning with the UK under Margaret Thatcher and the USA under Ronald Reagan.[57] In the global South, the transformation was effected under pressure from bilateral aid donors and international financial institutions such as the World Bank and IMF, which made the implementation of extensive privatisation programmes a condition of their continuing loans and debt relief. This global transfer of power and resources to the private sector has gone hand in hand with a sustained ideological assault on the ability of the state to provide the structures necessary for growth, development or poverty eradication. In most circumstances, this contention has been supported by claims as to the greater efficiency of the private sector in delivering public goods – claims which have long been shown to be fallacious, even in research by the World Bank and IMF themselves.[58] Where the debate has taken place within the donor-driven political economy of international development, it has also incorporated the 'good governance' agenda which confers special privileges on transnational capital in view of the supposed inability of Southern governments to abide by globally accepted standards of transparency or probity. As Dinah Rajak notes in her rich ethnography of CSR and global corporate citizenship, persistent attacks by donors and NGOs on official corruption in the global South result in the usurping of state powers by business being represented as a 'virtuous act stepping into the vacuum left by a government's moral abdication of responsibility'. If governments are perpetually unwilling or unable to deliver for their people, according to the dominant narrative, TNCs have a 'hegemonic duty of care' which requires them to take over the task.[59]

This argument, with its echoes of Kipling's 'white man's burden', has acquired particular significance in the context of the international community's assumed responsibility for achieving the Millennium

Development Goals (MDGs) agreed by government leaders in the UN Millennium Declaration of 2000. In keeping with the spirit of the time, the declaration spoke of giving 'greater opportunities to the private sector' to contribute to the shared programme of poverty reduction encapsulated in the MDGs, a contribution that would be made primarily by means of CSR initiatives and public-private partnerships. Now, as argued in the B20 business lobby's report to the G20 summit in 2011, the private sector is considered crucial to delivering the MDGs not so much through its marginal CSR commitments but as a result of the core business activities it undertakes on its own behalf – as in the private sector's 'central role in agri-food production systems', which will be able to meet the MDGs' hunger target if only capital is granted the freedom to operate without restriction or interference.[60] When properly understood, according to this narrative, the private sector and the free market are the essential guarantors of public goods. Milton Friedman, who famously argued that business should not be distracted by any supposed responsibility to society, need never have worried.[61]

From the corporate perspective, too, CSR has been redefined as a central business opportunity rather than as a restriction on, or adjunct to, a company's core operations. The mantra of 'responsible competitiveness' was invented to alert TNCs to the potential of embracing markets that could be considered to offer social or ecological externalities, with headline attractions such as the prospective $500 billion market in low carbon technologies, or the $40 billion to be secured by guaranteeing women equal access to health, education and employment in the Asia/Pacific region alone.[62] At its most crude, the integration of CSR into a company's core activities may still manifest itself in the use of social investments to win favours: staff at Chevron Texaco, for instance, admitted that the company had timed its announcement of a $50 million development partnership with USAID and UNDP in Angola in order to coincide with negotiations to renew its stake in the country's most prized oil concession, and a subsequent USAID report confirmed that the company's well-timed pledge had been instrumental in winning it the 20-year extension desired.[63] In its more sophisticated versions, however, the concept of responsible competitiveness envisages companies expanding into new markets on the grounds that they can offer technological solutions to (and profit from) even the most stubborn social or humanitarian challenges.[64] The reinvention of the poorest masses at the 'bottom of the pyramid' as a vast, untapped market of expectant consumers is one of the more bizarre variations on the theme.[65]

Capital's final rehabilitation was confirmed at the UN's Rio+20 Conference on Sustainable Development, held in Rio de Janeiro in June 2012 to mark the twentieth anniversary of the original Earth Summit described earlier in this chapter. Study after study published in the intervening years had pointed to the depth of ecological crisis already in evidence across the world and the urgent need to halt the endless pursuit of capitalist expansion that would drive the planet beyond the point of no return, yet this systemic threat received scarcely a mention at the summit itself. Just as for the WSSD in Johannesburg ten years before, BASD was convened again as 'the voice of business' in the Rio+20 process, bringing together the ICC, World Business Council for Sustainable Development and Global Compact as well as a number of sectoral industry associations. Repeating its WSSD performance, BASD held a dedicated Business Day in Rio on 19 June 2012 which was attended by over 800 participants and concluded with the message that 'business is the primary investor in, and the primary solution provider for, sustainable development'. The official Rio+20 outcome document, 'The Future We Want', confirmed the ancillary role to which the state had been relegated, as it encouraged governments to introduce 'regulatory and policy frameworks that enable business and industry to advance sustainable development initiatives' – especially in the context of progress towards delivering the capitalist 'green economy', which had been one of BASD's priorities in the run-up to the summit.[66] As BASD commented in its final assessment of the conference's conclusions, 'We are gratified that the final Rio+20 outcome document identifies the private sector and inclusive markets as principal parts of any solution for sustainable development.'[67]

The ultimate delusion thus promulgated by CSR is that there is no longer any conflict between capital and the broader interests of society. This overturns a basic understanding that stretches back to Adam Smith himself, who warned at the end of the first book of *The Wealth of Nations* that the interest of those who live by profit is 'always in some respect different from, and even opposite to, that of the public'.[68] If, however, there is now no contradiction between the corporate pursuit of profit and the broader goals of society as a whole, then capital can indeed be entrusted with the lead role in delivering public goods.[69] Much of civil society has been co-opted into this delusion, not only through active involvement in the CSR programmes of business but also in the refusal of many NGOs to join with grassroots movements mobilising against TNCs, privatisations or other acts of dispossession. This collaborationist turn on the part of NGOs – increasingly pronounced in recent years – has contributed to the closing down of critical space, as corporations have been able to point to their partnerships with 'respectable' civil society (especially NGOs from the global North) as a means of marginalising more radical opposition to their operations or to the system as a whole.[70] In this way CSR becomes a mechanism for restricting the parameters of the possible and denying more radical visions of change: 'CSR here ensures that subversive alternatives suffer the fate of utopias – they are dismissed as impossible however attractive we find them.'[71]

Back in the real world, the conflict between capital and other societal groups remains as strong as ever. The three sectors explored in the following chapters – extractives, garments and food – demonstrate the different ways in which the ongoing process of neoliberal globalisation has brought communities into conflict with capital, and the ways in which they have mounted resistance against it. This will in turn reveal those alternatives to capitalism that CSR would dismiss as impossible, but which continue to assert themselves regardless.

5

Extractives:
Dispossession through
Devastation

N o economic sector offers such a stark reminder of the
devastation that capital causes in its relentless pursuit of
profit than the extractive sector. Encompassing oil, gas and
mining in their various forms, the extractive industries are unrivalled
in the intensity of social and environmental devastation they cause to
local communities and regions. The 'resource curse' that has blighted
so many economies which become over-reliant on their natural
wealth endowment is a constant threat, and only the most incautious
commentator would suggest that foreign investment from extractive
transnationals offers host countries unalloyed benefit. Yet at the same
time, few sectors are heralded as being so important for the long-term
prospects of their host economies, if only the involvement of private
capital (and especially foreign capital) can be properly managed. For
the countries of Africa, a continent which still relies on fuels and
mining products for two thirds of its total merchandise exports, the
successful exploitation of strategic natural resources is still seen as
critical to future economic prospects.[1]

The unique threat posed by the extractive industries to host
populations was affirmed by Professor John Ruggie in the early
days of his mandate as UN Special Representative on human rights
and transnational corporations (TNCs). In his first interim report of
February 2006, in which he presented an overview of the 65 cases of

corporate human rights abuse he had examined from 27 countries around the world, Ruggie noted:[2]

> The extractive sector – oil, gas and mining – utterly dominates this sample of reported abuses with two thirds of the total ... The extractive industries also account for most allegations of the worst abuses, up to and including complicity in crimes against humanity. These are typically for acts committed by public and private security forces protecting company assets and property; large-scale corruption; violations of labour rights; and a broad array of abuses in relation to local communities, especially indigenous people ... The extractive sector is unique because no other sector has as enormous and as intrusive a social and environmental footprint.

This identification of the extractive industries' complicity in crimes against humanity and other human rights abuses was confirmed by the United Nations Conference on Trade and Development (UNCTAD) in its *World Investment Report* for 2007. Such abuses have often been committed by private security forces guarding oil, gas and mining installations on behalf of the companies that own them, but UNCTAD also highlighted the issue of corporate complicity when companies rely on state forces to provide security more generally: 'While these forces may be under the control of a host-State entity, TNCs might still be held accountable for their behaviour when they support their actions either by paying their salaries, or providing intelligence or other services such as transportation.'[3] The examples catalogued in this chapter provide numerous examples of such complicity.

Human rights lawyers have developed a hierarchy of three forms of corporate complicity in order to distinguish the different ways in which such companies might be held accountable for violations from which they ultimately derive an advantage. 'Silent complicity' is held to exist where companies fail to speak out against clear patterns of human rights abuse in the areas where they operate. 'Beneficial complicity' pertains when a company is the beneficiary of human rights abuses committed by state or other forces, irrespective of whether it is possible to prove the company's own connection to the abuses themselves. 'Direct complicity' occurs when a company provides assistance of any sort to another actor (public or private) which then commits a human rights violation. This form of complicity is understood to exist even if the company may not have itself wished for the human rights violation to take place: 'it is enough if the corporation or its agents knew of the likely effects of their assistance'.[4] This triple hierarchy of silent, beneficial and direct complicity has gained increasing currency over recent years, and is now incorporated even within 'soft' initiatives such as the UN's Global Compact. It bears special relevance to the extractive industries, in that the intensity of their interventions (and the resistance to them) involves them in all three types of complicity on a regular basis. Before providing examples of such complicity, however, it is important to recognise some of the features that distinguish the extractive industries from other transnational operations, and the underlying reasons for the sector's over-representation in the corporate catalogue of shame.

Boom and Bonanza

To begin with, the vast profitability of the extractive industries marks them out from other sectors. On size alone, no other sector comes close: the ten most profitable corporations from the extractive sector recorded between them profits of over $250 billion in 2011 – vastly more than even the $160 billion registered by the top ten financial services companies. Seven of the ten largest non-financial corporations in the world are oil and gas companies – three of them (PetroChina, Petrobras and Gazprom) from BRICS states (Brazil, Russia, India, China, South Africa).[5] The commodity price boom has delivered a bonanza for these companies, which are posting record profits year on year as a result.

For oil and gas companies, the inexorable rise in the price of crude oil and natural gas has driven profits upwards. Average prices of crude oil have quadrupled from 2002 levels, even if they are still lower than the dramatic spikes of 2008, when prices threatened to reach $150 a barrel. As a result, the six supermajors (ExxonMobil, Shell, Chevron, BP, Total and ConocoPhillips) recorded profits of over $150 billion between them in 2011. ExxonMobil's profits of $41.1 billion were up 35 per cent on the previous year, though still behind the all-time record $45.2 billion for any corporation it posted in 2008. Shell saw a 54 per cent increase on 2010 earnings to $28.6 billion, while BP returned to profit once more following the 2010 Deepwater Horizon disaster in the Gulf of Mexico, which forced the company to divert $20 billion to a compensation fund for the tens of thousands of victims who had suffered from the spill.

For the mining sector, the twenty-first century has seen an even greater explosion in profits. Net profits for the world's leading mining companies doubled from $6 billion in 2002 to $12 billion the following year. By 2005 the figure had climbed to $45 billion, and by 2007 it had reached $80 billion. In 2010, after two years' brief dip due to the global economic recession, net profits for the world's top 40 mining companies registered a record $110 billion. The following year the figure was $133 billion – well over 20 times its 2002 level. These astronomical profit increases reflect revenue records that were sustained above pre-crash levels even in 2008 and 2009, and which broke through the $700 billion mark in 2011. These levels are forecast to remain high, as 'insatiable demand' stoked by strong growth in emerging markets continues to drive up commodity prices, in turn stimulating record levels of capital investment on the part of mining companies keen to cash in on the boom.[6]

Nor is this purely a question of scale: profit margins for the mining sector have also been consistently high over recent years, despite the economic crisis: no lower than 15 per cent in any year since 2004, the top 40 mining companies saw a return to pre-crash levels in 2010 with a combined net profit margin of 25 per cent. In terms of profit rates, similarly, the return on capital employed for the top 40 companies rebounded to 18 per cent in 2010 from 9 per cent the year before, if not yet back to the 22 and 23 per cent registered for 2007 and 2006, respectively. These profits have been made possible not only as a result of the boom in commodity prices, but also because the companies concerned have managed to retain such a significant proportion of the resource rents for themselves.[7] For decades, many governments that had fallen under the structural adjustment programmes of the World Bank and the International Monetary Fund were compelled to implement major reforms to their mining sectors in favour of foreign investors, reducing taxes and royalties to such an extent that they barely provided any benefit to the host countries at all. As confirmed by one 2005 UNCTAD report on the experience of African countries, 'while programmes designed to deregulate the mining sector can claim some success in attracting FDI [foreign direct investment] in recent years, a positive developmental impact has failed to materialize'. In the blind rush for higher FDI volumes, no structures had been put in place to ensure the reinvestment of profits or their fiscal absorption for purposes of development, leading the report to conclude that 'some of the largest recipients of FDI have also been those with the greatest capital flight, underscoring the perverse profit-investment nexus that has built up under adjustment programmes'.[8]

A key component of this nexus, highlighted by numerous studies over recent years, is the power of the extractive industries to sidestep their tax obligations in both host and home economies alike. Ten of the largest extractive industry corporations surveyed in one 2011 report (ExxonMobil, Shell, BP, Chevron, ConocoPhillips, Glencore, Rio Tinto, BHP Billiton, Anglo American and Barrick) were found to be operating through a network of 6,038 subsidiaries between them, over 2,000 of which were incorporated in secrecy jurisdictions where company accounts and beneficial ownership details were not publicly available. As a result of abusive transfer pricing facilitated by such arrangements in the oil industry, an estimated $110 billion 'disappeared' into corporate coffers through mispricing of crude oil imports in the European Union (EU) and USA between 2000 and 2010.[9] A celebrated UN study of tax avoidance in Chile during the ten years 1993–2002 revealed that most copper mining companies had been paying no taxes at all, despite combined sales of more than $34 billion; in fact, as a result of accumulating a further $2.6 billion in tax credits from the government, the companies had become a net liability on the state.[10] Similar findings from the mining sector in other Latin American countries reveal how widespread the practice of tax avoidance and trade mispricing has become, often with the active collusion of the World Bank. Tax holidays negotiated in secret with African governments have further combined with tax avoidance and evasion by transnational mining corporations to deprive the peoples of Africa of billions of dollars in tax revenue.[11]

The bare fact of natural resource abundance does not of itself bring down a resource curse on the host economy, even though it is widely attested that 'point' resources exploited from a narrow base such as oil, gas and minerals are more associated with worse economic and developmental outcomes than 'diffuse' resources such as agricultural land held under equitably distributed ownership.[12] The deciding factor as to whether a country can benefit from its natural resource wealth lies in the policies and institutions through which it captures and invests the rents generated, and in the political will to stand up to external forces that would appropriate the natural resources for themselves. This is increasingly being realised in practice through the greater confidence of governments to renegotiate the terms on which foreign companies from the extractive industries are granted access to operate in their territories: as noted in Chapter 3, fully 93 per cent of the regulatory changes introduced at the national level in the extractive industries during 2010 tightened obligations on foreign investors, including stricter performance requirements, new tax regimes and the renegotiation of contracts.[13] In addition to high profile moves by Latin American countries such as Ecuador, Bolivia, Venezuela and Argentina to renegotiate the licences of foreign extractive companies in recent years, the Africa Mining Vision adopted by African Union ministers in 2008 stressed the need for countries to reclaim a higher share of natural resource rents for their own development in future, criticising African governments' failure to do this in the past as 'due either to a lack of state capacity or the subversion of that capacity to produce overly investor friendly outcomes'. Zambia, for example, which had previously dropped its mineral royalty rate to just 0.6 per cent under pressure from the World Bank, raised the rate to 3 per cent in 2008 and then to 6 per cent in the country's 2012 budget, as well as increasing corporation tax on mining companies to 30 per cent from its previous concessional rate and clamping down on tax avoidance in an attempt to close loopholes that were costing the country $2 billion in lost revenue annually;[14] Tanzania, South Africa and the Democratic Republic of Congo have also attempted similar reforms in recent years. The resurgence of resource sovereignty has also led more countries to guard the use of their natural wealth for their own domestic development needs: China's move to restrict exports of rare earths (of which it produces over 90 per cent of the world's supply) as well as other minerals and metals such as bauxite, magnesium and zinc caused consternation in rival countries, leading the EU and USA to challenge the restrictions through the dispute settlement mechanism of the World Trade Organisation (WTO).[15]

Herein lies another key reason why the extractive industries are a cause of such violence and dislocation to host populations, in that control over other countries' strategic natural resources remains a key determinant of twenty-first-century imperialism (while any form of resource sovereignty on the part of host countries is portrayed, perversely, as an act of aggression). Western powers have made no secret of their continuing resolve to appropriate the world's natural resources for their own use in the post-colonial era, as stated bluntly in the first ever declaration of the G8 (at that time, the G6) in 1975: 'We are determined to secure for our economies the energy sources needed for their growth.' In more recent times, the EU's Raw Materials Initiative, launched in 2008, aims to ensure continued European access to natural resources around the world, noting that the EU is 100 per cent dependent on external sources for most of the metals and minerals used in high technology manufacturing, in addition to already being 85 per cent dependent on imports for its consumption of crude oil. The initiative, which remains the baseline policy for all member states of the EU, seeks to prevent emerging economies from using their natural resources for their own development, requiring them instead to abolish export restrictions and investment controls so as to surrender the required mineral wealth to European corporations.[16] The 'fair access' language in which the strategy is couched cannot disguise either the imperialist nature of the initiative or the increasing anxiety with which European policy makers view their own continent's dwindling resource base.

The USA is even more explicit in characterising its global resource needs as strategic national interests. The Pentagon's 2010 Quadrennial Defense Review highlights the threat of future adversaries' impeding US access to energy resources around the world, and stresses the need for US armed forces to retain sufficient military superiority to guarantee worldwide access in future and defeat 'anti-access' forces in the field. The idea was further developed in the Pentagon's 2012 paper on the Joint Operational Access Concept, which noted: 'As a global power with global interests, the United States must maintain the credible capability to project military force into any region of the world in support of those interests. This includes the ability to project force both into the global commons to ensure their use and into foreign territory as required.' The paper cited the 2001 invasion of Afghanistan and the deployment for the invasion of Iraq two years later as examples of the US military's ability to overcome anti-access forces in recent times, but cautioned that 'such unopposed operational access will be much less likely in the future'. The willingness of the USA and its allies to pursue their natural resource interests through the use of military force has been amply confirmed by internal US and UK government documents that have been brought to light showing that the Iraq war was indeed fought to secure access to that country's vast oil reserves.[17] Once employed, the mere threat of such overwhelming military aggression casts its shadow over all future initiatives and interventions; as Voltaire remarked 250 years ago, brute force needs to be exercised only occasionally *pour encourager les autres*.[18]

Shell in the Niger Delta

Few cases demonstrate the threat posed by the extractive industries as clearly as Shell's longstanding involvement in the Niger Delta. Despite being the source of Nigeria's vast oil wealth, the communities of the Niger Delta have not benefited from the revenues generated from their territories, instead experiencing intense social and ecological devastation over several generations. The region thus exemplifies the 'paradox of plenty' experienced by so many communities suffering under the natural resource curse: a fount of great riches for others, but itself mired in desperate poverty and racked by violence. A dedicated UN report on the 'appalling' human development situation facing the 30 million inhabitants of the Niger Delta recorded the deep levels of popular distrust towards government and oil companies alike as a result of decades of corruption, dispossession and neglect.[19]

Shell traces its presence in Nigeria back to 1937, when it was awarded monopoly rights to exploration across the country by the British colonial government. The company's engagement in oil exploration and production in the Niger Delta dates from the late 1950s, shortly before Nigeria won its independence. Even today, Shell remains the dominant force among foreign oil companies operating in Nigeria, with a 30 per cent stake in the joint venture shared between the state-owned Nigerian National Petroleum Corporation (55 per cent), Total (10 per cent) and Agip (5 per cent). Shell also operates the Bonga deepwater oil and gas project 120 kilometres offshore in the

Gulf of Guinea, which was to expand the company's production in Nigeria by 25 per cent when it came online in 2005, as well as holding the largest foreign share in the liquefied natural gas plant at Bonny Island. In all, Shell's Nigerian operations account for around 12 per cent of the company's total global production.[20]

Shell's long-term domination of the Nigerian oil industry means that the company is centrally involved in the Niger Delta, including in the deterioration of the security situation there. A leaked internal security report commissioned by Shell in 2003 dismissed the company's claims to neutrality in the high-intensity conflict then costing over 1,000 lives a year in the Delta, concluding that Shell had become 'an integral part of the Niger Delta conflict system' as a result of its 50-year involvement, and that the manner of its operations itself 'creates, feeds into, or exacerbates conflict'.[21] The report warned that Shell would be forced to abandon its onshore operations within five years if it failed to address the underlying causes of conflict with local communities. As predicted, Shell was repeatedly forced to suspend operations in the Niger Delta over the following years due to actions by local movements and militant groups seeking to reclaim control of the region's natural resource wealth. Nigeria's output of crude oil fell by over 28 per cent in the period 2006–09 as a result of these suspensions.

In order to guarantee the free flow of oil and revenue from the region, Shell has nurtured close relationships with armed groups in the Niger Delta, both public and private, over a period of many years. Shell's relationship with the Nigerian armed forces was cemented during the period of military rule in the 1990s, and brought to international attention as a result of Shell's collusion in the violent suppression of the Movement for the Survival of the Ogoni People, which had mobilised hundreds of thousands of Ogoni people in protest against the devastation of their communal lands by oil spills and fires. The full extent of the environmental damage caused to Ogoniland has recently been confirmed by a further UN report, which concluded that the Ogoni people continue to suffer from widespread oil contamination as a daily reality, even though the production of oil in Ogoniland has been suspended for the past two decades; in the same week as the report was published, Shell admitted liability for two massive oil spills that had devastated the Ogoni village of Bodo in 2008 – although independent consultants calculated that Shell's estimate for the size of the spills was at least 60 times too low.[22] Shell's close involvement with the Nigerian state in its suppression of the Ogoni people included calling in armed assistance to deal with Ogoni demonstrations against Shell and helping to plan raids on communities suspected of opposing the company's operations, according to confidential documents released in 2009.[23] Shell had already admitted that it paid Nigerian army units for their operations against the Ogoni people, and that it had imported weapons to arm the Nigerian police forces responsible for protecting Shell facilities in Ogoniland.[24]

Shell was universally condemned over the Nigerian state's torture and execution of nine Ogoni human rights activists including Ken Saro-Wiwa, president of the Movement for the Survival of the Ogoni People, and Dr Barinem Kiobel in 1995. Shell was formally accused of collaboration in the deaths of the nine men in a suit brought against the company under the US Alien Tort Statute, which also accused Shell of complicity in a series of other human rights violations against the Ogoni people. Shell eventually settled the case out of court in 2009, preferring to pay $15.5 million to the victims' families by way of 'reconciliation' rather than admit culpability. A parallel suit brought by the family of Dr Kiobel alleged that Shell 'knowingly instigated, planned, facilitated, conspired and cooperated in' attacks by the Nigerian military on unarmed Ogoni people, and that Shell supported the operations of armed units financially and through the purchase of ammunition.[25] Shell has been accused of further collusion with armed forces in the increased militarisation of the Niger Delta over the past ten years. In addition to maintaining its own 1,200-strong internal police force, buying in the services of private military and security companies and allegedly making payments to rival armed gangs in the Delta, Shell has reportedly hired a further 1,300 government troops to protect its vast network of oil fields, wells, pipelines and gas plants, and continues to provide the Nigerian military with significant logistical assistance in its operations.[26] These operations are characterised by extreme violence and human rights violations, including extrajudicial executions, torture and the destruction of people's homes. Shell's attempts to disclaim responsibility for these abuses were undermined by the 2010 WikiLeaks publication of a confidential cable from the US embassy in Abuja, in which Shell's Vice-President for sub-Saharan Africa, Ann Pickard, was reported to have boasted of the company's penetration of all relevant Nigerian government ministries with seconded Shell employees, and its resulting knowledge of all government plans and actions.[27]

Shell is guilty not only of persistent ecological degradation in the Niger Delta, but also of direct complicity in the violation of human rights there. In response to the international outcry against its activities, which saw activists picket Shell petrol stations across the world, the company launched a sophisticated public relations offensive based on a new corporate social responsibility (CSR) policy, including active engagement with human rights organisations such as Amnesty International, which appointed former Shell senior executive Sir Geoffrey Chandler to chair its UK Business Group. The resulting collaboration enabled Shell to position itself as a champion of business ethics, yet in its dedicated 2009 report into what it termed the 'human rights tragedy' of the Niger Delta, Amnesty International's researchers concluded that Shell had 'failed to respect the human rights of the people of the Niger Delta' over a period of decades.[28] A further case accusing Shell of polluting land and waterways in the Niger Delta was brought to court in the Netherlands by Nigerian farmers in October 2012 – the first time a Dutch company has been sued in a Dutch court on charges of environmental damage abroad.[29]

Far from being a unique case, Shell's disregard for the lives and livelihoods of the local communities in which it operates is representative of the oil industry as a whole. US oil company Chevron has also operated in Nigeria for over 50 years, and has been the target of sustained protest by indigenous communities based in the Niger Delta over the destruction caused by its operations. As with Shell in Ogoniland, Chevron was formally accused of collusion with Nigerian security forces in the violent suppression of peaceful protest by members of the Ilaje community, including the murderous attack in 1998 on villagers staging a non-violent demonstration on Chevron's Parabe oil platform off the Nigerian coast. According to testimony presented in the subsequent court case, Chevron called in the Nigerian military and the infamous 'kill and go' mobile police force to put down the protest, flying them to the platform on Chevron-contracted helicopters and supervising the attacks, in which two demonstrators were shot dead, others wounded and many more detained and tortured. In a series of rulings in August 2007, US federal judge Susan Illston confirmed that there was evidence of Chevron's being directly involved in the human rights violations, noting that Chevron and the Nigerian armed forces enjoyed a 'much closer relationship than the traditional relationship between private parties and law enforcement officials', with Nigerian security forces on Chevron's payroll and engaged in extensive security work for the company. The case was finally closed in Chevron's favour by the US Supreme Court in April 2012, however, following a jury trial four years earlier. In addition to the company's own admission that its policies of supporting some communities over others have fuelled conflict in the Niger Delta, Chevron's operations have continued to cause social and environmental devastation, including an unprecedented gas well fire in 2012 which burned out of control for several weeks.[30]

Nor is this level of confrontation between oil companies and local communities in any way restricted to Nigeria. The same story can be told of BP's operations in Colombia, where the British oil giant's role in the construction of the 720-kilometre OCENSA pipeline led to charges of complicity in human rights violations carried out by paramilitary and state forces against local Colombian communities. In addition to direct payments to the Colombian military to protect its installations, BP had contracted Defence Systems Colombia, a subsidiary of the British private military and security company Defence Systems Limited (later renamed ArmorGroup, and bought in 2008 by G4S), to provide extra protection and security services, including counter insurgency training for the Colombian police. Defence Systems Colombia was implicated in passing intelligence identifying groups opposed to BP's presence to the Colombian army's notorious XVIth Brigade, intelligence which was subsequently linked to extrajudicial executions and disappearances.[31] In July 2006, BP paid out an undisclosed sum to settle a legal suit accusing the company of profiting from the reign of terror and causing severe environmental and social damage to communities living in the path of the OCENSA pipeline. A further claim was brought against BP in 2008.

Many equally high profile cases of social and environmental conflict have highlighted the impact of oil companies' operations around the world: Unocal's complicity in the murder, rape and forced displacement of Burmese villagers during the construction of the Yadana gas pipeline, which led to the company paying out undisclosed sums in compensation; Talisman's presence in Sudan, which led to its being sued in the USA under the Alien Tort Statute for complicity in human rights violations; Texaco's destruction of the Amazonian rainforest in Ecuador, eventually settled by an Ecuadorian court in an unprecedented $18 billion judgment in favour of the indigenous communities – a judgment that is now itself being contested by Chevron, Texaco's owner since 2001; plus the cases of Occidental in Colombia, ExxonMobil in Indonesia, Total in Burma, BP's Baku-Tbilisi-Ceyhan pipeline and countless other examples. Increasing attention is also turning to the impact of new oil majors, in particular China National Petroleum Corporation (CNPC) and its subsidiary PetroChina.[32] In 2011, the Norwegian government's advisory Council of Ethics recommended that Norway's state pension fund divest its PetroChina holdings as a result of CNPC's involvement in two new pipelines being constructed in Burma, which had already led to widespread human rights abuses, while in 2012 Dutch pension fund ABP – the world's third largest pension fund – divested its interests in PetroChina over CNPC's continuing presence in Sudan.

Mining Emergencies

The mining sector has long rivalled the oil sector in witnessing the most egregious cases of social and environmental abuse by TNCs. As with oil, the damage caused by mining operations is devastating for local communities, many of which have lived in relative isolation from the global economy before the arrival of the corporations concerned.[33] As a consequence, mining operations regularly represent long-term human rights emergencies for the communities which bear the brunt of their impacts, while companies such as Anglo American, BHP Billiton and Rio Tinto have become bywords for corporate conflict. Ongoing environmental and human rights disasters such as the Grasberg gold and copper mine in West Papua or the Ok Tedi mine in neighbouring Papua New Guinea have been matched in intensity by the Cerrejon open-cast coal mine in Colombia, the expansion of mining operations in the Philippines, Barrick in Tanzania, Vedanta in India and countless other confrontations in countries as far afield as Bangladesh, Uzbekistan, South Africa, Argentina and Zambia. As with the oil majors, the traditional dominance of the imperial mining giants from the North (especially Britain, Canada and Australia) is being challenged by new players from the global South: Brazil's Vale is now the world's second largest mining company by market capitalisation behind BHP Billiton, while China Shenhua has taken fourth place behind Rio Tinto, ahead of both Xstrata and Anglo American.

Few countries exemplify the threat caused by mining operations as clearly as Peru, which has seen an unprecedented surge both in corporate activity and community resistance over recent years as indigenous peoples' movements have mounted sustained campaigns of opposition to the expansion of extractive operations in their territories. The brutal force with which such protests have been put down was brought to global attention in June 2009, when police commandos opened fire on thousands of indigenous protesters demonstrating against the dispossession of their lands in the Amazonian region of Bagua, and unknown numbers lost their lives. As a result of the drive by former president Alan García to secure foreign investment into the extractive industries from 2006 onwards, metals, minerals and fuels now represent over 70 per cent of Peru's total exports.[34] The successor government of Ollanta Humala has continued the investment strategy of his predecessor, despite being elected in 2011 on a left-nationalist platform which promised to balance market-friendly economic growth with policies of social inclusion.

The Río Blanco project in the northern region of Piura offers just one example of the many social conflicts between local communities and mining companies in Peru over recent years. British mining company Monterrico Metals acquired sole rights to the concession in 2003, and established the project in the name of its wholly owned Peruvian subsidiary Minera Majaz. The Río Blanco copper deposit was estimated to be one of the largest undeveloped copper resources in the world, and Monterrico promoted the mine as being able to produce around one million tonnes of copper and 10,000 tonnes of molybdenum over the first five years of its life.[35] Local communities registered their opposition to the project from the outset out of concern for the environmental damage it would cause to an area previously untouched by mining operations, and noted that Monterrico had failed to obtain the community approval required under Peruvian law before embarking on any exploratory activity – a judgment confirmed by Peru's national ombudsman, the Defensoría del Pueblo.[36] A referendum held in September 2007 across the three districts of Piura that would be most affected by the proposed mine returned an overwhelming vote of more than 90 per cent against the initiation of any mining activity. An equally emphatic referendum result five years earlier in the neighbouring district of Tambogrande had led to the permanent withdrawal of Canadian mining corporation Manhattan Minerals from the region, although not before the main leader of the opposition to that mine had been murdered. Monterrico Metals was bought in 2007 by a Chinese consortium, Xiamen Zijin Tongguan Development Co. Ltd, and moved its head office to Hong Kong, although the company remains incorporated in the UK.

The lengths to which Monterrico was prepared to go in order to suppress local opposition to its Río Blanco project were revealed in legal proceedings against the company for its part in the detention and torture of more than 30 indigenous Peruvian protesters over a period of three days at the mine site in August 2005, one of whom, Melanio García Gonzales, bled to death from his injuries. The protesters had been detained following a mass demonstration against the mine by thousands of local farmers from across the region, which was met by armed police from Peru's special operations unit as well as private security guards employed by Monterrico to protect the mine. Hooded and handcuffed, the protesters were beaten, abused and threatened with death; in addition, the two women among those captured were sexually abused. Testimony received from Río Blanco employees confirmed the protesters' allegation that the mine's manager had personally directed the police in their brutality against those detained, with witnesses claiming that he had been in regular contact throughout the three days with Monterrico's chief operating officer, Ray Angus. The claimants in the case also alleged that the company had engaged in a wider campaign of intimidation over a period of months designed to suppress local opposition to the mine. In July 2011, three months prior to the case coming before the High Court in London, Monterrico agreed to settle by means of compensation payments to the farmers, but without admitting liability for complicity in the abuses.[37]

In the drive to expand their operations in Peru, Western mining companies have relied heavily on the violent suppression of legitimate protests by state and private forces, rendering them complicit in the human rights violations committed on their behalf. Six anti-mining demonstrators were shot dead by police in June 2011 at Juliaca airport in the south-east region of Puno, where a long-running protest involving 17,000 people had just succeeded in winning the revocation of a local mining licence granted to Canadian company Bear Creek. At the other end of the country, a 60-day state of emergency was announced in December 2011 in order to allow security forces to overcome mass mobilisations against Newmont Mining Corporation's proposed Conga open-cast gold mine, a controversial plan which had already caused Peru's deputy environment minister to resign in protest. Two further demonstrators were killed by police and dozens more injured in May 2012 during actions against Xstrata's Tintaya copper mine in the south of the country, prompting the government to declare a state of emergency there too and raising fears that the presidency of Ollanta Humala would degenerate into the same conflict-ridden crisis as that of his predecessor.

Yet there are signs that foreign companies have played more than a passive role in the suppression of anti-mining resistance in Peru. US embassy cables released through WikiLeaks in 2011 revealed details of mining company executives meeting with Western diplomatic representatives in August 2005, shortly after the abuses at Monterrico's Río Blanco mine described above, in order to 'coordinate efforts' against the new wave of community protests around the country. At one such meeting, jointly hosted by the US and Canadian ambassadors and attended by representatives from the UK, Australian and Swiss embassies, one mine executive called for diplomatic pressure to be applied to Peru's Ministry of Education in order to secure the removal of radical teachers who might be fomenting anti-mining sentiment in key regions – and for the same pressure to be applied to the Catholic Church in respect of radical priests or bishops. US ambassador Curt Struble called on the mining executives to provide evidence of any non-governmental organisation (NGO)-funded groups or individuals involved in advocating violence against mine operations, so that the evidence could be used to warn off the NGOs concerned. The embassy representatives promised the mine executives that they would work together as a diplomatic lobby group to exert pressure in favour of foreign mining interests on the Peruvian government, the Catholic Church and other political party leaders.[38]

Strategic Philanthropy

The other strategy recommended by US Ambassador Struble to the executives present at the meeting was that they should try to win over public opinion by highlighting the civic projects undertaken by foreign mining companies in Peru, such as the building of roads, wells, schools and clinics for use by local communities. Public relations offensives of this kind are a familiar response on the part of the extractive industries, which have developed sophisticated programmes of 'strategic philanthropy' to deflect criticism of their operations over the years. Even more important, however, are the CSR programmes which oil, gas and mining companies have established in order to address the reputational damage caused by their complicity in human rights violations by public and private security forces, and to offset international moves towards the introduction of binding frameworks of accountability.[39]

The most significant move in this respect was the formulation of the Voluntary Principles on Security and Human Rights in 2000. According to Bennett Freeman, who led the process within the US State Department, the initial impetus for the Voluntary Principles stemmed from US and UK government concern at the economic and political threats posed by the corporate human rights scandals of the 1990s in 'key countries' such as Nigeria, Indonesia and Colombia, and the consequences of not being able to maintain operations in such countries in the future.[40] The Voluntary Principles were first drafted by the US State Department in consultation with the UK government's Foreign and Commonwealth Office, and then finalised with extractive companies and international NGOs in what has been characterised as a 'closed-door process' leading to the 'privatised negotiation of global corporate standards of behaviour'.[41] By 2012, a total of 20 companies were listed as participants in the Voluntary Principles initiative, along with seven national governments and eleven international NGOs. Yet the legitimacy of this 'private club' has repeatedly been called into question, while studies of the initiative's impact at ground level have confirmed not only the ineffectiveness of the Voluntary Principles in addressing corporate complicity in human rights violations, but also their role in deflecting public pressure away from more fundamental questions of community consent, resource wealth distribution and the extractive industries' right to operate in situations of conflict. The most telling criticism of the Voluntary Principles is that they ultimately serve to legitimise the presence of extractive companies in such situations, including their right to provide lethal and non-lethal equipment to both public and private security forces engaged in guarding their property, on terms dictated by the companies themselves.[42]

While the Voluntary Principles refer to the most serious cases of human rights violations, a number of other initiatives show how the extractive industries have led the way in initiating voluntary CSR schemes as a means to escape calls for binding frameworks that might restrict their autonomy. The International Council on Mining and Metals (ICMM), established in 2001 as the leading CSR vehicle for the mining industry, requires members to sign up to its Sustainable Development Framework and ranks their performance in published annual assessments; run wholly by industry represen-tatives for their own purposes, it has never enjoyed wider legitimacy – not least because of candid statements by founder members as to the true reasons for the ICMM's existence (see below).[43] Despite widespread calls for mandatory measures to ensure the transparency of extractive companies, whose poor record on tax avoidance has already been noted above, former UK prime minister Tony Blair remained loyal to corporate interests and announced at the World Summit on Sustainable Development in Johannesburg in 2002 that the new Extractive Industries Transparency Initiative (EITI) would be a voluntary scheme only. Other such non-binding initiatives include the Global Mining Initiative, Kimberley Process, Initiative for Responsible Mining Assurance, Environmental Excellence in Exploration (E3), International Cyanide Management Code for the Gold Mining Industry, and more.

In addition, it is now standard practice for major oil, gas and mining companies to publish their own CSR reports in an attempt to present a positive face to the public in both home and host countries alike. Extractive companies from the global South have also recognised the importance of being seen to play the game: Brazilian mining giant Vale has produced sustainability reports for many years, while CNPC released its first annual CSR report in 2007 and has since then also published country-specific reports on the company's operations in Kazakhstan, Sudan and Indonesia. Chinese recognition of the need for such public expressions of concern for social and environmental issues has doubtless been heightened by the rising number of local protests against its extractive companies' operations around the world: in March 2012, as many as 25,000 protesters from indigenous communities across Ecuador converged on the capital Quito in opposition to a $1.4 billion Chinese investment in what would be the country's first large-scale mining project, while villagers in south Kyrgyzstan agreed to suspend their protests against two Chinese gold mining companies in August 2011 only when local authorities promised to set up a special commission to investigate their grievances.

There is ample evidence that the social investment and CSR programmes of extractive companies are a deliberate distraction from the brutal reality of their industries, as confirmed by statements from within the oil industry that 'CSR is about managing perceptions and making people inside and outside the company feel good about themselves'.[44] Company chiefs have at times been equally candid: speaking to the London Business School in 2006, former Rio Tinto chairperson Paul Skinner declared that the mining industry's zeal for CSR over the previous ten years had been a strategy not only for dealing with the reputational risk it faced, but also for opening up new avenues to resources; Skinner particularly stated that this latter purpose of 'gaining access to land, capital and markets' had been the goal behind the founding of the ICMM. Former Anglo American chairperson Sir Mark Moody-Stuart similarly reminded his company's 2006 AGM of the importance of risk management through engagement in initiatives such as the EITI and ICMM, in order to ensure 'our continuing access to land and resources'.[45]

The full scale of the conflict between the extractive industries and society – and the delusion wrought by the sector's CSR initiatives – was brutally revealed in the massacre of 34 South African mineworkers at the Lonmin platinum mine in Marikana in August 2012. The mine had long been known for the appalling conditions in which workers (many of them migrants supplied as contract labourers by intermediary brokers) are forced to live and work, as well as the negative social and ecological impacts of its operations on rural communities nearby. Lonmin had received a $100 million loan and $50 million equity investment in 2007 from the World Bank's private sector arm, the International Finance Corporation, on the understanding that it would be introducing a new CSR programme with beneficial results for the workforce and for surrounding communities at Marikana. Yet an independent report into conditions at the mine released just two days before the August 2012 massacre accused Lonmin of failing to address any of the longstanding issues that had plagued the site for years, and concluded that any genuine signs of corporate citizenship were still 'illusions on a far horizon'.[46] In light of these failures, and in particular the chronically low levels of pay for what remain very hazardous jobs, around 3,000 rock drill operators at the Marikana mine went on strike on 10 August 2012. The Lonmin management refused to engage in dialogue with the strikers, escalating tension until the deadly confrontation of 16 August, when South African police opened fire on protesters with automatic weapons, killing 34 in a series of attacks that echoed the darkest days of the apartheid era.[47] The rock drill operators eventually returned to work in late September after agreeing to a 22 per cent wage increase; by this time, however, workers in other sectors had embarked on their own campaigns of strike action in pursuit of fairer pay – including casualised farm workers in the fruit and wine sector, whose actions forced the South African government to raise their minimum daily wage by over 50 per cent. Capital has consistently used CSR programmes to 'manufacture amnesia' in post-apartheid South Africa, not only 'seducing South Africans into forgetting, absolving, effacing old scars' but also masking corporate malpractice in the present.[48] The Marikana massacre is a brutal reminder that direct conflict with the extractive industries' insatiable drive for profit remains a daily reality for millions of people across the world.

6

Garments: Capitalism's False Promise

If the extractive sector is the site of the most intense confrontations between transnational corporations (TNCs) and local communities, the garments sector is the most familiar example in the public eye for capital's continuing exploitation of labour – and especially women's labour. As a result of ongoing struggles by trade unions in garment factories of the global South and parallel campaigns in countries of the North, it is now commonly recognised that the relocation of clothes production outside the core capitalist economies has allowed brand names and retailers to maintain high profits at the expense of workers' rights. As a result, the garments sector has become the defining example of how the process of globalisation has enabled capital to drive down wage costs and labour standards while evading all prospects of binding regulation.

The garments sector has long been important to national development strategies in that it has traditionally acted as a 'gateway' industry providing a first step on the ladder for countries seeking to diversify their economies into manufacturing. As a labour-intensive industry requiring limited education or prior training of its workforce, many countries in the global South have enjoyed a comparative advantage in the garments sector, and have used it as a means to developing skills which could then be transferred to higher-value industries. Garments have long represented an important proportion of total export earnings in some of the world's poorest countries, accounting for around 80 per cent of manufacturing exports in Bangladesh and Cambodia, for instance. Moreover, the rapid growth of the garments industry in both countries owed much in its initial stages to contracts with international clients seeking to capitalise on low labour costs and increasingly responsive supply times. In many respects, the relocation of garments manufacturing to new countries represented the most hopeful side of the globalisation ideal, with consumers in the rich North promised ever lower prices and communities in the global South standing to benefit from their country's integration into the global economy through new employment opportunities. There was an additional gender dimension to these new job prospects, as the 'feminisation of labour' associated with the spread of the garments industry brought with it the promise of economic empowerment and social emancipation for the millions of young women from poor rural backgrounds whom the sector was expected to recruit.

Yet the promise of the globalised garments industry has not materialised, as a direct result of its imprisonment within the framework of global supply chains dominated by capitalist relations of production, or 'networked capitalism'.[1] The garments sector is a stark example of a buyer-driven value chain controlled by brands and retailers that are able to dictate terms to suppliers as a result of their overwhelming market power, ensuring that they also capture the greater part of all gains arising from globalised production.[2] Consequently, as this chapter will show, the emancipatory potential of employment in the garments sector has been largely negated as a result of TNCs' drive to keep labour costs low and their requirement that supplier factories meet increasingly unrealistic production deadlines. These demands have led to women employed in the garments sector being condemned to insecure, low paid and dangerous jobs, their working lives characterised by exploitation rather than empowerment. Only the struggles of the workers themselves, backed up by worldwide campaigns against the brands and retailers ultimately responsible for their abuse, have managed to challenge the power relations that underpin the system.

Global Competition

Intensified competition at the international level has also played a role in undermining the prospect of positive outcomes in the garments sector, particularly as a result of the phasing out of the Multi-Fibre Arrangement (MFA) in 2005. The MFA was originally designed in the early 1970s as a protectionist shield for clothing manufacturers in the global North in the face of competition from new producers in the South, especially China and India. While it certainly restricted those countries from expanding their exports into the markets of Europe and North America, a further consequence of the quota system imposed by the MFA was that companies from the newly industrialised Asian economies were forced to look to new production bases in a broader range of countries if they wished to take full advantage of the increasing opportunities to supply Western consumers. As a result of this 'quota hopping', the managed trade regime of the MFA was responsible for the spread of the garments industry to new countries whose export quotas had not been exhausted, and thus also responsible for starting some of those countries off on the road to industrialisation. By the same token, however, the eventual phasing out of the MFA in 2005 under the World Trade Organisation's (WTO's) Agreement on Textiles and Clothing removed restrictions on exports from countries such as China and India, and thus militated against the continued spread of production bases in other countries around the world.

The full effects of the MFA phase-out are still being worked out in practice, not least because the WTO allowed for the continued use of protectionist measures against Chinese exports for several years after 2005. However, China swiftly doubled its share of both the US and European Union (EU) textiles and clothing markets, as expected. Companies that had previously sourced garments widely from across the world were able to consolidate their operations in a more limited number of countries, leading to significant job losses as factories closed in export bases such as Costa Rica, Guatemala, Mexico and Honduras. In the Dominican Republic, one in three factories closed and 70,000 jobs were lost in the garments sector between 2004 and 2007, while South Africa saw the value of its garments exports to the EU and USA crash by 75 per cent over the same period. Other countries of sub-Saharan Africa were also badly hit by the immediate effects of the MFA phase-out: within the first year alone, Kenya recorded job losses in the garments sector of almost 10 per cent, Lesotho of 26 per cent and Swaziland of a catastrophic 43 per cent.[3] Women were particularly affected, as the feminisation of labour turned swiftly into a feminisation of unemployment: in Mauritius, for example, 88 of the country's 292 garments factories closed between 2004 and 2009, with a loss of over 17,000 jobs; while the national unemployment rate for men remained at under 6 per cent, the rate for women soared to 16.5 per cent after the phase-out of the MFA, and remained high thereafter as many women were unable to find alternative work in other sectors.[4] Even in those countries that managed to survive the phasing out of the MFA regime without such losses, the resulting increase in competition exerted downwards pressure on wages and working conditions, particularly for women. In Cambodia, Vietnam and Sri Lanka, the differential between women's and men's wages widened in the immediate post-MFA period, surging to a 55 per cent gender gap in the case of Sri Lanka. Even while total employment in the garments sector increased in Bangladesh, Cambodia, India and Pakistan after 2004, working conditions were found to have declined for women in all four countries.[5]

While terms and conditions of employment remain a terrain of struggle, the basic structure of the global garments industry looks set to stay. Contract manufacturing is now so established that most well known brands run the vast majority of their operations through outsourcing, either directly with supplier factories or through trading intermediaries such as Hong Kong-based supply chain managers Li & Fung. Almost all of Nike's brand apparel (and all of its footwear) is produced by independent contract manufacturers from outside the USA, in a network of 700 factories across 45 countries, predominantly in Asia and Latin America, involving over 800,000 workers. Puma operates a similar system involving 300,000 workers in some 350 factories, again mostly in Asia. Gap's extensive network demonstrates the full spread of contract manufacturing across the world, as the company has suppliers in South Asia (188 factories), China (186), South-East Asia (180), North Asia (57), Latin America and Caribbean (53), North Africa and Middle East (20), Europe (20), North America (18) and sub-Saharan Africa (5). The employment generated by such outsourcing is small in absolute terms, but significant in particular contexts; in Cambodia, for instance, factories producing garments for international clients (the majority of which are owned by companies from elsewhere in Asia) still account for around half of the country's total manufacturing employment.[6]

Brands Under Attack

The first wave of stories revealing exploitation in global supply chains serving the clothes industry swept across the world during the 1990s.[7] A series of media exposés in the USA revealed sweatshop conditions, poverty pay and child labour as standard practice in factories manufacturing goods for household names such as Gap, Kathie Lee Gifford (sold exclusively by Wal-Mart), Nike and Disney. These revelations created the impetus for the brands to launch their own corporate social responsibility (CSR) initiatives as a defensive strategy to protect their reputations from increasingly vocal public outrage, with Levi-Strauss introducing its code for business partners as early as 1992.[8] Few companies experienced such an onslaught as Nike, which soon found itself the target of a worldwide campaign. In a May 1998 speech to the National Press Club in Washington DC, Nike's chief executive Phil Knight admitted that 'the Nike product has become synonymous with slave wages, forced overtime, and arbitrary abuse', and pledged to introduce a code of conduct which would cover the company's suppliers in all countries. Indeed, one of the successes of the early campaigns on the garments sector was that responsibility for labour rights was understood to extend throughout the supply chains of the brands and retailers, applying not only to each company's own employees but also to the workers employed in its supplier factories, and to anyone further subcontracted by those factories in turn.

In addition to individual company codes, the garments industry responded to the wave of criticism it faced during the 1990s by embracing a number of multi-stakeholder initiatives in order to 'engage' with its critics. Foremost among these were the Ethical Trading Initiative (ETI) in the UK and the Fair Labor Association (FLA) in the USA; established in 1998 and 1999 respectively, both initiatives were strongly backed by their respective governments, and both encompass more than just the clothing and footwear industries. The ETI was founded with support from the UK government's Department for International Development (DFID), which has sustained it with close to $10 million in funding over the first 15 years of its existence, and the initiative now boasts over 70 corporate members plus a number of trade union and non-governmental organisation representatives.[9] The FLA was set up in direct response to a call from then US President Bill

Clinton for the industry to establish a partnership with its detractors and bring them 'inside the tent'; headquartered in Washington DC, today it also has offices in China, Switzerland and Turkey. Other multi-stakeholder initiatives in the garment industry include WRAP (Worldwide Responsible Apparel Production, subsequently rebranded Worldwide Responsible Accredited Production), an initiative of the American Apparel and Footwear Association; the Fair Wear Foundation in the Netherlands, with a membership of 80 companies from seven European countries; and the MFA Forum launched in 2004 in order to explore ways of mitigating the losses caused by the phasing out of the MFA quota system. In addition, there have been a number of country-specific initiatives such as the Better Factories Cambodia programme, started by the International Labour Organisation (ILO) in 2001, and the Joint Initiative for Corporate Accountability and Workers' Rights (JO-IN) instigated by the ETI and piloted in Turkey, in collaboration with five other organisations with experience of implementing voluntary codes of conduct, from 2004 to 2007.

Yet at the same time as the garments industry was busy proliferating codes of conduct to profess its commitment to social responsibility, brands and retailers were intensifying their pressure on the factories in their supply chains to deliver cheaper goods at higher quality and with faster turnaround times. Few corporations have exemplified this aggressive approach better than Wal-Mart, the world's largest retailer, whose disregard for the rights of its own workforce is legendary.[10] A Pulitzer-winning series of articles on the 'Wal-Mart effect' in the *Los Angeles Times* in 2003 revealed the company's use of a 'Plus One' strategy in its procurement of clothing from factories around the world, with suppliers required to offer Wal-Mart lower prices or higher quality year on year if they wished to retain the retail giant's business. According to the head of its global procurement division, Wal-Mart would pit supplier factories against each other and drive down prices by 'putting our global muscle on them'. Factory owners in Bangladesh stated that Wal-Mart had demanded price cuts of up to 50 per cent, while the country's trade minister complained that Wal-Mart's 'every day low prices' approach represented the 'biggest threat' to Bangladesh's prospects of success.[11]

Nor is the practice of demanding price cuts from supplier factories year on year in any way restricted to Wal-Mart. Indeed, according to one industry insider, 'Most companies negotiate using historic data ... Example: you made that shirt for US$2.00 – make this one for US$1.90. Very little science goes into the negotiation and certainly 90 per cent of the companies that work this way will not give a toss on what the labour rates are in the factory, as long as the external audits do not put them under the country laws of paying the "minimum wage".'[12] A series of job advertisements posted on the website of the UK's leading retailer Tesco during 2012 confirmed the continuing importance of this approach in the current era, promising new recruits that they would be initiated into the company's 'four ways of buying', namely: 'buy for less, someone else pays, use less, re-engineer'.[13] One of the adverts, for an assistant buyer of ladies' casual wovens and denim in Tesco's own-label F&F fashion range, which sources from countries such as Kenya, Sri Lanka and Bangladesh, informed applicants: 'You will negotiate, with the support of the Buyer, to achieve "buy for less" and "sell for less" plans.' According to Terry Green, former head of clothing at Tesco, this hard-nosed approach would not necessarily mean a drop in wages for workers in the company's supply chains, in that they would still be able to earn enough to live if they increased their productivity levels – a standard claim made by buyers, many of which have developed their own productivity projects in countries such as China, Bangladesh and India to support their claim, but rejected by trade unions and other commentators as having potentially adverse effects on job security, working conditions and, indeed, pay.[14]

The result of this aggressive cost-cutting by brand buyers has been a dramatic decline over the past two decades in the unit prices of clothes leaving the factory floor. The factory price for cotton knit shirts, for instance, was driven down by over 20 per cent in Mexico, El Salvador, Pakistan, Peru, Turkey and Bangladesh during the ten years 1994–2004, by over 30 per cent in Haiti, Guatemala, Dominican Republic and Egypt, and by over 50 per cent in Honduras and Nicaragua.[15] This collapse in prices was further exacerbated in the four years immediately following the phase-out of the MFA, during which period the average unit prices for clothes exports to the USA fell by an additional 29 per cent in Sri Lanka, 25 per cent in Cambodia, 13 per cent in India, 11 per cent in Bangladesh and 6 per cent in Pakistan and Vietnam.[16] Then, as their sales began to be hit by financial crisis and recession from 2008 onwards, Western retailers embarked on their own discount campaigns in an attempt to offset declines in consumer spending, driving down factory prices still further: in Bangladesh, according to the country's Export Promotion Bureau, the average price for woven and knitted garments fell another 3 per cent between 2010 and 2011 as a result of this downwards pressure from retailers, while production costs increased by around 10 per cent.[17] Control over the value chain has granted brands and retailers the power to determine factory prices, without reference to the increasing squeeze on suppliers trying to make ends meet.

To consumers in the West, this meant ever cheaper clothing over a sustained 20-year period, defying inflation and giving rise to a throw-away fashion culture unknown to previous generations.[18] In the USA, the price of women's clothing fell by over 17 per cent between 1992 and 2010, compared to a 55 per cent rise in the consumer price index as a whole.[19] The UK clothing sector experienced significant price deflation in the first decade of the twenty-first century, as supermarkets tripled their share of the clothes market and other 'value' retailers such as Primark burst onto the scene, leading to a 23 per cent fall in the retail price of clothing and footwear in the ten years from 1999 to 2008 (and a 38 per cent fall in the case of women's clothes).[20] Brands and retailers at all points of the spectrum have seen vastly increased profits during this period as a result of driving down factory prices: Gap, for instance, posted sales of around $14.5 billion in both 2002 and 2010, but saw its profits increase two and a half times from $478 million to $1.2 billion in the same period. Nike's profits more than tripled from $663 million in 2002 to $2.1 billion in 2011, with its profit margin increasing in the same period from 6.7 per cent to 10.2 per cent. Primark, which now has stores in Belgium, Germany, the Netherlands, Portugal and Spain as well as in the UK and Ireland, increased sales from £654 million in 2002 to £3 billion in 2011, and profits from £72 million to £309 million. The world's largest fashion retailer Inditex, which owns brands such as Zara and Massimo Dutti, quadrupled its profits from €438 million in 2002 to €1.9 billion in 2011; Inditex's founder Amancio Ortega was pronounced the world's third richest man in August 2012, with a personal fortune estimated at $46.6 billion.[21]

Exploitation Without End

While Western consumers and retailers have benefited from the globalisation of garments production, those producing the goods have been excluded from the feast. The enforced decline in factory prices has steadily increased pressure on workers' terms and conditions, as factory owners pass on retailers' more stringent requirements on price and response times to the workforce. As detailed below, suppressed wages have fallen far behind the cost of living, at a time when prices of basic foodstuffs and other essentials have escalated dramatically in all producer countries. In addition, the earlier demands of 'lean retailing', with its emphasis on constantly updated consumer preferences, product proliferation and rapid stock replenishment, have now been superseded by 'fast fashion', where producers are required to meet even quicker response times but now with the added pressure of supplying distinguishably new designs rather than replenishment orders.[22] As a consequence, working hours have become longer and less predictable as corporate profits and consumer convenience are granted absolute priority over the needs of the producer workforce.[23]

The true cost of the deflationary pressure on workers' wages became clear during the first decade of the twenty-first century, as new exposés revealed a standard pattern of exploitation in garments factories around the world. Bangladesh is regularly cited as the most extreme example of this pattern, as the country competes in the global market by offering buyers the lowest labour costs in the world. As a result of undercutting the factory prices of competitor countries, Bangladesh has become the second largest exporter of ready-made garments behind China, supplying clothes to many of the world's best known retailers such as Wal-Mart, Tesco, Primark, Marks & Spencer, H&M and Carrefour. The importance of the sector to the Bangladeshi national economy is reflected in the unparalleled political power of the garment factory owners, many of whom also hold leading positions in parliament. By the same token, trade unionists and other activists who stand up against this power do so at great personal risk, as evidenced by the sustained campaign of violence and intimidation against them by Bangladeshi state security forces, including the special police force for the garments sector that was set up in 2010. In addition to the violent suppression of protests and industrial action, trade union leaders and labour rights activists have faced personal threats and violence from security forces, including the arrest of hundreds of trade unionists during 2010 and the torture and murder of leading labour rights activist Aminul Islam in April 2012.[24]

Workers in the Bangladeshi garments industry have responded to the downwards pressure on wages with sector-wide mobilisation and action. The minimum monthly wage for garment workers was set at 1,662 taka by the government in 2006 – its first increase since 1994 – in response to months of coordinated protests by workers across Bangladesh, but then remained unchanged for the next four years, despite rampant inflation raising prices on all daily necessities. Sustained industrial action in 2010 secured a further 80 per cent increase to 3,000 taka a month, but even this victory left the legal minimum well short of the 5,000 taka baseline identified as necessary by Bangladeshi trade unions, let alone the actual cost of living for families living in the capital, Dhaka. As a result the situation soon became critical once more, leading to renewed clashes between workers and factory owners that closed down over 300 factories in the Ashulia industrial district outside Dhaka for an entire week during June 2012. Yet the defining moment for the Bangladesh garments industry came with the collapse of the eight-storey Rana Plaza building in the Dhaka subdistrict of Savar on 24 April 2013, killing over 1,100 workers who had been at work at a number of garments factories on the upper floors. The wave of international outrage generated by the disaster focused attention on the local factory owners for failing to heed warnings that the building was unsafe, and also on the Western brands sourcing clothing from the factories, whose perennial demand for cost-cutting was understood to be instrumental in denying workers the basic guarantees that would have prevented the building's collapse. It remains to be seen whether the commitments on building safety, higher wages and trade union representation made by the brands and the Bangladesh government in the immediate aftermath of the Rana Plaza disaster will lead to a new era for an industry whose competitive edge in the global market has until now been based on the most extreme exploitation of its workforce.

Similar tensions are apparent in the garments sector in Cambodia, another source country increasingly favoured by Western brands such as Gap, H&M and Zara because of its low factory prices and labour costs. Despite the ILO's Better Factories Cambodia programme, the garments industry in that country is blighted by chronically low pay levels and by working weeks regularly in excess of 70 hours. Cambodia has the lowest garments sector wage of any country in South-East Asia, at a level estimated to be under half a living wage. Combined with poor working conditions, persistently long hours have led to the mass fainting of workers witnessed in Cambodia's garment and shoe factories during the past few years, with incidences ranging from dozens to hundreds of workers collapsing at any one time. Around 90 per cent of the workforce in the garments industry is made up of young women migrants from rural Cambodia, where paid jobs are rare and poverty is widespread, and while trade union density is relatively high in the garments sector, the right to freedom of association is undermined by a climate of intimidation and harassment of trade union leaders. Over 200,000 Cambodian garment workers have taken part in strikes over wage levels and factory conditions in recent years, winning additional allowances that effectively raised the basic $61 minimum wage to $83 a month from September 2012. In light of rising living costs in Cambodia, however, trade union leaders branded the increases insufficient to prevent future unrest.[25]

While the wage suppression strategies of Bangladesh and Cambodia represent the globalised garments industry at its most extreme, the trend towards exploitation is standard across all countries that have managed to survive the ending of the MFA regime by attracting foreign investment on the basis of low labour costs. In Vietnam, workers have identified low wages and the prevalence of the piece-rate system as the issues of most pressing concern within the garments industry, and recent years have seen a rising wave of industrial action as high inflation tightens the squeeze on already low incomes.[26] Foreign-owned factories from elsewhere in Asia have been particularly affected by the unrest, leading the government to amend the country's Labour Code to introduce a minimum wage for the first time in Vietnamese law and to increase the provision for maternity leave from four to six months as of May 2013. Indonesia's garments sector has seen similar waves of protests over low wages, social security benefits and the outsourcing of jobs to companies supplying contract workers. In the wake of a one-day strike across the country's industrial zones in October 2012, the head of the Indonesian Chamber of Commerce responded to the call for an increase in the minimum wage, saying: 'This is part of what makes Indonesia attractive. Our wages are more competitive than China, and we have to keep conditions appealing to investors.'[27] In Sri Lanka, tens of thousands of women workers protested during 2011 at the government's proposed imposition of a new private sector pension scheme, which would have fallen particularly hard on workers in the garments industry; the protests were violently suppressed by the police, with one protester killed by live ammunition, but the government eventually agreed to withdraw the legislative bill that would have set up the scheme. Even Burma has seen its first signs of labour unrest in the garments industry following decades of military rule, with a number of sit-down protests for better pay and working conditions during 2012.[28]

The garments sector in Pakistan presents a different profile to those already described, in that it has attracted limited foreign investment from elsewhere in Asia and the vast majority of its factories are therefore domestically owned. Pakistan also differs from most other countries in that women have until now constituted a minority of the workforce in the garments sector, but factories are increasingly seeking to employ women workers as part of a strategy to reduce labour costs, as female sewing machine operators typically earn a third less than their male counterparts.[29] While Pakistan's textiles industry is relatively modernised and capital-intensive, the country's garments sector remains a more traditional cottage industry, with most of its 2 million workers employed in small production units and often (especially in the case of women) as temporary contract labourers with no employee benefits such as maternity leave, transport or day care facilities. Pakistan's minimum wage was increased in 2010 from 6,000 to 7,000 rupees a month, and to 8,000 rupees in 2012; yet this is calculated to be less than half of what is required as a living wage in the country, given the effects of inflation and the continuing depreciation of the Pakistani rupee against the US dollar. Moreover, in the absence of any government enforcement many factories in Pakistan are known to flout national wage rules, meaning that large numbers of workers do not receive even the minimum determined at the state level. The failure to enforce basic regulations extends to all areas of industrial safety, with government inspections known to be ineffective, at best. It was revealed that the Ali Enterprises garments factory in Karachi which burned down on 11 September 2012 at the cost of 258 lives had no fire exits or safety equipment, and that workers had been unable to escape as a result of being locked in the factory. Another fire in an illegal shoe factory in Lahore on the same day killed a further 25 workers.[30]

India and China are similar to Pakistan insofar as they also boast vertically integrated garments industries linked to domestic sources of cotton and the production of textiles. An estimated 35 million people are employed in India's textiles and garments sectors combined, with many women in the garments sector working in small home-based units within the informal economy, where pay and conditions are at their lowest and abuses such as child labour still widely reported. As with Pakistan, foreign investment into the sector has been minimal, and Europe remains the principal export market. In India's case, however, around two thirds of all textile and garment production is directed towards the country's vast domestic market – a market which has already been targeted by international brand retailers such as DKNY, Gant and Marks & Spencer, which has 24 stores across ten Indian cities. The huge sales potential represented by China's burgeoning middle class is of even greater interest to foreign retailers, in that the country's fashion market tripled in size to $60 billion between 2000 and 2010, and is predicted to triple again by 2020.[31] Nike and Adidas each have over 6,000 stores in China, while latecomers Inditex opened 75 new stores there during 2010 alone and Japanese clothing retailer Uniqlo has voiced its intention to open 100 new stores in the country every year. China's own garments industry has experienced significant upgrading in recent times, with wages now rising as the country moves up the value chain. While higher production costs will not dent China's domination of the global clothing market for several years yet, brands have already begun looking towards additional source countries such as Vietnam, Bangladesh and Cambodia in an attempt to keep their profit margins high.[32] The unprecedented mobility offered to capital by outsourced production networks makes the job security of supplier workforces an irrelevance.

Ethical Impasse

The yawning gulf between buyer practices and corporate rhetoric indicates how the CSR programmes introduced in the 1990s have functioned as smoke screens to hide the reality of how TNCs operate in the globalised garments sector. Codes of conduct introduced by the brands and retailers have perpetuated the power relations that define the industry, and provisions to promote the rights to freedom of association and collective bargaining have been commonly undermined.[33] A new torrent of exploitation exposés in the media during the 2000s eventually turned the spotlight onto the multi-stakeholder initiatives themselves, raising questions not only as to their effectiveness but also their legitimacy as buyer-dominated bodies perpetuating an unequal system to the benefit of transnational capital. The independent assessment of the ETI published in 2006 found that the only tangible benefits seen by workers as a result of the initiative were in the field of health and safety, while fundamental conditions of employment such as worker income, job security and freedom of association had remained largely untouched by the introduction of the ETI base code.[34] Similarly, an academic review of 805 factory audits that had been carried out by the 'corporate-influenced' Fair Labor Association between 2002 and 2010 found that they were far more competent at uncovering 'minimal' violations in health and safety, wages and benefits than the most serious abuses of workers' rights such as freedom of association, which went largely unreported.[35] The unpublished draft evaluation of the MFA Forum, which was eventually discontinued in 2011, noted that it had struggled to define its objectives as an initiative and to make any tangible progress in the countries where it had tried to set up national working groups, such as Bangladesh, where the overwhelming power of the employers' association and the intimidation of local trade unionists exposed the Forum's hopes to start up a genuinely participatory dialogue as unrealistic.[36] The JO-IN initiative piloted in Turkey between 2004 and 2007 exposed a similar flaw in the multi-stakeholder approach, in that – like most such projects – it represented a collaboration between corporations and campaigners from the USA and Europe in which local workers and trade unions played little part. In addition to the obvious question of legitimacy raised by such exclusivity, which extended even to withholding the identities of the supplier factories from those local trade unions that were involved in the initiative, the project was rendered ineffective as a result of being viewed by Turkish workers as an employers' initiative, and therefore untrustworthy. The suggestion that one could transplant alien traditions of social dialogue into the hostile context of Turkish industrial relations was acknowledged as a stumbling block in the final report of the initiative itself.[37]

While many criticisms have been levelled at multi-stakeholder initiatives, the audit-based approach to improving pay or working conditions has come under particular attack for failing to secure any lasting structural improvements. Accounts of 'audit fraud' were common from the start, including individual workers being schooled in how to deliver the desired responses to visiting auditors, factory owners keeping false sets of documentation in order to mislead inspectors, and other such obfuscations; one report noted that there are even software packages and training courses in China for factories to learn how to keep multiple sets of staff records in order to pass audits.[38] By 2006, the practice of ethical auditing was so discredited that the ETI itself was talking of a sector in crisis, noting that audits were 'ineffective at identifying many of the most serious labour problems'. By the end of the decade, social auditing had been rejected by most serious commentators as a basis for genuine improvement in workers' rights, with the ETI's own communications manager dismissing it as an approach 'which we all know fails to drive any change for workers'.[39] The fact that it continues regardless has been ascribed to the fact that ethical auditing is now an $80 billion industry in its own right, with a vested interest in self-perpetuation.[40]

Cross-Border Resistance

As the private governance model of voluntary codes and social auditing has now been rejected as a meaningful solution to the continuing problems of exploitation in the globalised garments industry, the focus has shifted onto the power relations underpinning the system and the model of networked capitalism itself. While international campaigns against the brands and retailers continue to call for systems of accountability for corporations profiting from exploitative supply chains, there is now universal recognition of the need for functioning trade union structures within the factories themselves as the indispensable mechanism for defending and advancing workers' rights. In this respect, genuine freedom of association and collective bargaining rights are critical at the individual factory level, while the development of broader forms of 'associational power' through mobilisations by trade unions and other workers' organisations at the national level has been shown to be the most effective way of securing better terms and conditions, including wage increases, across the industry as a whole.[41]

Yet the central contradiction of all outsourced production networks is that while workers and their trade unions may confront the immediate failure of factory owners and national governments to guarantee decent working conditions and a living wage, ultimate responsibility rests not at the national level but with the buyers and retailers that control the global supply chain and dictate the terms of its operation. Those who hold power over the value chain are removed from the locus of production itself, and thus insulated from any direct challenge on the part of labour – this being the essential advantage of all outsourced production, reinforced in the final analysis by the ease with which buyers can end a relationship with any particular supplier and take their business elsewhere. Faced with this most extreme form of capital mobility, individual associations of workers are constrained in what they can achieve at the factory or national level, and can only hope to mitigate the worst excesses of the system. As Jeroen Merk describes it, 'even if workers succeed in organising themselves and want to enter into collective bargaining, they discover that they are bargaining with the wrong people, namely local capital itself subordinated to the dynamics of global capitalism'.[42]

As a strategy to counter the elusiveness of buyer power and the underlying threat of relocation, trade unions and other workers' rights organisations from across Asia have launched a cross-border campaign for a living wage in the garments industry: the Asia Floor Wage. Living wage campaigns demand a needs-based entitlement in place of the market-based minimum wage customarily set by national wage boards, calculated so as to provide workers with an income to cover all basic necessities as well as a small amount of discretionary income. From its first international planning meeting in 2007, the Asia Floor Wage Alliance has extended this principle to cover differences between national economies, setting a floor wage according to purchasing power parity (PPP) in US dollars (calculated at 540 PPP $ for 2012), which can then be applied to each country in the region as a guide to what the living wage might represent. The wage is calculated so as to provide sufficient income to cover food and non-food expenditure for a household of three consumption units (for example, two adults and two children), to be earned within each country's maximum working week and in no case exceeding the ILO's standard limit of 48 hours. This then provides a benchmark for labour rights activists in each country to use in their collective bargaining and other mobilisations, with the aim of preventing capital from playing off workers in different countries against each other.

The cross-border campaign for an Asia Floor Wage is a necessary response to the extreme form of capital mobility inherent in the networked capitalism of the global garments industry. By basing its demands upon the needs of the worker and her family rather than the market, it contests the appropriation of surplus value that is at the heart of the capitalist system, and thus forms 'part of a process of subordinating capitalism to an alien logic, the logic of human development'.[43] Yet even the most successful challenge to the foundations of capitalist production will be limited in what it can achieve if it does not seek to transcend the confines of a global system that is stacked against the workers. In this respect, the most important contribution made by movements for a living wage is, like other such mobilisations, the class consciousness that workers gain from taking action together in pursuit of their common interest, and the potential this creates for an eventual exit from the 'impasse of capitalism'.[44] Even more significantly, therefore, the cross-border organisation of garments industry workers in the Asia Floor Wage Alliance is a vehicle by which to develop an international class consciousness over and against the very real challenges posed by globalisation to transnational solidarity itself.[45] As already noted by Marx and Engels in the *Communist Manifesto*, the individual victories of organised labour in securing wage increases or other gains are of secondary importance when compared to these longer-term structural developments: 'The real fruit of their battle lies, not in the immediate result, but in the ever-expanding union of the workers. This union is helped on by the improved means of communication that are created by modern industry and that place the workers of different localities in contact with one another.'[46] The potential for expanding this union on a global scale is greatly enhanced today by virtue of the communications revolution, but to have any long-term effect the international labour movement must still direct its challenge to the globalised capitalist system itself. Otherwise, as Marx noted to the General Council of the First International in June 1865, it will simply be 'applying palliatives, not curing the malady'.[47]

It is now commonly agreed that the era of constantly falling consumer prices for clothing is over. With the cost of raw materials and freight rising, retail prices for garments are starting to increase once more in line with other goods. Workers are already being told that they cannot hope for wage increases as long as factory margins are squeezed by the rising cost of inputs – just as in deflationary periods the same workers were told that they could not expect wage increases as long as factory prices for their outputs were in decline. Nothing could indicate better the political economy of a sector where profits accrue to those who wield the greatest power over the value chain: where brands and retailers can switch suppliers with ease and at no cost to their own operations, capital will always retain the whip hand. This is why the garments industry represents such an important case study, in that it exemplifies the networked structure of globalised production, distribution and consumption that has come to characterise the capitalist world economy in the twenty-first century. The same structural iniquities can be observed in other value chains where the lion's share of the profits is captured by the brands and retailers, yet in some sectors alternative models have been developed as a direct challenge to the system itself. One of the most powerful of these is to be found in the food sovereignty movement, which has developed a comprehensive framework for the production, distribution and consumption of food which aims to confront and, eventually, supplant the capitalist food regime. That alternative forms the subject matter of the next chapter.

7

Food: The Final Frontier

The global food regime exemplifies in its starkest form the challenge posed to the peoples of the world by the endless process of capitalist accumulation. As with the garments sector, the production, distribution and consumption of food are already dominated by a small number of giant transnational corporations who seek to determine what is grown and what is eaten in all corners of the globe. As with the extractive sector, capital has become increasingly aggressive in its attempts to appropriate the natural resources necessary for its further expansion: land, seeds, water and the genetic building blocks of life itself. These 'new frontiers' of primitive accumulation have in turn generated a modern day gold rush of hedge funds, pension funds, sovereign wealth funds and private equity funds desperate to buy into the latest asset classes following the bursting of their dotcom and housing bubbles. The renewed 'scramble for Africa' is just the most visible example of a phenomenon that is tearing across the planet as a whole.

The direct challenge posed by such speculative activity has galvanised a worldwide movement of peasant farmers, fisherfolk, landless workers and indigenous peoples determined to defend their lands and their livelihoods from the depredations of foreign investors. More than just a force of resistance, however, the movement has developed its own positive framework of food sovereignty to set against the dominant capitalist model of dispossession and exploitation. The principles of food sovereignty, described more fully below, provide the framework under which communities retain the right to develop their own models of farming on agroecological lines, and to explore constructive alternatives to a global system that has delivered great gains to agribusiness but failed in all social and ecological respects.[1]

The full extent of that failure was brought to international attention in 2009 when the UN's Food and Agriculture Organisation (FAO) reported that, for the first time in human history, over a billion people were officially classified as living in hunger. The FAO stressed that this scandal was not a result of limited food supplies, in that the previous two years had seen record levels of cereal production, but a direct consequence of poverty and economic disempowerment of those who could no longer afford the food available.[2] The backlash that met the publication of the one billion figure led the FAO to suspend further statistical pronouncements on global hunger until 2012, when its annual *State of Food Insecurity* report recorded instead that 868 million people should be considered 'chronically undernourished'. Yet the FAO itself acknowledged that this headline figure 'should be deemed a very conservative indicator of hunger' as it relates only to those who fail to secure the minimum intake of calories required to support a 'sedentary' lifestyle. When set against the minimum level of calories needed to sustain a lifestyle of 'normal activity', the FAO estimated that 1.52 billion people are without enough food, while for the level needed to sustain 'intense activity' the FAO estimated that as many as 2.56 billion people have an inadequate food intake – substantially more than the corresponding figure for the same category in 1990.[3]

The conclusion that more working people around the world are now suffering from insufficient food than 20 years ago corresponds to the indicators of growing inequality and reduced share of national income returning to labour that were noted in Chapter 2. Yet the ultimate scandal is that the majority of those suffering from extreme poverty are to be found among the world's rural populations – precisely those who, as food producers, should be benefiting from rising prices – just as three quarters of all those living with chronic hunger are from smallholder farming communities, landless rural families or communities dependent on herding, fishing or forest resources. In a global food regime that has increasingly favoured the spread of industrial agriculture over sustainable local farming, those who live off the land have been rendered most vulnerable. As food commodities fetch record prices on global markets, those growing the food are denied even the basic minimum to eat.[4]

Extractive Agriculture

The struggle for power over agricultural production is as old as the history of colonialism itself. As recounted so vividly in Eduardo

Galeano's *Open Veins of Latin America*, the sugar cane plantations established in north-east Brazil and across the Caribbean from the sixteenth century onwards provided the model for an extractive capitalism which still today regards local communities and ecosystems as nothing more than sources of profit to be exploited, exhausted and abandoned in favour of new ventures elsewhere. Predicated upon the inexhaustible supply of slave labour from Africa, the sugar trade enriched not only the Portuguese, Spanish, Dutch and British directly involved in it, but also made possible the development of European industry as a whole – and even when slave labour was no longer available, the model remained intact and was replicated across other commodities such as cacao, cotton, coffee and the fruit plantations of Central America, each time bringing 'monoculture, the burning of forests, the dictatorship of international prices, and perpetual penury for the workers'.[5] The irresistible appeal of an agricultural system directed purely towards capital accumulation laid the foundations for today's *latifundia* and corporate plantations, and for the new expropriations that have become a defining characteristic of twenty-first-century globalisation.

Corporate control over the global food regime extends to more than just land. Industrial agriculture has created a complex system of interlocking oligopolies that spans seeds, agrochemicals, biotechnology, trading, retailing and consumer goods companies. Just three transnational corporations – Monsanto, DuPont and Syngenta – control between them over half the world's entire commercial seed market; all three are also ranked in the top ten list of world agrochemical companies, which Syngenta dominates with close to 20 per cent market share, and all three are major players in the biotechnology industry. The four largest commodity traders – ADM, Bunge, Cargill and Louis Dreyfus: the 'ABCD companies' – enjoy significant power over world trade in grains, oilseeds and palm oil. The top ten food processing corporations control 28 per cent of the global market, with Nestlé far and away the largest single company, followed by PepsiCo and Kraft Foods. In addition, the world's largest ten food retailers have more than doubled their share of the global market over the last decade as the major supermarket chains of Europe and the USA have sought to expand their operations away from their domestic bases. This intensity of market concentration means that a group of no more than 40 transnational corporations effectively control the global food regime from farm to fork, and have amassed spectacular profits as a result of their market domination. In 2010, as food price inflation and volatility once again reached record heights, the world's four largest agrochemical companies (Bayer, Dow, Syngenta and Monsanto) and three largest grain traders (ADM, Bunge and Cargill) made profits between them of $20 billion.[6]

At the same time, however, the majority of the staple crops needed to feed the planet's burgeoning population are grown not by transnational corporations but by farmers using traditional methods; indeed, 400 million of the 525 million farms that are estimated to exist across the world are classified as small farms, under two hectares in size. These smallholdings are known to have higher yields than large, plantation-based farms, as well as far greater potential for poverty reduction through increased returns on labour, with evidence that for every 10 per cent rise in yields there is a 7 per cent reduction in poverty in Africa, and over 5 per cent in Asia.[7] Yet instead of supporting the development of small-scale farming for subsistence or local trading, there has been a marked bias over the past 40 years towards the expansion of industrial agriculture dominated by transnational corporations, for use predominantly in growing cash crops for export, cattle feed or agrofuels. While small-scale farming still accounts for the majority of staples produced for human consumption, an increasing proportion of the total 1.5 billion hectares of land currently in use around the world for crop production is taken up by plantation-style monocultures dependent upon high volumes of agrochemical inputs.

The primary vehicle through which the global shift towards industrial agriculture has been realised was the Green Revolution, which engineered the expansion of corporate control over the farming systems of Asia and Latin America from the 1950s onwards. Based on the development of new, high-yielding varieties of staples such as maize, wheat and rice, the Green Revolution brought about a dramatic intensification of agriculture as farmers turned their land over to monocultures of the new varieties in place of traditional systems of intercropping, with two or three harvests per year instead of one. Millions adopted the intensive use of agrochemicals such as fertiliser and pesticides for the first time, sourcing them from corporate suppliers together with the new seeds in input 'packages' financed with credit from willing government elites. The Green Revolution thus saw an increased standardisation of farming, as industrialised agriculture fought against variation in natural ecosystems in order to raise the productivity of land and labour alike, as well as an increased integration of farming into corporate production networks both upstream (in the provision of seeds and agrochemicals) and downstream (in food processing, distribution and retail).[8] In addition, greater restrictions were then placed on the saving and sharing of seeds as a result of the global extension of intellectual property rights over plant life, as national governments were required by the World Trade Organisation's (WTO's) Trade-Related Aspects of Intellectual Property Rights (TRIPs) Agreement to provide effective protection for patent holders, including through legal mechanisms to enforce their rights against any farmers deemed to be infringing them. The fact that patents have been granted on natural life forms already known by indigenous peoples for centuries but now claimed by transnational corporations for their own – the practice otherwise known as biopiracy – only underlines the threat posed by the new restrictions.[9]

These developments brought a spectacular increase in profits for the companies concerned, whose products were marketed so successfully across Asia and Latin America that those two regions now account for higher sales of agrochemicals than Europe and North America combined.[10] Yet any broader success claimed by the Green Revolution in terms of distribution or hunger reduction was quickly revealed to be a mirage. While the total amount of food available per person across the world rose by 11 per cent between 1970 and 1990, and the estimated number of people living in hunger fell, these headline figures concealed more disturbing realities. Per capita food production did increase during this period by 8 per cent in South America and by 9 per cent in South Asia (both key areas for the new technologies of the Green Revolution) but the number of hungry people in each region rose by 19 per cent and 9 per cent, respectively – a potent reminder, if one were needed, that hunger in the modern era is a consequence of distribution rather than shortages of food. The global reduction in the number of people going hungry, on the other hand, was overwhelmingly due to progress achieved through rural reforms in China, which had not pursued Green Revolution policies. Taking

China out of the equation, the number of hungry people in the world increased during the Green Revolution by 11 per cent.[11]

The long-term social and ecological problems caused by increased dependence on high-input, intensified agriculture have further undermined the Green Revolution's claim to success. As well as a serious loss of biodiversity, intensive monoculture farming gradually led to a decline in productivity growth rates as land was no longer permitted to lie fallow and regenerate, while the increased use of pesticides and fertilisers brought its own inevitable consequences in the form of soil degradation, water pollution and increased emissions of nitrous oxide, one of the most potent greenhouse gases.[12] The impact on farmers was equally devastating. In the early stages of the Green Revolution, many peasant farmers who could not afford the 'packages' of seeds, fertiliser and pesticides were displaced from their smallholdings, leading to an increased concentration of land ownership in the hands of richer farmers, and rising inequality in rural areas.[13] Those who were able to obtain credit to buy the packages saw benefits from higher yields in the early years, but soon found themselves driven deeper into debt as a result of rising agrochemical prices, declining soil fertility and a need to apply ever more inputs. Rural households were forced to sell off livestock and land in an attempt to escape bankruptcy, and over a quarter of a million farmers committed suicide in India between 1995 and 2010 as a result of desperation in the face of such debt.[14] Those who were drawn into planting genetically modified seeds as part of the second wave of the Green Revolution soon discovered that the promises of the biotechnology corporations were as hollow as those of their predecessors, as farmers were eventually forced to spend more and more on pesticides to fight off new attacks. In the Indian state of Andhra Pradesh, where the government eventually banned Monsanto from operating, nine out of every ten farmers who committed suicide had been growing genetically modified cotton. Many killed themselves by drinking the pesticides that had condemned them to indebtedness in the first place.[15]

A New Green Revolution

Despite such warnings from recent history, there are now moves to initiate a new Green Revolution in those parts of the world that have not yet been wholly incorporated into industrial agriculture.[16] In particular, there has been a concerted effort on the part of donor institutions to extend the principles into Africa, a continent which successfully resisted earlier attempts to win it over to the Green Revolution. Leading the charge, the Rockefeller Foundation together with the Bill and Melinda Gates Foundation established the Alliance for a Green Revolution in Africa (AGRA) in 2006 as a vehicle for the pro-capitalist transformation of African farming through private investment and agricultural intensification – a political project that offers a striking parallel with the funding of the first Green Revolution by the Rockefeller and Ford Foundations as an explicitly anti-communist venture in the period after the Second World War.[17] Reflecting the growing power of philanthrocapital to determine the orientation of public bodies, AGRA subsequently received donor support from a number of government agencies including the UK's Department for International Development (DFID), USAID and the official international development agencies of Sweden and Denmark. Together with other G8 members, DFID and USAID have also joined forces in the New Alliance for Food Security and Nutrition, which has pledged to deepen the involvement of transnational corporations in African agriculture by leveraging over $3 billion of investment through a series of public-private partnerships that will integrate smallholder farms into the global operations of companies such as Cargill, DuPont, Monsanto, Syngenta, Unilever, Yara, Diageo and SABMiller. DFID announced in September 2012 that it would be contributing an initial $600 million to the New Alliance over three years, for use in Ethiopia, Ghana, Tanzania and Mozambique; the programme has since expanded to include several other African states.[18]

Africa's 33 million small farms account for around 80 per cent of the continent's agricultural production, which is in turn responsible for 75 per cent of total employment; the stakes could therefore not be higher from the point of view of the 239 million Africans categorised by the FAO as chronically undernourished.[19] From the perspective of the global agribusiness industry, on the other hand, Africa's farmers offer an important market both as consumers and as producers. As consumers, farmers must be integrated into the use of 'improved' inputs such as agrochemicals and hybrid seeds, on the understanding that they will become dependent on such inputs in the same way as their Asian counterparts during the first Green Revolution. To this end, the main programme of AGRA is the promotion of networks of local agro-dealers to sell farmers the chemicals and seeds provided by the transnational corporations, extending the companies' reach into new areas they were previously incapable of accessing; the importance of these networks is shown by revelations such as that coming out of Malawi, where 100 per cent of Monsanto's seed and herbicide sales have been achieved through AGRA's agro-dealer network, which has taken over the agricultural extension services previously delivered by the state.[20] As producers, farmers are increasingly incorporated into the supply chains of major agribusiness companies as outgrowers operating under contract, in a form of networked capitalism similar to that described for the garments industry in the previous chapter. This integration of African agriculture into the international food regime is the ultimate aim of many of the other initiatives being rolled out for the private sector across the continent, such as the new 'agricultural growth corridors' being trialled in countries such as Tanzania and Mozambique, establishing the presence not only of agribusiness but of mining and forestry companies as well.[21] In practice, farmers are often involved in such initiatives simultaneously as consumers and producers, as they purchase the corporate input packages precisely so that their output might meet the needs and standards of the supply chains in question. For its part, agribusiness gains access to the rich biodiversity of Africa's traditional seed heritage, now privatised and commodified for corporate profit.[22]

Critical to the success of the new Green Revolution is Africa's willingness to abandon resistance to the introduction of genetically modified (GM) crops into its agricultural systems.[23] South Africa has traditionally stood alone as the sole country on the continent to have permitted commercial GM production, although Egypt and Burkina Faso have also in recent years allowed the commercialisation of GM maize and cotton. The promotion of GM technology has been a central theme in the efforts of many donors to dictate the direction of African agriculture, with the Gates and Rockefeller Foundations again leading the way as active funders of research into GM crop varieties (the senior programme officer responsible for supervising AGRA within the Gates Foundation is Robert Horsch, a pioneer of genetic engineering who worked for Monsanto for 25 years). The capitalist motivation in promoting GM crops has been clear from the outset, as it is well understood that farmers incorporated into GM agriculture are dependent on corporate sales for the seeds and accompanying chemicals to continue their plantings. This corporate interest is equally evident in the membership of the bodies pressing for the adoption of GM technology in Africa: the African Agricultural Technology Foundation (AATF), which leads the promotion of GM crops across the continent, was designed by representatives from USAID, DFID and the Rockefeller Foundation working in close collaboration with biotechnology corporations Monsanto, Pioneer Hi-Bred, Aventis CropScience and Dow.[24]

There has been marked resistance to the new Green Revolution within Africa, in relation to the threat of GM crops, the incorporation of smallholder farming into transnational supply chains and the privatisation of Africa's own genetic wealth. African civil society groups meeting at the 2007 World Social Forum in Nairobi published a statement rejecting attempts to expand corporate dependency within African farming by means of AGRA and other initiatives, and affirming the right of African peoples to determine their own paths to the future.[25] Looking back over the first six years of AGRA's operations, the African Centre for Biosafety criticised the embedding of its technological programme within corporate power structures, 'laying the groundwork for the commercialisation of African agriculture and its selective integration into global circuits of accumulation'.[26] Mamadou Cissokho, Honorary President of the West African farmers' movement ROPPA, wrote an open letter to the President of the African Union prior to the G8's food summit in May 2012 rejecting AGRA, the New Alliance for Food Security and Nutrition and the 'Grow Africa' initiative of the World Economic Forum as 'seriously compromising' the legitimate agricultural development programmes formulated by West African states in conjunction with peasant farmers and other agricultural producers.[27] The same charge could be laid against the myriad other initiatives planned for African agriculture by global elites on behalf of foreign investors, too numerous to mention here.[28]

Land Grabbing

Nowhere is the drive for capitalist expansion seen more clearly than in the rush to dispossess farming communities of their land for use in the corporate production of food, agrofuels and agro-industrial crops, or simply for speculation. As many commentators have emphasised, the expropriation of land from the peasantry is a recurrent historical phenomenon, with the term 'land grabbing' already found in Marx's account of the displacement of rural labour through which large-scale agriculture was first introduced into England.[29] In the present context, capital's accelerated appetite for land acquisition reflects the relative scarcity of other asset classes in which it can be so profitably invested, together with the recognition that commodity prices are likely to remain high into the long-term future, as the rising demand for food is exacerbated by the challenges of climate change, water scarcity and the steady loss of millions of hectares of cultivated land to soil degradation and urbanisation each year.

While estimates vary as to the total number of deals done, at least 83 million hectares of land in the global South have been acquired in transnational agricultural investments (not including mining, forestry or tourism) since the year 2000.[30] Very often it is the most fertile land that is appropriated by investors, who are typically granted long leases or concessions lasting for anything up to 99 years. Foreign investors have targeted agricultural land in as many as 84 countries across the world, with a significant bias towards African states such as Sudan, Mozambique, Tanzania, Ethiopia, Madagascar, Zambia and the Democratic Republic of Congo (listed in order of total land area covered in reported deals). In Asia, investors have particularly focused their attention on the Philippines, Indonesia, Lao PDR and Cambodia, which alone has seen concessions covering two million hectares (over 10 per cent of the country's total land mass) granted to agro-industrial businesses, including several from China and Vietnam.[31] Brazil and Argentina are the two countries that have been most closely targeted in Latin America, while European capital has also pursued large-scale land acquisition in Russia, Ukraine and Kazakhstan. Even if the phenomenon of land grabbing is familiar from history, there is no doubting the scale of its current ambition.

The precise interest in land acquisition differs between investors. The rush to agrofuels has been responsible for around a third of all large-scale land grabs recorded during the first ten years of the twenty-first century, with private companies registered in the UK and Netherlands particularly active in land acquisition for the production of jatropha, the agrofuel crop behind three quarters of all non-food land grabs. Apocalyptic projections suggest that plantations of jatropha and other agrofuel crops could expand to encompass 20 per cent of all arable land by 2050 – a development whose destructive impact would be 'unprecedented in contemporary capitalism'.[32] Other deals have involved foreign agribusiness firms taking over farmland to produce staples such as rice, maize and wheat; non-food cash crops such as cotton (especially prevalent among land acquisitions in Ethiopia, for example); or so-called 'flex crops' such as soya bean, sugar cane and oil palm, which can be used for a range of food and non-food purposes. Others have seen investors establish agro-industrial plantations to produce high-value crops such as rubber, while others again have acquired land for tree plantations, or to log existing forests. Private equity funds, pension funds and sovereign wealth funds have invested substantial sums in agricultural land with a view to long-term financial returns, while hedge funds have engaged with an eye to more aggressive speculation.[33] Yet the common thread binding together all these forms of capital investment is the neocolonial drive to accumulate by means of the dispossession of those currently living off the land.

As hinted above, the global land rush is not simply a matter of capital from the global North being invested in the global South: China's acquisition of agricultural land around the world has been well documented in media reports, but Malaysia, South Africa, India, United Arab Emirates and South Korea also rank in the top ten countries signing transnational land takeovers, and individual countries can have a large presence in particular regions or states (Brazilian and Argentinian agribusiness in other parts of Latin America, for example, or Saudi Arabia in Sudan). Equally, countries can be both victims and aggressors at one and the same time: as local communities mobilise to resist land grabs in 130 separate districts across India, Indian enterprises have moved to acquire agricultural land in countries such as Gabon, Liberia, Madagascar, Indonesia, Lao PDR, Cambodia and Ethiopia, where Indian enterprises represent the second largest body of investors and where the forced eviction of communities to make way for new agricultural projects has led to serious human rights abuses.[34] In addition, much land acquisition takes place within borders: while large transnational takeovers receive most media attention, national elites are often responsible for a significant proportion of land deals in their countries, especially the acquisition of farms that are large by local standards but inconsiderable when compared to the typical size of foreign investments.[35]

The violence with which land is expropriated for capital without the free, prior and informed consent of the people living on it can often involve the forced eviction and displacement of whole communities. In Cambodia, dozens of rural and indigenous communities have been forcibly evicted to make way for new agribusiness projects, with over 400,000 people affected in the past decade.[36] In Colombia, farmers of the Afro-Colombian, indigenous and mestizo communities have been forced from their lands in terror attacks by right-wing paramilitary groups linked to agribusiness, in order to establish oil palm, banana and agrofuels plantations on their territories.[37] Similar mass evictions to make way for agricultural land grabs have been reported in recent years from Uganda, Honduras, Guatemala and many other countries, in addition to the vast number of instances where farmland has been expropriated for the extractive industries or other investments.[38] Around a third of the total land surface covered in reported deals is in forested areas, raising further concern as to the ecological damage that could arise if those forests are logged or otherwise destroyed to expand plantation agriculture. Olivier De Schutter, UN Special Rapporteur on the Right to Food, has argued that states have a duty to protect communities already living on the land, and to prioritise 'development models that do not lead to evictions, disruptive shifts in land rights and increased land concentration'. According to De Schutter, agricultural deals that imply a significant shift in land rights 'should represent the last and least desirable option, acceptable only if no other investment model can achieve a similar contribution to local development and improve the livelihoods within the local communities concerned.'[39]

Resistance and Alternatives

The accelerated spread of land grabbing has inspired significant resistance among local communities threatened with the loss of their lands and livelihoods. In addition to the Indian mobilisations mentioned above, there have been major demonstrations against agricultural land dispossessions in countries as diverse as Cambodia, China, Colombia, Cameroon, Ethiopia, Sierra Leone, Uganda and

Poland, to name a few. In August 2012, farmers protesting against the theft of thousands of hectares of farmland in Isabela province in the Philippines shut down production at the Green Futures bioethanol plant constructed by Philippine, Japanese and Taiwanese investors.[40] In Madagascar, where Korean industrial giant Daewoo had secured an extraordinary 99-year concession to 1.3 million hectares of arable land (half the island's total) in order to grow food crops and palm oil for the Korean market, mass protests in the capital Antananarivo led to the overthrow of the government and cancellation of the deal.[41]

Such resistance is representative of the broader movement of peasant farmers and landless workers that has formed over recent decades to contest the expansion of the capitalist food regime. At the national or sub-national level, the Sundanese Peasants Union (SPP) in West Java, National Union of Peasant Farmers (UNAC) in Mozambique, Karnataka State Farmers' Association (KRRS) in India and South Korean farmers' unions are among the most well known examples.[42] In Brazil, the Movimento dos Trabalhadores Rurais Sem Terra (Landless Rural Workers' Movement, or MST) has developed over 30 years through land occupations and the establishment of new rural settlements to become a powerful force on the national political scene, winning land titles for over 350,000 families and establishing cooperatives, schools and agroecological training courses in order to confront the power of agribusiness.[43] The achievements of the Zapatista uprising in sustaining its settlements in Chiapas, Mexico since the revolt of 1994 mirror those of the MST, with improvements in living standards, education and women's rights for the 150,000 indigenous people who live there.[44]

The peasant farmers' movement is most visible at the international level in the presence of La Vía Campesina, the autonomous movement which brings together 150 local and national organisations from 70 countries, representing a total of 200 million farmers. In the 20 years since its founding, La Vía Campesina has developed into one of the most high profile social movements, launching major campaigns externally for agrarian reform and the right to seeds while internally demanding gender parity at the highest levels of its representative structures, in recognition of the persistent marginalisation of women in farming systems the world over.[45] Yet the most significant element in the history of La Vía Campesina has been its promotion of food sovereignty as the framework for confronting and, eventually, supplanting the corporate food regime. As will be explored more fully in the final chapter, the concept of sovereignty is essentially opposed to the disempowerment inherent in corporate globalisation, in that it reclaims authority over natural resources and the means of production from transnational capital, relocating legitimate authority within the democratic structures of the community, however constructed and contested. La Vía Campesina presented the seven principles of the food sovereignty framework to the World Food Summit held in Rome in 1996 (see box) and has since worked to develop those principles further while building the food sovereignty movement worldwide. A critical moment in this development came in 2007 with the Nyéléni Forum for Food Sovereignty held in Sélingué, Mali, which brought together over 500 representatives of social movements from around the world committed to the construction of an alternative paradigm to the capitalist food regime. The concluding declaration of the forum affirmed food sovereignty to be 'the right of peoples to healthy and culturally appropriate food produced through ecologically sound and sustainable methods, and their right to define their own food and agriculture systems'.[46] The forum also committed its members to further action to promote the concept of food sovereignty in all regions of the world, to resist the 'corporate-led global capitalist model' of agriculture and to strengthen the food sovereignty movement by means of a series of planned actions coordinated at the international level. The first European Food Sovereignty Forum, held in Austria in August 2011, explicitly linked its final declaration to the Nyéléni forum in its call to reclaim control of the food system from transnational capital and establish food sovereignty in Europe.[47]

Taken together, the principles advanced by La Vía Campesina and others in the food sovereignty movement represent a comprehensive rejection of the capitalist food regime. In addition, insistence on the right to food was conceived as a counterhegemonic challenge to the concept of 'food security', which relegates food to a commodity to be traded on open markets, and hunger to a welfare issue to be dealt with through the distribution of food aid. Indeed, the 'food security' paradigm, by focusing solely on the consumption rather than the production and distribution of food, deliberately sidesteps any analysis

Box 7.1   The seven principles of food sovereignty

As presented by La Vía Campesina to the 1996 World Food Summit, Rome.

1. Food: a basic human right

Everyone must have access to safe, nutritious and culturally appropriate food in sufficient quantity and quality to sustain a healthy life with full human dignity. Each nation should declare that access to food is a constitutional right and guarantee the development of the primary sector to ensure the concrete realisation of this fundamental right.

2. Agrarian reform

A genuine agrarian reform is necessary, which gives landless and farming people – especially women – ownership and control of the land they work and returns territories to indigenous peoples. The right to land must be free of discrimination on the basis of gender, religion, race, social class or ideology; the land belongs to those who work it.

3. Protecting natural resources

Food sovereignty entails the sustainable care and use of natural resources, especially land, water, seeds and livestock breeds. The people who work the land must have the right to practise sustainable management of natural resources and to conserve biodiversity free of restrictive intellectual property rights. This can only be done from a sound economic basis with security of tenure, healthy soils and reduced use of agrochemicals.

4. Reorganising food trade

Food is first and foremost a source of nutrition and only secondarily an item of trade. National agricultural policies must prioritise production for domestic consumption and food self-sufficiency. Food imports must not displace local production nor depress prices.

5. Ending the globalisation of hunger

Food sovereignty is undermined by multilateral institutions and by speculative capital. The growing control of multinational corporations (MNCs) over agricultural policies has been facilitated by the economic policies of multilateral organisations such as the WTO,

World Bank and the IMF [International Monetary Fund]. Regulation and taxation of speculative capital and a strictly enforced Code of Conduct for MNCs is therefore needed.

6. Social peace

Everyone has the right to be free from violence. Food must not be used as a weapon. Increasing levels of poverty and marginalisation in the countryside, along with the growing oppression of ethnic minorities and indigenous populations, aggravate situations of injustice and hopelessness. The ongoing displacement, forced urbanisation, oppression of smallholder farmers and increasing incidence of racism against them cannot be tolerated.

7. Democratic control

Smallholder farmers must have direct input into formulating agricultural policies at all levels. The United Nations and related organisations will have to undergo a process of democratisation to enable this to become a reality. Everyone has the right to honest, accurate information and open and democratic decision-making. These rights form the basis of good governance, accountability and equal participation in economic, political and social life, free from all forms of discrimination. Rural women, in particular, must be granted direct and active decision-making on food and rural issues.

of the power relations inherent in the globalised food regime. In the words of agroecologist Michel Pimbert:

The mainstream definition of food security, endorsed at food summits and other high level conferences, talks about everybody having enough good food to eat each day. But it doesn't talk about where the food comes from, who produced it, or the conditions under which it was grown. This allows the food exporters to argue that the best way for poor countries to achieve food security is to import cheap food from them or to receive it free as 'food aid', rather than trying to produce it themselves. This makes those countries more dependent on the international market, drives peasant farmers, pastoralists, fisherfolk and indigenous peoples who can't compete with the subsidised imports off their land and into the cities, and ultimately worsens people's food security.[48]

Food sovereignty restores the social, geographical and ecological relations between food production and consumption, insisting that everything we eat is food from somewhere, not food from nowhere.[49] The food sovereignty framework also affirms the importance of diversity in farming practices the world over, both to preserve indigenous social and cultural life forms and also to mitigate the unprecedented loss of biodiversity caused by industrial agriculture, currently running at extinction rates of up to 1,000 times the historical background rate.[50] To this end, all peasant farmers' movements that are members of La Vía Campesina have introduced programmes of transition to agroecological forms of farming that are designed to diversify genetic resources while reducing dependence on external chemical inputs – the basis of a new 'agrarian revolution', according to the movement's many supporters.[51] Those alternatives are in turn being taken up at the highest levels of global governance: Olivier De Schutter, UN Special Rapporteur on the Right to Food, presented a compelling case for scaling up agroecological programmes in his report to the UN Human Rights Council in December 2010, in which he noted the unparalleled achievements of agroecological farming in raising yields.[52] The most systematic study of this to date, which surveyed 286 projects in 57 countries, found that farming according to agroecological principles increased productivity by 79 per cent on average across all categories of farm systems, with some systems more than doubling their output levels. The same study found that agroecological farming had also increased water use efficiency, improved the accumulation of organic matter in the soil and reduced pesticide use.[53]

De Schutter also drew attention to the startling potential of agroecological farming in combatting global warming. The Rodale Institute's ten-year study comparing organic agriculture with fields under standard tillage using chemical fertilisers found that the organically farmed fields could sequester (capture) up to 2,000lb of carbon per acre per year from the atmosphere. By contrast, fields relying on chemical fertilisers lost into the atmosphere almost 300lb of carbon per acre per year. If organic agriculture were practised on all 434 million acres of cropland in the USA, the study concluded, nearly 1.6 billion tons of carbon dioxide would be sequestered per year, mitigating close to one quarter of the country's total fossil fuel emissions. If traditional systems of mixed farming were adopted worldwide, similar calculations estimate that approximately two thirds of the excess carbon dioxide currently in the earth's atmosphere would be captured within 50 years.[54] De Schutter concluded his 2010 report to the United Nations by calling on all states to prioritise agroecological farming in their plans to reduce rural poverty and to combat climate change. This was also the conclusion of the comprehensive study of agricultural practices undertaken over a four-year period by 400 scientists under the banner of the International Assessment of Agricultural Knowledge, Science and Technology for Development (IAASTD), as well as numerous UN reports that have promoted agroecological, small-scale farming over industrial agriculture.[55] Despite this, large-scale agricultural investments continue to threaten smallholder farming across the world, as transnational corporations seek to capture the lucrative markets of food production and land control.

The CSR Response

Finding itself under renewed attack for being the root cause of food insecurity, ecological devastation and climate change, capital has again responded by establishing voluntary CSR mechanisms by which to suggest that it shares the same concerns and aspirations as other societal groups, and thereby to maintain its lead agency. To this end, the seven Principles for Responsible Agricultural Investment were formulated as a voluntary code of conduct for investors by staff of the World Bank (which has actively supported large-scale land acquisitions by agribusiness companies across the world)[56] and three UN agencies: the United Nations Conference on Trade and Development, the International Fund for Agricultural Development, and the FAO. The principles were drawn up without any consultation process and were universally dismissed as no more than a corporate charter to legitimise land grabbing, with even World Bank officials eventually acknowledging that their purpose seemed 'to promote investor interest rather than to help countries formulate strategies and implement regulations that would protect local rights'.[57] The FAO Committee on World Food Security refused to endorse the Principles for Responsible Agricultural Investment at its 2010 plenary session, and directed attention instead to the Voluntary Guidelines on the Responsible Governance of Tenure of Land, Fisheries and Forests, which were being developed through a broad process of consultation with the private sector, governments and civil society.[58] These guidelines, which were subsequently endorsed by the FAO Committee on World Food Security in 2012, represented the first international effort to ground traditional land tenure, land use and resource management issues within a human rights framework, and reminded governments of their duty to prevent forced evictions that might violate their existing obligations under national and international law. Yet once again, the endorsement of guidelines that ultimately create the conditions for the continuation of large-scale land acquisitions stands in direct opposition to the repeated calls for an end to land grabbing that have come out of the international farmers' movement and other social movements from around the world. And while there are still opportunities for political contestation around the implementation of the guidelines, the fact that they are voluntary rather than binding on either states or transnational corporations further undermines any potential benefit to be gained from their more progressive elements.[59]

In a similar vein, the earlier Voluntary Guidelines to Support the Progressive Realisation of the Right to Adequate Food in the Context of National Food Security, adopted by the FAO Council in 2004, ostensibly represented an acceptance of the state's obligation to guarantee the right to food.[60] However, fierce opposition from the USA, UK and other states to the inclusion of binding human rights language in the final text had ensured that the guidelines would be no more than discretionary policy recommendations for governments to adopt or ignore as they choose. Moreover, the right to food was reinterpreted in the guidelines (notably Guideline 4, on 'market systems') as a policy goal to be advanced through further expansion of the neoliberal world trade system and by the incorporation of 'the widest number of individuals and communities' into that system.[61] The successful role played by transnational corporations and their apologists in defusing any potential challenge from the guidelines to the dominant food regime reveals how decisively the language of rights can be appropriated to legitimise the programme of capitalist expansion – an important reminder of the limitations of any rights-based approach that fails to recognise the political dimension of the struggle over global governance.[62]

CSR and global governance mechanisms have again conspired to legitimise capital's incursion into new frontiers of accumulation. In this context, the political development of the food sovereignty movement has assumed additional importance as a bulwark against more than just the expansion of the global food regime.[63] For the food sovereignty framework offers more than simply an ecologically and socially sustainable form of agriculture: food sovereignty represents a challenge to the capitalist system itself, and an indication of what broader alternatives to capitalism might look like when freed from the tyranny of the market. In the Declaration of Maputo which came out of its fifth international conference in 2008, La Vía Campesina formally recognised the food crisis not as a sectoral crisis but as a crisis of the capitalist system, along with the converging crises in climate, energy and finance.[64] Such an anti-systemic orientation confirms the international farmers' movement as part of the broader anti-capitalist current which has developed over the past four decades, and which has been dramatically strengthened by the global economic meltdown of 2008 onwards. The final chapter explores that current, the alternatives it has articulated and the hope it offers for the future.

8

Beyond Capitalism

The movement to reclaim popular sovereignty over natural and economic resources was a response to the assault of neoliberal globalisation, as people found themselves increasingly dispossessed by the new powers granted to transnational capital. As the global justice movement crystallised in the wake of the 1994 Zapatista uprising and the mass demonstrations against the World Trade Organisation (WTO) in Seattle in 1999, its principal points of reference remained the leading institutions of globalisation: the G8, the International Monetary Fund (IMF), World Bank, WTO and World Economic Forum, and the movement manifested itself most publicly in its mobilisations against those institutions' summit meetings. Alternative spaces constructed physically in the World Social Forum from 2001 onwards, and virtually through the spread of electronic communications, allowed for a deepening of the critique of globalisation and the development of international networks of resistance. The mood of the movement was captured in several publications confronting the principles of globalisation and seeking to reclaim democratic power through a reassertion of popular sovereignty (for more on which, see below).[1]

The economic meltdown of 2008 onwards has matured the movement beyond simply an attack on neoliberal globalisation, so that it now recognises itself as an anti-systemic movement and readily expresses itself as anti-capitalist.[2] Neoliberalism is now understood as the logical expression of capitalism in the era of globalisation, not an aberration from which a kinder, gentler version of the system can be restored. Anger on the streets of Spain, Greece and Portugal is openly directed at the capitalist system and its political represen-tatives; likewise, the popular uprisings of 2011 in Tunisia, Egypt and Yemen confronted the regimes that had imposed programmes of neoliberal reform on their peoples while guarding the riches of privatisation for their immediate circle. The Occupy movement that flared into existence across the world during 2011 and 2012 was explicitly directed against the forces of capital, as expressed in its physical occupations of the headquarters of finance capitalism (Wall Street, the London Stock Exchange and the European Central Bank) as well as its symbolic challenge to the 1 per cent on behalf of the 99 per cent. However inchoate and diverse it may be, the main current of the global justice movement has now declared itself in opposition to the capitalist system, and thus reopened the debate over alternatives beyond that system.

As with the alter-globalisation movement before it, this anti-systemic articulation is a reflection of many thousands of existing struggles being fought by social movements, trade unions and local communities across the world. While those mobilising at the core of the capitalist system often receive the greatest attention from the global media, their challenge has in recent times been more limited in its achievements, as mature capitalist societies famously enjoy a highly developed capacity to contain the desire for meaningful change.[3] Whether that situation will survive the growing political unrest caused by the current wave of austerity and unemployment sweeping Europe and North America is increasingly doubtful, given the numbers of people affected. Yet it has typically been historical agents from outside the core capitalist economies that have mounted the most powerful challenges to the system over the past 100 years, leading to revolutions that have successfully assumed power in such countries as Mexico, Russia, Turkey, China, Vietnam, Cuba, Nicaragua and Iran.

Continuing this trend, it is Latin America that has led the way in developing real alternatives to the neoliberal capitalist model in the twenty-first century.[4] Here, the resurgence of popular struggles has transformed the hopes of a continent, with social movements rising up against programmes of privatisation and dispossession, repeatedly unseating governments through mass mobilisations and strike action, and creating the potential for long-term, structural change.[5] Where social movements have created their own political parties, they have won power at the national level to turn that potential into a reality. The Movement for Socialism (MAS) that swept Evo Morales to a landslide victory in the 2005 presidential election in Bolivia, and the 'citizens' revolution' that did the same for Rafael Correa in Ecuador the following year, showed how such forces could break the stranglehold on electoral politics and set about redefining the institutions of the capitalist state.[6] The popular base of grassroots support that elected the late Hugo Chávez to four successive presidencies, and enabled him to withstand the US-backed coup attempt against him in 2002, secured a mandate for even more far-reaching change in Venezuela. These experiences have the significance of being more than theoretical blueprints, as they represent actually existing programmes in countries that have chosen to pursue a democratic transition away from capitalism. Even if the programmes are context-specific and not instantly replicable in other environments, therefore, they offer important intimations of what is possible when social movements mobilise for radical structural change.[7]

Alternative Realities

Seen against the backdrop of the preceding 40 years in Latin America, during which all attempts to develop more equitable societies were brutally crushed in every country save Cuba, the resurgence of alternative social and economic models for the twenty-first century is a truly historic development. The election of centre-left governments in Argentina, Chile, Uruguay, Brazil, Nicaragua, El Salvador, Guatemala, Peru and Paraguay generated a 'pink tide' across the region that has complemented and supported, in turn, the more radical programmes of Bolivia, Ecuador and Venezuela. While the USA has not abandoned its attempts to intervene in other states of the western hemisphere (witness US support for failed insurrections in Bolivia as well as Venezuela, and for the successful coup which overthrew the government of Manuel Zelaya in Honduras in 2009), it has shown itself increasingly powerless to withstand the pressure for change. Most symbolically, this includes the growing demand for an end to the isolation of Cuba: in June 2009, despite dogged US opposition, foreign ministers from across Latin America voted to revoke the 1962 decision suspending Cuba's membership of the Organisation of American States (OAS), having already welcomed the country into the Rio Group of Latin American and Caribbean countries in November 2008. The 2012 Summit of the Americas ended in disarray as an increasingly isolated

President Obama confounded even his Colombian hosts by refusing to agree to Cuba's inclusion in the next hemispheric summit in 2015, with only the right-wing Canadian government of Stephen Harper prepared to support the USA in its intransigence. Yet the high point of defiance to US hegemony came with the founding of the Community of Latin American and Caribbean States (CELAC) in December 2011: a pan-regional body to which the USA and Canada are not invited, and which some hope will in time replace the US-dominated OAS. More pointedly still, the presidency of CELAC for 2013 was given to Cuba.

Each of the Latin American states that form part of the 'pink tide' has implemented its own programme of social and economic reforms. The government of the Workers' Party in Brazil, for instance, under the presidencies of first Luiz Inácio ('Lula') da Silva and then Dilma Rousseff, had won power through a broad alliance which included the manufacturing elite in the south east of the country and major landowners from the poorer regions. While it thus pursued a programme of capitalist expansion (particularly in the agro-industrial sector) that has provided the basis for the outward turn of Brazilian corporations into the global economy, it also raised the minimum wage and boosted expenditure on social welfare programmes, reducing both unemployment and poverty levels at home.[8] In Argentina, where the revolt of the unemployed *piqueteros* and other social movements had overthrown the government in 2001 under the slogan '¡Que se vayan todos!' ('Get rid of the lot of them!'), the subsequent presidencies of first Néstor and then Cristina Kirchner also combined an export-driven model of capitalist expansion with an extension of relief programmes for the poor and unemployed.[9] Such programmes have seen states adopt a more interventionist role in the economy, and particularly the sectors of infrastructure and finance, but they have sought not to disturb the existing framework of capitalist relations, actively promoting the interests of capital at home and abroad. While they may have challenged the worst excesses of neoliberalism through progressive programmes of redistribution, these governments have not addressed the structural causes of exploitation and inequality in their respective countries, so that any welfare gains made during periods of social democratic rule can be easily reversed in future. By contrast, the more radical transformations under way in Bolivia, Venezuela and Ecuador are directed towards transcending the capitalist structures and institutions which they have inherited from history, in paths of transition towards new forms of democratic socialism for the twenty-first century. It is this ambition which has made the programmes in each of the three countries such an important focus for all movements seeking to explore progressive alternatives in the real world.

Bolivia has seen a combination of political, social and economic reforms that have already brought with them significant changes. While indigenous people constitute two thirds of Bolivia's population, they had effectively been marginalised into a political minority over a period of centuries; addressing this disenfranchisement was one of the primary demands of the social movements whose mobilisation saw Evo Morales elected as the first indigenous president in the country's history. The redefinition of the country as the Plurinational State of Bolivia in its new constitution was the first step in a process of decolonisation designed to restore indigenous sovereignty and control over the country's natural resource wealth, especially its large reserves of natural gas. The new constitution, which was drafted by a constituent assembly and approved in 2009 by popular referendum, also restricted future land titles to a maximum of 5,000 hectares; agrarian reform has so far seen over 10 million hectares of land taken out of the hands of large landowners and redistributed to indigenous peoples and peasant communities, with further areas declared public lands for conversion into protected forests. Yet it is the structural economic reforms vis-à-vis transnational capital that represent the most significant lessons for other countries seeking to restore sovereignty over their future. Within four months of assuming office, Morales nationalised the country's oil and gas resources, requiring all foreign companies operating in the energy sector to renegotiate their contracts with the government; the state now retains 82 per cent of rents from the most productive fields, and government income from hydrocarbons has increased more than tenfold, from just $173 million in 2002 to $2.2 billion in 2011. National economic growth has been higher under the Morales administration than at any other time in the past 30 years – a vindication of the government's decision to ignore the advice of the IMF and its US backers – and financial reserves have mushroomed to over $12 billion. As a result of such changes and the public investment programmes they have made possible, per capita income more than doubled in Bolivia between 2005 and 2011; unemployment fell from 8.2 per cent to 5.7 per cent through the creation of half a million new jobs; the number of municipalities with telecommunications coverage tripled from 110 to 324 (out of a total of 339), while the number of households with gas connections increased by 835 per cent. Extreme poverty was reduced from 38.2 per cent of the population in 2005 to 24.3 per cent in 2011.[10]

As Morales had done in Bolivia, so too Rafael Correa required foreign oil companies operating in Ecuador to renegotiate their contracts with the government, replacing production sharing agreements with fixed tariffs and thereby ensuring that all extra revenue from future oil price increases would automatically accrue to the state. Correa also introduced a number of popular financial reforms, foremost among which was to bring the Central Bank under government control and force it to repatriate $2 billion in reserves held outside the country – money which was then used to fund a major programme of domestic investment, including loans to stimulate solidarity-based financial cooperatives. Private banks lost an exemption which had previously allowed them to pay income tax at 13 rather than 23 per cent, and were also forced to hold at least 60 per cent of their liquid assets inside the country, which saw the repatriation of hundreds of millions of dollars in the first year alone; in the same vein, a tax was introduced on all capital leaving the country, which raised as much as 10 per cent of government revenue by 2012. Following an audit carried out by an international commission into Ecuador's illegal or 'odious' foreign debt, the government defaulted on $3.2 billion of government bonds in December 2008 and February 2009, buying them back later at a significant discount and thereby clearing a third of the country's total debt burden at a stroke.[11] The right to recover illegitimate debt had been one of the items included in Ecuador's new 2008 constitution, which was drafted by a constituent assembly in a similar way to Bolivia's. The constitution declared national control over oil, mining, transport and other economic sectors that had previously been privatised, and affirmed the rights of the country's large indigenous population by identifying Ecuador for the first time as a plurinational state, as well as introducing the concept of '*buen vivir*' ('*sumak kawsay*' in Quechua) as a post-capitalist corrective to Western models of development.[12] According to the constitution, this concept of 'living well' commits Ecuador to guaranteeing a number of rights to its people and communities, including the rights to food (through national promotion of food sovereignty), water, health, education, habitat and labour; the rights of Mother Earth, or *Pachamama*, are also enshrined. While supporting the new constitution as a positive step in Ecuador's decolonisation process, indigenous movements grew increasingly suspicious of the government's commitment to their rights, particularly in relation to their free, prior and informed consent to extractive industry operations in their territories.[13] Correa's achievements were sufficient in the minds of Ecuador's electorate, however, to secure him a third successive presidency by a large margin in February 2013.

Venezuela has articulated the most explicit commitment to building a new socialism for the twenty-first century, particularly in the pronouncements and programme of Hugo Chávez, who was first elected president in 1998, seven years before either Morales or Correa. As an initial step in the construction of a social base from which to launch his 'Bolivarian revolution', Chávez convened a constituent assembly to rewrite the country's constitution, which was adopted by popular referendum at the end of 1999. A new hydrocarbon law reasserted state ownership of Venezuela's all-important oil wealth, requiring foreign corporations to enter into joint ventures as minority partners with the national oil company Petróleos de Venezuela SA, and raising royalties from a maximum of 16.7 per cent to a standard 30 per cent. Using the increased government revenues generated by these reforms, Chávez embarked on a massive programme of public investment and social spending which brought startling results: the number of households recorded as living in extreme poverty fell by 16 per cent in just three years between 2003 and 2006; with the help of the Cuban government, which sent doctors to work in poor neighbourhoods throughout Venezuela, the number of primary care physicians in the public sector increased from 1,628 to 19,571 in the period between 1999 and 2007, bringing healthcare to millions who had previously been denied access; and as a result of successive educational missions and the provision of free primary school education, enrolment rates rose for all levels of schooling, and illiteracy was effectively eradicated. Venezuelan society has been further democratised by the massive expansion of the cooperative sector: while there were just 1,000 cooperatives in the country in 1998, by 2007 that number had risen to 180,000 – many of them set up by women with the aid of low-interest loans from Venezuela's new Bank for Women (Banmujer) established on International Women's Day 2001.[14]

Following Chávez's third election victory in 2006, the reform programme was radicalised by means of a wave of nationalisations that gradually extended state control over the manufacturing, service and agricultural sectors. Finance was included in this assertion of national sovereignty, with the return to public ownership of the Banco de Venezuela from Spain's Grupo Santander. The government acquired 90 per cent of the country's cement industry, returned Venezuela's largest steel mill to state hands and nationalised all the country's gold mines; it also bought up the major fertiliser producer Fertinitro and the Spanish-owned seed company Agroisleña, which had enjoyed an almost complete monopoly of commercial seed and agricultural supplies across the country. In addition, the government has redistributed an estimated 4 million hectares of land since 2005 to peasant farmers and collectives as part of its programme of 'agrarian socialism', and introduced a new labour law in 2012 that extended workers' rights, especially the rights of women workers.[15] The net result of 14 years of Chávez's presidency was that unemployment halved, per capita gross domestic product (GDP) more than doubled, the number of people living in extreme poverty fell to 8.5 per cent, and Venezuela now boasts the lowest inequality levels of any country in the region. While the greatest achievement of the Bolivarian revolution may be the political transformation made possible by reclaiming the state from the country's US-backed oligarchy, the social and economic empowerment of millions of ordinary Venezuelans is a further testament to what can be achieved through the progressive application of state power.

Latin America's new assertiveness in rejecting neoliberal capitalism has been confirmed in a number of victories at the regional level. As described in Chapter 3, the US programme to roll out the North American Free Trade Agreement (NAFTA) across the western hemisphere so as to create a Free Trade Area of the Americas (FTAA) was the lead item on the agenda of the Summit of the Americas held in Québec in 2001; by the time of the 2005 Summit, concerted popular resistance and government opposition from Brazil, Argentina and Venezuela had left the initiative dead in the water. In its place, several states from Latin America and the Caribbean have now joined the Bolivarian Alliance for the Americas (ALBA), originally set up by Venezuela and Cuba in 2004 as an alternative to the FTAA and designed to operate according to principles of cooperation, solidarity and complementarity rather than the explicitly pro-corporate motivation of free trade agreements.[16] Those same principles were extended across the Atlantic in the Caracas-London agreement with former mayor Ken Livingstone, whereby the poorest Londoners enjoyed half-price bus fares subsidised by cheap Venezuelan oil in return for London providing the Venezuelan capital with technical expertise on a range of urban issues such as transport planning, waste disposal and environmental management.[17] Equally important politically has been the initiative to set up regional cooperation bodies such as the Union of South American Nations (UNASUR) and the regional development bank Banco del Sur (Bank of the South), which was signed into agreement in September 2009 by the presidents of Argentina, Brazil, Paraguay, Uruguay, Bolivia, Ecuador and Venezuela as an alternative source of finance to the IMF.

While Latin America maintains a united front in the face of US imperialism, however, the 'pink tide' has ebbed in a number of places. Electoral reversals have restored right-wing governments in Chile and Guatemala, while Paraguay's president Fernando Lugo was ousted by a 'parliamentary coup' in June 2012. The defeat of the FTAA did not prevent the USA from forcing through the Central America Free Trade Agreement (CAFTA) on the peoples of Central America, whose governments also followed Colombia and Peru in negotiating a far-reaching free trade agreement (FTA) with the EU. Chile, Peru and Mexico are parties to the negotiations towards the Trans-Pacific Partnership (TPP), the super-FTA that aims to create a new free trade area between the Americas and Asia. And at the national level, as noted above, several of the 'pink' governments have actually augmented the power of capital both nationally and internationally, maintaining their socially progressive credentials through pro-poor welfare programmes, but at the expense of any structural change.

Even in the more radical social and economic reforms of Bolivia, Ecuador and Venezuela, there are calls to move beyond revolutionary symbolism to a redistribution of power that breaks more decisively with the capitalist past. The leaders of those governments have affirmed the need for long periods of transition if their countries are to create the material conditions to achieve such a rupture: Álvaro García Linera, intellectual theorist and vice-president in the Morales government, has written of the need for many decades before Bolivia can develop a sufficient industrial base from which to graduate to socialism.[18] García Linera has also confronted another of the central contradictions facing those Amazonian states that depend on exploiting their natural resource wealth while at the same time holding to principles of ecological integrity and safeguarding indigenous peoples' rights.[19] In his widely studied essay, 'Geopolitics of the Amazon', García Linera defends Bolivia's pursuit of 'extractivism' as the only realistic means of generating the material resources necessary to sustain wealth redistribution and to construct a path towards industrial development which will eventually allow the country to overcome its dependency on natural resource extraction.[20] By way of an alternative solution, in order to prevent the ecological disaster that would result from its exploitation of the substantial oil reserves in the rainforest of the Yasuní national park, Ecuador had offered to leave the area untouched if it were compensated for the loss of revenue by the international community at large. While the proposal generated some interest, only a tiny fraction of the $3.6 billion demanded had been received by 2013, and the plan was abandoned. Critics had already countered that the government should not be contemplating oil exploration in a designated UN biosphere reserve, and that the compensation scheme represented an abdication of Ecuador's autonomous responsibility to protect its ecological heritage (Article 407 of the country's new constitution prohibits extractive operations in protected areas, save in exceptional circumstances).[21]

For all the undoubted challenges still facing those countries that have embarked on more radical reform programmes, the Latin American experience offers important lessons for those seeking alternatives to capitalism. In particular, the recognition that each country must define its own historical path to the future is a decisive step away from the sectarian dogmatism that scarred the twentieth century. As Marta Harnecker concludes in her study of the various transitions to socialism under construction in Latin America, a new left culture is needed which promotes unity around values such as solidarity, humanism, celebration of difference and respect for the environment at the same time as it 'turns its back on the view that hunger for profit and the laws of the market are the guiding principles of human activity'.[22] A similar call could be made for solidarity towards those countries and communities in other parts of the world that are experimenting with their own mix of market and socialist principles. It is otiose to suggest any abstract restriction on those experiments, or to attempt to collate the various alternatives into any form of blueprint. However, it is still useful to note broad themes around which the alternatives congregate, as a means to developing shared principles and a common orientation beyond values alone.[23] Drawing on the many different manifestos and charters that have been constructed in the wake of the global economic meltdown to challenge the neoliberal capitalist programme, the final section of this book focuses on three such principles of convergence: popular sovereignty, common ownership and social production, as a means to moving beyond the poverty of capitalism and towards a better world.

Popular Sovereignty

The assertion of popular sovereignty as a bulwark against corporate globalisation has been a recurrent theme in this book, but it is one that is ambiguous as to its point of reference. National sovereignty, such as that increasingly exercised by many states over their natural resource base, has been the most obvious form of resistance to the new imperialism of transnational capital, opening up the political space for states to determine their own economic policies free from the constraints of international financial institutions or trade rules. Reasserting such sovereignty at the national level has also signalled the possibility of a return of the 'developmental state', actively intervening to govern the market in the interest of accelerating national development and balancing private and public goals.[24] This renewed interest in the role of the state as a force for progressive redistribution marks a recognition of the relative success of those economies that adopted intervention-ist strategies in the decades immediately after the Second World War. The accomplishments of Latin American and East Asian states in implementing industrial policies are traditionally held up as the most positive examples of the developmental state in action, but the newly independent nations of Africa also registered significant achievements in the brief period between their liberation from colonial rule and the oil shocks of the 1970s. Countries such as Ghana, Gabon, Botswana and the Republic of Congo all posted strong average growth rates in the years between 1960 and 1973, while no fewer than 22 African countries recorded annual per capita growth of at least 2.3 per cent (the rate needed to double per capita GDP within a period of 30 years).[25] Contrasted with the dismal performance of their economies under the structural adjustment programmes of the World Bank and IMF, it is small wonder that these years of national sovereignty are still regarded as Africa's 'golden decade'.[26]

Yet for all its importance as a defence against neoliberal capitalist globalisation, the restoration of state sovereignty brings its own contradictions, as is revealed in closer inspection of the historical record. The grand bargain made with those corporations which were identified as 'national champions' in countries such as India, Brazil and Turkey, that they should be supported with state subsidies and protected from external competition until such time as they could stand on their own two feet, built up the power of national capital to such a level that it could successfully resist any pressure to direct its operations or investments towards public goals.[27] The pro-capitalist orientation of governments such as Taiwan, Singapore and South Korea meant that they were ruthless in their repression of popular democratic movements, crushing trade union rights and other freedoms and declaring martial law for years at a time. While advocates for the return of the developmental state are adamant that such brutality would be unacceptable this time around, expanding the power of national capital through government support still reproduces the dynamics of exploitation and dispossession within the borders of the nation state. As noted above, this has once again been the popular experience of national champions in emerging economies such as China, Brazil and India, which have developed so as to be almost indistinguishable in power and size from corporations originating from the core capitalist economies, whether operating at home or abroad.

The inadequacy of restoring sovereignty at the national level alone points to the need for democratic structures by which to establish working forms of social sovereignty as well. The significance of globalisation's challenge was not that states lost the political space to determine their own policies, but that labour and local communities were disempowered by the state and capital combined; in Étienne Balibar's formulation, 'the heart of the crisis of sovereignty is the *disappearance of the people*'.[28] The restoration of sovereignty is thus the recovery of democracy itself – yet simply calling for popular sovereignty throws open the question as to how such sovereignty might be defined or established in practice: as described above, those Latin American movements that have initiated programmes of democratic transition away from capitalism have confronted the inevitable clash of sovereignties where national interest and community resistance collide. Social sovereignty is understood to operate not just through the agency of those in authority, but through establishing structures of decision making which allow for the continuing participation of those who are supposed to hold ultimate power.[29] In this respect, the constituent assemblies convened to draft new constitutions in Bolivia, Ecuador and Venezuela (and recently also in Tunisia and Iceland) can be seen as participatory mechanisms to overcome the tensions inherent in constructing a national programme out of many differing agendas. Yet for popular sovereignty to function on more than a symbolic basis, there need to exist structures of ongoing democratic engagement, such as the communal councils and workers' councils established as the building blocks of participatory democracy in Venezuela. These councils operate on the basis of delegation from the bottom up, where spokespeople remain fully accountable to their peers and can be recalled as soon as they cease to voice the decisions of the collective – leaders who 'lead by obeying', in the Zapatista formulation. This is in sharp contrast to the disempowering experience of parliamentary representation the world over, 'where citizens drop their ballots in the box every so many years and then never hear anything more from the representative for whom they voted'.[30] At the farthest extreme, the development of seats of power that are increasingly distanced from the people – whether in federal superstates or regional bodies such as the European Union – is a particular challenge for all those dedicated to restoring sovereignty to levels that are closer to popular control.[31] The dialectic between state and popular sovereignties will continue to play itself out in various forms of political struggle across the world, but the need to deepen processes of democracy to encompass more direct forms of participation is clear.[32]

Most challenging of all is the imperative to establish any form of social sovereignty through which to contest the power of capital at the global level. Hopes that the World Social Forum might develop beyond its original conception as an 'open space' towards a coordinated political movement have not materialised beyond the 'assemblies of convergence' designed to articulate connections between the myriad issues presented to each forum, and to plan themed days of action to take place over the ensuing year.[33] Indeed, it remains unclear what such a movement would look like at the supranational level beyond the vague 'distributed network' of the multitude posited by Hardt and Negri, in which every struggle 'remains singular and tied to its local conditions but at the same time is immersed in the common web'.[34] The global trade union movement offers an enduring model of functioning structures that provide international coordination and solidarity at many levels, but it is unclear whether it would ever be possible (or desirable) to replicate its bureaucratic hierarchies in and between the new social movements. Yet the need for such a challenge from below is irrefutable, given the confirmedly capitalist orientation of the states that are constructing the new world order described at the beginning of this book. Today's resurgence of emerging nations was originally prefigured in the 1955 Bandung conference of Asian and African states that led to the birth of an independent Non-Aligned Movement prepared to condemn the twin imperialisms of Washington and Moscow alike. Sixty years later, the challenge to global civil society is to build a 'Bandung of the peoples' that will confront the new imperialism of global capitalism from a democratic base constructed out of the convergence of all the many struggles for freedom across the world.[35]

Common Ownership

Closely linked with the recovery of popular sovereignty is the issue of common ownership. As noted in previous chapters, the neoliberal stage of global capitalism has seen an intensified drive for primitive accumulation by means of a new wave of dispossessions that recall the enclosures of the commons from earlier history. The accelerated privatisation of public goods, assets and utilities has gone hand in hand with capital's physical appropriation of natural resources, and has been a prelude to the commodification of people's rights for sale on the open market. In addition, the increased financialisation of household budgets that has often accompanied privatisation now offers banks and other financial institutions direct access to the incomes of those forced to pay for water, healthcare, education, housing and other public services.[36] In emergency situations, the impact of paying for such services can be catastrophic: over 60 per cent of bankruptcies in the USA are due to medical bills (up from just 8 per cent at the start of the 1980s), while across the world 25 million households are driven into extreme poverty each year as a result of selling off assets to pay for medical treatment.[37] Popular opposition to this new wave of enclosures can be seen in mass movements against privatisations the world over, prominent among them the water and gas wars fought (and won) by social movements in Bolivia; the victory of Iraqi oil workers in their fight to defend the country's oil wealth from privatisation at the hands of US and UK occupation forces; the mobilisations of the Anti-Privatisation Forum in South Africa and the diverse struggles mounted in Colombia, Peru, El Salvador, Greece, Spain, South Korea, India and many other countries besides. The global campaign against water privatisation registered a significant victory when the United Nations General Assembly officially recognised the human right to water and sanitation in July 2010, in the face of dogged opposition from the governments of the USA, UK, Canada, Australia and New Zealand, and their determination to define water as an economic good.[38]

There has also been wholesale rejection of capital's attempt to privatise the global public good of knowledge through its intensifying 'intellectual property' regime and the enforcement of patents, trademarks and copyrights as the mechanism for corporations' collection of rent on 'their' property.[39] For instance, the movement for seed sovereignty that has gained international momentum in recent years explicitly denies the possibility that the biological commons can be 'owned', just as farmers' refusal to abandon centuries-old traditions of seed sharing represents an act of defiance through which to assert the primacy of use value over exchange value, and of common ownership over the market.[40] The development of open source software for free use by all is another assertion of knowledge as a public good in the face of privatisation, and one which has been replicated in other open access systems such as the alliances for patent-free medical research that have flourished between scientists, the sharing of cultural resources via Creative Commons licences, or the 'free culture' movement that argues for a commons beyond all forms of licensing.[41] Even the car pooling schemes now in operation in many countries around the world represent simple examples of the principle of common ownership that stand in direct opposition to the restrictions of capitalist enclosure.[42]

The revival of interest in common ownership has been further reflected in the success of the cooperative movement and other forms of social economy in recent years. Launching its 'Blueprint for a Cooperative Decade' in February 2013 as an explicit alternative to the failed model of contemporary capitalism, the International Cooperative Alliance (ICA) noted that many mutually owned banks had managed to thrive during the financial crisis even as their investor-owned competitors crashed around them, and that consumer cooperatives had proved similarly resilient. As happened most dramatically in Argentina during the 2001 economic crisis, new workers' cooperatives have been created out of the bankruptcies of investor-owned businesses: in France, 128 firms on the point of closure were converted into workers' cooperatives in 2010 and 2011, while the total number of French worker-owned cooperatives grew during 2007–11 by 9 per cent. The importance of cooperatives in countries outside the core of the capitalist world system is particularly noteworthy: an estimated 250 million farmers in the global South belong to a cooperative; in India, the consumer needs of two thirds of rural households are covered by cooperatives; in China there are 180 million cooperative members; while 40 per cent of African households belong to a cooperative. Nor are sustainability and resilience the only benefits offered by mutual ownership: the active participation in the running of cooperatives that ownership affords also contributes to the creation of social capital and to democratic control over economic resources, as well as advancing awareness of the principle of cooperation as an alternative to capitalist competition.[43] Charges that cooperatives are structurally exclusive communities of self-interest, with limited solidarity towards those outside their membership, do not do justice to the principles that inspire the movement – as shown in the positive conclusions reached by the authors J.K. Gibson-Graham in their critical examination of the Basque country's powerful Mondragón group.[44] In the British context, too, the Cooperative Group was the first (and, at time of writing, the only) supermarket chain to announce a full boycott of all products emanating from Israeli settlements in the Occupied Palestinian Territories, or from Moroccan companies operating in Occupied Western Sahara.[45]

Cooperatives are not the only form of social economy. Mutual benefit societies operating in the health and social protection sectors provide coverage on a non-profit basis to over 170 million people worldwide, while other forms of association that do not distribute cash surpluses to their members (as cooperatives do) combine further social and economic functions with mutual ownership. All share some form of democratic control by their members as an integral aspect of their common ownership structure, and thus differ from social enterprises that may also be directed towards social purposes but are not run according to participatory principles.[46] In addition, the solidarity economy (a concept with roots stretching back to the Spanish Civil War but most familiar from Latin America, France and Québec) has developed across the world to encompass a wide range of innovative community initiatives such as local exchange trading systems, social currency schemes, community-supported agriculture programmes and community food groups, all developed through democratic grassroots agency. The solidarity economy is often more explicitly directed towards confronting the dominant capitalist system rather than simply existing alongside it, as the social economy has tended to do, and typically expresses itself through more activist participation; in this respect, the concept is linked to the resurgence of the 'popular economy' as developed in various countries of Latin America and Africa in recent years.[47]

While such forms of common ownership typically operate within community economies, however constituted, others require democratic control of structures at higher levels of society, including public ownership by the state. The most pressing issue facing the core capitalist economies in the wake of the 2008 financial crash was not how to create space for alternative models of finance such as local credit unions and social investment funds, attractive though they may be, but how to deal with a banking sector that had grown to dominate the economy and was now holding it to ransom. The widespread call to nationalise the banks and bring finance under democratic control was rejected in favour of the worst possible resolution, whereby taxpayers' money was used to bail out the financial system but without introducing any form of popular control over the system they had bought. The absurdity of offering infinite sums of public money to underwrite a private banking sector that cannot be allowed to fail has prompted calls for full nationalisation even from the right of the political spectrum, just as leading US economists of the Chicago School had argued at the time of the Great Depression.[48] In the UK, where the state bought an 82 per cent stake in the Royal Bank of Scotland but refused to take control of its operations (a situation described as 'the worst of all worlds' by subsequent business secretary Vince Cable), the Thatcherite former chancellor Nigel Lawson called for the full nationalisation of the bank and its reconstitution as a lender to small businesses.[49] Several other European countries had already moved to take banks into public ownership and control: two of the four largest Dutch banks, ABN Amro and SNS Reaal, were nationalised in the wake of the financial crisis; of the other two, Rabobank is one of Europe's leading cooperatives, leaving only ING in private hands. Like several other administrations, however, the Dutch government announced its intention to return the nationalised banks to private ownership once they had been stabilised, thus creating the conditions for repeated financial crises in years to come. Instead of nationalisation being seen as a necessary evil to be reversed as soon as circumstances allow, the fact that many banks are already in public ownership should be understood as an opportunity to re-establish banking as a public utility 'so that the distribution of credit and capital would be undertaken in conformity with democratically established priorities, rather than short term profit'.[50] Failed attempts to cajole the private financial sector into socially productive practices only underline the importance of ownership as the sole means of guaranteeing control.

Restoring public ownership over finance may be a necessary step in establishing popular control over the economy, but it is far from sufficient. Other strategic sectors of the economy must also be taken into common ownership if there is to be any transition away from the destructive practices described in previous chapters, with the aim of moving beyond a capitalist system predicated upon private ownership of the means of production, distribution and exchange. The extent of nationalisation and the terms under which public control is reasserted are matters for political forces in each country to determine, as shown in the varied examples from Latin America given above. That there is no corresponding mechanism at the international level through which to reclaim control over transnational capital is a further reason why the reassertion of popular sovereignty remains such a priority in any future restructuring of the global political economy. Beyond simply restoring democratic control over the commanding heights of the economy, however, there must also be a parallel process to make public ownership responsive to the needs of society. The shortcomings of many twentieth-century experiences of state ownership are all too familiar from our current historical vantage point, and those who advocate new forms of common ownership are under no illusion that the past exists in order to be repeated. Social ownership requires a further democratisation in the relations of production, so that working people are no longer alienated from the products of their labour but are able to participate in decisions to be made concerning the production in which they are engaged and its purpose in society – again, the model already familiar from workers' cooperatives. This is in turn a programme for developing an alternative consciousness beyond capitalism, raising awareness that economic activity can be directed towards social ends rather than the pursuit of profit – in other words, towards social production.[51]

Social Production

Common ownership is not just a matter of democracy or sovereignty; in practical terms, ownership confers the power to decide what is produced, how it is produced and in what quantities. Social production is production for use, not profit, and thereby opens up the possibility of a radical transformation of the economy away from the destructive tendencies of capitalism towards socially constructive purposes. The various forms of social and solidarity economy already conform to this orientation insofar as they prioritise the delivery of social goods ahead of profit and assert the primacy of people over capital in the distribution of revenues. Yet for social production to be a possibility in the broader economy, it is necessary to decommodify the social and economic spheres and challenge the profit motive at the heart of the capitalist system. This process of decommodification is already evident in the myriad political struggles around the world aimed at reclaiming the commons, resisting privatisation and asserting the priority of public good over private gain. As explained by Dennis Soron and Gordon Laxer:

> The goals of radical transformative decommodification are not to dismantle all markets, but to remove *capitalist markets*, extend democratic authority, and reorient society away from producing commodities for profit as dominant collective activities. Decommodification is a process that transforms activities away from production for profit for the purpose of meeting a social need, meeting a use value, or restoring nature. Decommodification pertains both to production of an economic good or service and to the removal from production of something of nature that had been used to generate profits. Decommodification is a process and a continuum. It is not an 'either/or' issue of having a society that has been wholly commodified or one that is fully decommodified. It is variable, and a matter of degree.[52]

The process of decommodification in turn hints at the full range of campaigns that must be undertaken to break the cultural hegemony of capitalism and redirect both production and consumption towards social need. For a start, such a process will necessarily entail a parallel decommodification of labour itself, so that working people are no longer reduced to the status of commodities within the system, but are understood as beings with social rights that exist independently of the market.[53] In its fullest form, this necessitates a positive revolution in working practices, with all members of society guaranteed the possibility of decent work by means of shorter hours at sufficient rates of pay to meet their basic needs; such a move in turn eliminates the vast wastage of unemployment, unlocking the latent potential of millions of workers in a virtuous cycle for socially beneficial production. In transition towards such a goal, the concept of a living wage calculated according to workers' needs rather than market rates, as discussed in Chapter 6, is one instance of how the process of labour decommodification can already begin to challenge the logic of capitalism from within; the movement for an unconditional basic income across Europe (accepted by the European Commission in January 2013 as a European Citizen's Initiative) is another. In its original conception, the fair trade movement sought to mount a similar challenge from within the existing international trading system to the dominant capitalist model of unequal exchange.[54]

Social production in turn opens up the possibility of new forms of social reproduction, whereby society can be recreated on an inclusive basis to take account of the changing politics of class, ethnicity and gender. Through its assault on the welfare state and its removal of public support for child rearing, care provision and other aspects of social existence, the neoliberal capitalist programme has intensified pressure on women as those who shoulder the greatest burden of social reproduction, and particularly on those women who are further marginalised by ethnicity or class.[55] The process of decommodification, by contrast, not only redirects production towards social use rather than profit, but also reinstates the principle of quality public service provision that is available and accessible to all. In the classic formulation of Gøsta Esping-Andersen, 'Stripping society of the institutional layers that guaranteed social reproduction outside the labour contract meant that people were commodified ... De-commodification occurs when a service is rendered as a matter of right, and when a person can maintain a livelihood without reliance on the market.'[56] While early models of decommodification failed to account for the gendered division of labour and the relative independence that can be achieved by women through paid work, more developed forms must necessarily confront the patriarchal foundations of a capitalist system that relegates reproductive work to a social status lower than that of productive work, and seeks to deny women the right to full participation whether they enter the commodified labour market or not.[57] The importance of such a gendered understanding is heightened in the global economic context, where the feminisation of waged labour has been one of the defining characteristics of neoliberal capitalist globalisation, as noted above.[58]

Social production also implies a comprehensive demilitarisation of the economy in order to end the scandal of the arms trade. The total amount wasted globally on military expenditure, currently running at $1.7 trillion every year, is only the most obvious cost of this uniquely anti-social form of production; the price paid in lives lost and livelihoods destroyed when the weaponry is put to use outweighs even the vast opportunity costs of society's continuing tolerance of the armaments industry.[59] Conversion to an arms-free economy is achievable without loss of jobs, given the existing level of state subsidies provided to the arms industry that could be transferred to socially productive alternatives.[60] The demilitarisation of production would then open the way to a demilitarisation of society itself – a transformation beyond the imagination of most countries, but already a reality for those states which have abolished their standing armies, including Costa Rica, Panama, Grenada, Iceland and Liechtenstein, or those which have never had military forces in their national histories, such as Mauritius, St Lucia, Solomon Islands, Samoa and several other island states.

Finally, social production opens up the possibility of an economic agenda that respects the limits of local and global ecosystems, including the realities of climate change. Such an agenda inevitably challenges capitalism's pursuit of endless expansion, as concluded by the *décroissance* (degrowth) movement in its response to the triple crisis of society, economy and ecology. The declaration that emanated from the first international conference on degrowth held in Paris in April 2008 called for a transition to a 'steady state' economy by means of a paradigm shift away from the general pursuit of growth and ever increasing consumption. That transition is understood to require a redistribution of wealth both within and between countries as an essential part of the process, with the aim of effecting an increase in consumption where there is still extreme poverty, and a reduction in consumption where there is currently excess. It will also necessitate a renewed localisation of economies, as demanded by earlier critiques of globalisation, restricting to a minimum the production of commodities for export and the profit driven transport of goods from one side of the planet to the other. Needless to say, no such transition is conceivable within the framework of global capitalism: as stated by the movement's preeminent theorist, Serge Latouche, 'nothing but a rupture with the capitalist system, its consumerism and its productivism, can avoid catastrophe'.[61]

Getting There

The principles sketched out above are deliberately broad, in that they seek to draw out common threads from the many different movements for transformative change currently in existence around the world.

Distinctions between common, public and collective ownership, for instance, have been deliberately elided in order to concentrate on what unites rather than what divides them.[62] This unifying political project also refrains from prioritising one model of collective action over another, or from prejudging the potential of any of the various challenges to the capitalist system. While this chapter has profiled some of the most dramatic instances of social movements rising up to assume control of the state in the twenty-first century, previous chapters have described non-statist and anti-statist challenges to capital: community confrontations with oil and mining corporations, worker mobilisations within transnational supply chains, cross-border campaigns for a living wage, local resistance to land grabbing, global movements for food and seed sovereignty, actions against FTAs and the institutions of neoliberal globalisation, and those autonomous uprisings that through their construction and defence of local alternatives have contributed to the production of a new global reality.[63] Any comprehensive account of the broader movement for social and economic justice must also include campaigns against privatisation and in defence of the commons, growing anti-austerity mobilisations across Europe, feminist critiques of patriarchal modes of production, movements against militarism and imperialism, ecological defence of the planet in the face of capitalist expansion, liberation movements of those peoples still living under colonial occupation, legal challenges demanding accountability and redress for corporate malfeasance, the tax justice movement and all existential attacks on the foundations of the corporation itself, most notably the principle of limited liability.[64] Building the strength and unity of these anti-systemic movements remains the overwhelming priority of any strategy for transcending capitalism in the future. Engaging actively in their struggles remains the overwhelming priority for the present.

Capitalism will continue to lurch from crisis to crisis as a result of its own internal contradictions, creating the objective conditions for its eventual demise and replacement by systems that are not predicated upon the continuing immiseration of classes, peoples and communities or the destruction of the planet on which we live. Despite such an assurance, however, it is still necessary for social movements and other progressive forces to assume the subjective role of lead agents in the process of historical development, rejecting the dominant orthodoxy that grants such agency to transnational capital. As already noted in the conclusion to Marx's *Poverty of Philosophy*, it is in political struggle that the broad mass of working people becomes united and develops consciousness of its own interests, not just over and against capital but as a class for itself.[65] The end goal of social empowerment is thus prefigured in the praxis of collective political action, if only that action is understood as being directed towards transcending the systemic barriers to change. The struggle for alternatives beyond capitalism is what makes another world possible. Even in the midst of crisis, that world is already coming into view.

Notes

Chapter 1

1. Karl Polanyi, *The Great Transformation: The Political and Economic Origins of Our Time*, Boston: Beacon Press, 1944; David Harvey, *A Brief History of Neoliberalism*, Oxford: Oxford University Press, 2005.

2. Amilcar Cabral, 'The Weapon of Theory', speech delivered to the first Tricontinental Conference of the Peoples of Asia, Africa and Latin America, Havana, January 1966; see also Frantz Fanon, *The Wretched of the Earth*, New York: Grove Press, 2004 (first published 1961); Eduardo Galeano, *Open Veins of Latin America: Five Centuries of the Pillage of a Continent*, New York: Monthly Review Press, 1973; Amiya Kumar Bagchi, *Perilous Passage: Mankind and the Global Ascendancy of Capital*, New Delhi: Oxford University Press, 2006.

3. Samir Amin, 'The Destructive Dimension of the Accumulation of Capital', in Gernot Köhler and Emilio José Chaves (eds), *Globalization: Critical Perspectives*, New York: Nova Science Publishers, 2003, pp. 1–15; David Harvey, *The New Imperialism*, Oxford: Oxford University Press, 2003; for the continuity of imperialist ambitions in the post-colonial era, see Mark Curtis, *The Ambiguities of Power: British Foreign Policy since 1945*, London: Zed Books, 1995.

4. Shaohua Chen and Martin Ravallion, 'The Developing World is Poorer than We Thought, but No Less Successful in the Fight against Poverty', Washington DC: World Bank, 26 August 2008; $2 a day in purchasing power parity represents 'the median poverty line found amongst developing countries as a whole'. Later estimates released by the World Bank suggested that the number living in extreme poverty subsequently dropped to 1.29 billion, prior to the global economic contraction of 2009; 'World Bank Sees Progress Against Extreme Poverty, but Flags Vulnerabilities', World Bank press release, 29 February 2012. For a broader analysis of the Bank's strategy, see Paul Cammack, 'What the World Bank Means by Poverty Reduction, and Why it Matters', *New Political Economy*, Vol. 9, No. 2 (2004), pp. 189–211.

5. See, for instance, the many articles on this theme contributed by John Bellamy Foster, Brett Clark and Richard York to the pages of *Monthly Review* (available at monthlyreview.org), or their joint book, *The Ecological Rift: Capitalism's War on the Earth*, New York: Monthly Review Press, 2010.

6. 'Nicolas Sarkozy se penche de nouveau sur la moralisation du capitalisme financier', *La Tribune*, 8 January 2009; the transcript of Brown's speech at St Paul's Cathedral on 31 March 2009 was released by 10 Downing Street as 'Prime Minister Gordon Brown Calls for Global Economy Founded on Family Values'; the transcript of Obama's news conference from London's ExCel centre on 2 April 2009 is available on www.whitehouse.gov.

7. Naomi Klein, *The Shock Doctrine: The Rise of Disaster Capitalism*, London: Penguin, 2007.

8. Wolfgang Münchau, 'US joins misguided pursuit of austerity', *Financial Times*, 6 January 2013.

9. It was no surprise, in this context, that the High-Level Panel appointed by the UN Secretary-General to advise on a new global development framework for the period after 2015 appointed UK prime minister David Cameron as co-chair but found no place for a single representative of the social movements actually engaged in fighting poverty from the grassroots; see Mark Tran, 'Ban Ki-moon names panel to lead global development agenda post-2015', *Guardian*, 1 August 2012; John Hilary, 'David Cameron is unfit to chair the UN development panel – and here's why', *Guardian*, 24 May 2012.

Chapter 2

1. 'After historic downgrade, US must address its chronic debt problems', Xinhua news agency, Beijing, 6 August 2011.

2. Ming Jinwei, 'Frustrating fiscal talks expose deficiencies of US political system', Xinhua news agency, Beijing, 1 January 2013.

3. For further discussion on the concepts of core, semiperiphery and periphery in world systems theory, see later in this chapter.

4. The interrelations between economic and political cycles are summarised in Barry K. Gills, 'Globalization, Crisis and Transformation: World Systemic Crisis and the Historical Dialectics of Capital', *Globalizations*, Vol. 7, Nos 1–2 (2010), pp. 273–286.

5. *The Global Economic Crisis: Systemic Failures and Multilateral Remedies*, New York and Geneva: United Nations Conference on Trade and Development, 2009, chapter 1; for David Harvey's account of the 'spatial fix' in the context of the current crisis, see his *The Enigma of Capital and the Crises of Capitalism* Oxford: Oxford University Press, 2010.

6. John Bellamy Foster and Fred Magdoff, *The Great Financial Crisis: Causes and Consequences*, New York: Monthly Review Press, 2009. Financial profits collapsed completely as a result of the 2007 crisis, but already by the end of 2010 represented 30 per cent of total US domestic profits once more; Kathleen Madigan, 'Like the phoenix, US finance profits soar', *Wall Street Journal*, 25 March 2011.

7. See, for example, the Pentagon's own assessment in its *Quadrennial Defense Review Report: February 2010*, Washington DC: Department of Defense, 2010; also Andrew F. Krepinevich, 'The Pentagon's Wasting Assets: The Eroding Foundations of American Power', *Foreign Affairs*, Vol. 88, No. 4 (2009), pp. 18–33.

8. Giovanni Arrighi, *The Long Twentieth Century: Money, Power and the Origins of Our Time*, London: Verso, 2nd edition, 2010; the 'sign of autumn' formulation is cited by Arrighi from Braudel's 1984 classic *Civilization and Capitalism*.

9. *The BRICS Report: A Study of Brazil, Russia, India, China and South Africa with Special Focus on Synergies and Complementarities*, New Delhi: Oxford University Press, 2012; for more on China's long-term ambitions, see Jenny Clegg, *China's Global Strategy: Towards a Multipolar World*, London:

Pluto Press, 2009; Giovanni Arrighi, *Adam Smith in Beijing: Lineages of the Twenty-First Century*, London: Verso, 2007; Li Mingqi, 'The Rise of China and the Demise of the Capitalist World-Economy: Exploring Historical Possibilities in the 21st Century', *Science & Society*, Vol. 69, No. 3 (2005), pp. 420–48.

10. *World Investment Report 2011: Non-Equity Modes of International Production and Development*, New York and Geneva: United Nations Conference on Trade and Development, 2011.

11. All based on GDP in terms of purchasing power parity (PPP). Estimates vary as to the relative positions of Brazil, Russia and Germany, but the positions of the top four are agreed.

12. Author's calculations from *World Investment Report 2011: Non-Equity Modes of International Production and Development*, New York and Geneva: United Nations Conference on Trade and Development, 2011. On the damage caused by 'investment' into the Caymans and British Virgin Islands, see Nicholas Shaxson, *Treasure Islands: Tax Havens and the Men Who Stole the World*, London: Bodley Head, 2011; on the use of round-tripping by Chinese firms, see Naomi Rovnick, 'Caribbean tax haven adds heat to China's hot money', *South China Morning Post*, 19 May 2011.

13. *International Trade Statistics Yearbook: Volume 1 – Trade by Country*, New York: United Nations, 2011; all figures refer to merchandise trade only.

14. Author's calculations from *UNCTAD Handbook of Statistics 2010*, New York and Geneva: United Nations Conference on Trade and Development, 2010 and *International Trade Statistics Yearbook: Volume 1 – Trade by Country*, New York: United Nations, 2011; see also *Economic Development in Africa Report 2011: Fostering Industrial Development in Africa in the New Global Environment*, New York and Geneva: United Nations, 2011.

15. John Hilary, 'Trade Liberalization, Poverty and the WTO: Assessing the Realities', in Homi Katrak and Roger Strange (eds), *The WTO and Developing Countries*, London: Palgrave Macmillan, 2004, pp. 38–62.

16. Raphael Kaplinsky, *Globalization, Poverty and Inequality: Between a Rock and a Hard Place*, Cambridge: Polity, 2005, especially chapter 7; Yilmaz Akyüz, *Trade, Growth and Industrialisation: Issues, Experiences and Policy Challenges*, Penang: Third World Network, 2005; Arslan Razmi and Robert A. Blecker, 'Developing Country Exports of Manufactures: Moving Up the Ladder to Escape the Fallacy of Composition?', *Journal of Development Studies*, Vol. 44, No. 1 (2008), pp. 21–48.

17. Paul Collier, *The Bottom Billion: Why the Poorest Countries are Failing and What Can be Done About It*, Oxford: Oxford University Press, 2007.

18. IMF Independent Evaluation Office, *IMF Involvement in International Trade Policy Issues*, Washington DC: International Monetary Fund, 2009; for the effects of IMF conditionality, see the report of the Structural Adjustment Participatory Review International Network (SAPRIN), *Structural Adjustment: The Policy Roots of Economic Crisis, Poverty and Inequality*, London: Zed Books, 2004; also Michel Chossudovsky, *The Globalisation of Poverty: Impacts of IMF and World Bank Reforms*, London: Zed Books, 1997.

19. Branko Milanovic, *Worlds Apart: Measuring International and Global Inequality*, Princeton: Princeton University Press, 2005, chapter 11 – the

statement refers to unweighted intercountry inequality, as the comparison when weighted by population is overwhelmed by India and China; see also Francisco H.G. Ferreira and Martin Ravallion, 'Global Poverty and Inequality: A Review of the Evidence', Policy Research Working Paper No. 4623, Washington DC: World Bank, 2008.

20. David Harvey, *Spaces of Global Capitalism: Towards a Theory of Uneven Geographical Development*, London: Verso, 2006; Samir Amin, *Capitalism in the Age of Globalization: The Management of Contemporary Society*, London: Zed Books, 1997; Giovanni Arrighi, Beverly J. Silver and Benjamin D. Brewer, 'Industrial Convergence, Globalization, and the Persistence of the North-South Divide', *Studies in Comparative International Development*, Vol. 38, No. 1 (2003), pp. 3–31.

21. For instance, Branko Milanovic, *The Haves and the Have-Nots: A Brief and Idiosyncratic History of Global Inequality*, New York: Basic Books, 2011; Graham Turner, *The Credit Crunch: Housing Bubbles, Globalisation and the Worldwide Economic Crisis*, London: Pluto Press, 2008; David Harvey, *The Enigma of Capital and the Crises of Capitalism*, Oxford: Oxford University Press, 2010.

22. Leslie Sklair, *Globalization: Capitalism & its Alternatives*, Oxford: Oxford University Press, 2002, chapter 3.

23. *World of Work Report 2008: Income Inequalities in the Age of Financial Globalization*, Geneva: International Labour Organisation, 2008.

24. Luci Ellis and Kathryn Smith, 'The Global Upward Trend in the Profit Share', Working Paper No. 231, Basel: Bank for International Settlements, 2007; see also Olivier Giovannoni, 'Functional Distribution of Income, Inequality and the Incidence of Poverty: Stylized Facts and the Role of Macroeconomic Policy', Geneva: United Nations Research Institute for Social Development, 2008.

25. Aviva Aron-Dine and Isaac Shapiro, 'Share of National Income Going to Wages and Salaries at Record Low in 2006', Washington DC: Center on Budget and Policy Priorities, 29 March 2007; Floyd Norris, 'As corporate profits rise, workers' income declines', *New York Times*, 5 August 2011.

26. Paul Krugman, *The Conscience of a Liberal: Reclaiming America from the Right*, London: Allen Lane, 2007, chapter 7.

27. Michael Greenstone and Adam Looney, 'Trends: Men In Trouble', *Milken Institute Review*, Third Quarter 2011, pp. 8–16; the median earnings for men with less than a high school education have declined by as much as 66 per cent in real terms over the same period.

28. Emmanuel Saez, 'Striking it Richer: The Evolution of Top Incomes in the United States (Updated with 2008 Estimates)', July 2010; revised version of Thomas Piketty and Emmanuel Saez, 'Income Inequality in the United States, 1913–1998', *Quarterly Journal of Economics*, Vol. 118, No. 1 (2003), pp. 1–39.

29. Stewart Lansley, *Unfair to Middling: How Middle Income Britain's Shrinking Wages Fuelled the Crash and Threaten Recovery*, London: Trades Union Congress, 2009.

30. Matthew Whittaker and Lee Savage, *Missing Out: Why Ordinary Workers are Experiencing Growth without Gain*, London: Resolution Foundation, 2011.

31. Daniel Dorling et al., *Poverty, Wealth and Place in Britain, 1968 to 2005*, Bristol: The Policy Press, 2007; *An Anatomy of Economic Inequality in the UK: Report of the National Equality Panel*, London: Government Equalities Office, 2010.

32. *Combating Poverty and Inequality: Structural Change, Social Policy and Politics*, Geneva: United Nations Research Institute for Social Development, 2010, p. 66.

33. *Global Wage Report 2010/11: Wage Policies in Times of Crisis*, Geneva: International Labour Organisation, 2010, p. 24; José Gabriel Palma, 'The Seven Main "Stylized Facts" of the Mexican Economy since Trade Liberalization and NAFTA', *Industrial and Corporate Change*, Vol. 14, No. 6 (2005), pp. 941–91.

34. R. Nagaraj (ed.), *Country Study: India*, In-Depth Background Paper for *Combating Poverty and Inequality: Structural Change, Social Policy and Politics*, Geneva: United Nations Research Institute for Social Development, 2010; James K. Galbraith, Deepshikha RoyChowdhury and Sanjeev Shrivastava, 'Pay Inequality in the Indian Manufacturing Sector, 1979–1998', Working Paper No. 28, Austin: University of Texas Inequality Project, 2004.

35. Ho-fung Hung, 'Sinomania: Global Crisis, China's Crisis?', in Leo Panitch, Greg Albo and Vivek Chibbers (eds), *The Crisis and the Left: Socialist Register 2012*, Pontypool: Merlin Press, 2011, pp. 217–34.

36. Ricardo Molero Simarro, 'Functional Distribution of Income and Economic Growth in the Chinese Economy, 1978-2007', Department of Economics Working Paper No. 168, London: School of Oriental and African Studies, 2011; Jean C. Oi, 'Development Strategies, Welfare Regime and Poverty Reduction in China', Country Overview Paper for *Combating Poverty and Inequality: Structural Change, Social Policy and Politics*, Geneva: United Nations Research Institute for Social Development, 2010.

37. James B. Davies, Susanna Sandström, Anthony Shorrocks and Edward N. Wolff, 'The World Distribution of Household Wealth', Helsinki: United Nations University World Institute for Development Economics Research, 2008; Anthony Shorrocks, James B. Davies and Rodrigo Lluberas, *Global Wealth Report 2012*, Zurich: Credit Suisse Research Institute, 2012.

38. For a personal view from a business journalist who has 'spent more than two decades shadowing the new global super-rich', see Chrystia Freeland, *Plutocrats: The Rise of the New Global Super-Rich and the Fall of Everyone Else*, London: Allen Lane, 2012; for more on the 'plutocratic oligarchy' in the countries of the periphery and semiperiphery, see Samir Amin, *Ending the Crisis of Capitalism or Ending Capitalism?* Cape Town: Pambazuka Press, 2011.

39. The Forbes ranking allocates each corporation a composite score according to an equal weighting of sales, profits, assets and market value; see the World's Biggest Public Companies for 2012 at www.forbes.com. For an earlier comparison using *Fortune* magazine lists, see Leslie Sklair and Peter T. Robbins, 'Global Capitalism and Major Corporations from the Third World', *Third World Quarterly*, Vol. 23, No. 1 (2002), pp. 81–100.

40. Tables showing the foreign assets and transnationality index of the world's top 100 non-financial companies – as well as the top 100 from developing

and transition economies – can be found on the UNCTAD website: www.
unctad.org/wir; see also *World Investment Report 2006: FDI from Developing
and Transition Economies: Implications for Development*, New York and
Geneva: United Nations Conference on Trade and Development, 2006.

41. Sylvia Pfeifer and Leslie Hook, 'Chinese demand for energy pumps up M&A
share', *Financial Times*, 7 November 2010.

42. *2010 Statistical Bulletin of China's Outward Foreign Direct Investment*, Beijing:
People's Republic of China Ministry of Commerce, 2011; Ken Davies,
'Outward FDI from China and its Policy Context', New York: Vale Columbia
Center on Sustainable International Investment, 2010.

43. *World Investment Report 2011: Non-Equity Modes of International Production
and Development*, New York and Geneva: United Nations Conference on
Trade and Development, 2011.

44. Peter Nolan, *Is China Buying the World?* Cambridge: Polity, 2012.

45. Gawdat Bahgat, 'The USA's Policy on Sovereign Wealth Funds' Investments',
in Xu Yi-chong and Gawdat Bahgat (eds), *The Political Economy of Sovereign
Wealth Funds*, Basingstoke: Palgrave Macmillan, 2010, pp. 228–44; Mitchell
Silk and Richard Malish, 'Are Chinese Companies Taking Over the World?',
Chicago Journal of International Law, Vol. 7, No. 1 (2006), pp. 105–131.

46. Li Hong, 'Chinese investment rejected again', *People's Daily Online*, 8 June
2009; Jameson Berkow, 'Canada rejects $5.9-billion Petronas bid for Progress
Energy', *Financial Post*, 20 October 2012.

47. Charles Arthur, 'US shuts out China tech firms over "security threat"',
Guardian, 9 October 2012.

48. See, for example, Andrew Newcombe and Lluís Paradell, *Law and Practice of
Investment Treaties: Standards of Practice*, Alphen aan den Rijn: Kluwer, 2009,
pp. 3–4, note 6. The major capital-exporting states were also, of course, the
principal importers of capital, as FDI formerly circulated mainly among the
countries of the North. The distinction between capital-exporting and capital-importing economies was based on relative rather than absolute weight;
see Gus Van Harten, *Investment Treaty Arbitration and Public Law*, Oxford:
Oxford University Press, 2007, pp. 13–14, note 6.

49. *North-South: A Programme for Survival; Report of the International Commission
on International Development Issues under the Chairmanship of Willy Brandt*,
London: Pan Books, 1980, pp. 31–2.

50. Jørgen Dige Pedersen, 'The Second Wave of Indian Investments Abroad',
Journal of Contemporary Asia, Vol. 38, No. 4 (2008), pp. 613–37. This is a
different challenge from that posed by Nigel Harris in his study *The End of
the Third World: Newly Industrializing Countries and the Decline of an Ideology*,
London: I.B. Tauris, 1986, which charted the rise and fall of 'Third Worldism'
as a reformist programme for national development. For 'accumulation by
dispossession', see David Harvey, *The New Imperialism*, Oxford: Oxford
University Press, 2003, chapter 4.

51. For the role of the semiperiphery, see Immanuel Wallerstein, *The Capitalist
World-Economy*, Cambridge: Cambridge University Press, 1979, especially
chapter 5; Giovanni Arrighi and Jessica Drangel, 'The Stratification of the
World-Economy: An Exploration of the Semiperipheral Zone', *Review*,
Vol. 10, No. 1 (1986), pp. 9–74; Christopher Chase-Dunn, 'Comparing

World-Systems: Toward a Theory of Semiperipheral Development', *Comparative Civilizations Review*, No. 19 (1988), pp. 29–66; and the essays in Owen Worth and Phoebe Moore (eds), *Globalization and the 'New' Semi-Peripheries*, Basingstoke: Palgrave Macmillan, 2009.

52. This is not to deny that there are deeper questions of intention surrounding the engagement of China and other emerging economies in the governance structures of the global economy; see Martin Hart-Landsberg, 'The US Economy and China: Capitalism, Class, and Crisis', *Monthly Review*, Vol. 61, No. 9 (2010), pp. 14–31; Gregory Chin, 'The Emerging Countries and China in the G20: Reshaping Global Economic Governance', *Studia Diplomatica*, Vol. 63, No. 2 (2010), pp. 105–24.

53. 'IMF nearly doubles funding capacity by pledges of over 430 bln USD', Xinhua news agency, Washington DC, 20 April 2012.

54. IMF Independent Evaluation Office, *The IMF's Approach to Capital Account Liberalization: Evaluation Report*, Washington DC: International Monetary Fund, 2005; the IMF has since conceded that the use of capital controls 'is justified as part of the policy toolkit to manage inflows'; see 'Capital Inflows: The Role of Controls', IMF Staff Position Note SPN/10/04, Washington DC: International Monetary Fund, February 2010.

55. Cited in Walden Bello, 'The Capitalist Conjuncture: Over-Accumulation, Financial Crises, and the Retreat from Globalisation', *Third World Quarterly*, Vol. 27, No. 8 (2006), pp. 1345–67.

56. Ruggiero cited in 'UNCTAD and WTO: A Common Goal in a Global Economy', UNCTAD press release TAD/INF/PR/9628, 8 October 1996.

57. 'Building Our Common Future: Renewed Collective Action for the Benefit of All', Final Declaration of the G20 Cannes Summit, 4 November 2011.

58. Paul Cammack, 'The Governance of Global Capitalism: A New Materialist Analysis', *Historical Materialism*, Vol. 11, No. 2 (2003), pp. 37–59; see also Nitsan Chorev and Sarah Babb, 'The Crisis of Neoliberalism and the Future of International Institutions: A Comparison of the IMF and the WTO', *Theory and Society*, Vol. 38, No. 5 (2009), pp. 459–84.

59. IMF Independent Evaluation Office, *Structural Conditionality in IMF-Supported Programs*, Washington DC: International Monetary Fund, 2007; Daniela Gabor, 'The International Monetary Fund and its New Economics', *Development and Change*, Vol. 41, No. 5 (2010), pp. 805–30.

60. The classic account of the 1976 crisis relates how imposition of conditionality on both developed and developing countries was tightened following the UK's earlier recourse to the IMF during the sterling crisis of 1967: Kathleen Burk and Alec Cairncross, *'Goodbye, Great Britain': The 1976 IMF Crisis*, New Haven: Yale University Press, 1992; see also Kevin Hickson, *The IMF Crisis of 1976 and British Politics*, London: I.B. Tauris, 2005, chapter 3.

61. William K. Carroll, *The Making of a Transnational Capitalist Class: Corporate Power in the 21st Century*, London: Zed Books, 2010; see also William I. Robinson, *A Theory of Global Capitalism: Production, Class, and State in a Transnational World*, Baltimore: Johns Hopkins University Press, 2004; Leslie Sklair, *The Transnational Capitalist Class*, Oxford: Blackwell, 2001.

62. Bilderberg has come out of the shadows a little in recent years, and now has its own official website on which the outline details of past conferences can

be consulted: bilderbergmeetings.org; see also the interviews with attendees and steering committee members in Ian Richardson, Andrew Kakabadse and Nada Kakabadse, *Bilderberg People: Elite Power and Consensus in World Affairs*, London: Routledge, 2011.

63. 'Framework for Advancing Transatlantic Economic Integration between the European Union and the United States of America', Agreement signed at the EU-US Summit of 30 April 2007 between Angela Merkel, José Manuel Barroso and George W. Bush.

64. On the ERT, see Belén Balanyá et al., *Europe, Inc: Regional and Global Restructuring and the Rise of Corporate Power*, London: Pluto Press, 2nd edition, 2003.

65. 'Forging a Transatlantic Partnership for the 21st Century', Joint statement by US Business Roundtable, the TransAtlantic Business Dialogue and the European Round Table of Industrialists, 18 April 2012.

66. 'World Economic Forum Annual Meeting 2012, Media Fact Sheet', www. weforum.org.

67. Ralph Miliband, 'State Power and Class Interests', *New Left Review*, No. 138 (1983), pp. 157–68; see also Miliband's earlier, more discursive treatment: *The State in Capitalist Society: The Analysis of the Western System of Power*, London: Weidenfeld & Nicholson, 1969.

68. Alex Callinicos, *Imperialism and Global Political Economy*, Cambridge: Polity, 2009.

69. *Cannes B20 Business Summit: Final report with appendices*, Paris: MEDEF, 2011.

70. Ruy Mauro Marini, 'Brazilian Subimperialism', *Monthly Review*, Vol. 23, No. 9 (1972), pp. 14–24; Srikant Dutt, *India and the Third World: Altruism or Hegemony?* London: Zed Books, 1984; Matthew Flynn, 'Between Subimperialism and Globalization: A Case Study in the Internationalization of Brazilian Capital', *Latin American Perspectives*, Vol. 34, No. 6 (2007), pp. 9–27; Patrick Bond, 'US Empire and South African Subimperialism', in Leo Panitch and Colin Leys (eds), *The Empire Reloaded: Socialist Register 2005*, London: Merlin Press, 2004, pp. 218–38.

71. For a more balanced survey of China in Africa, see Deborah Brautigam, *The Dragon's Gift: The Real Story of China in Africa*, Oxford: Oxford University Press, 2009; also Firoze Manji and Stephen Marks (eds), *African Perspectives on China in Africa*, Nairobi and Oxford: Fahamu, 2007; and Philip Snow's earlier *The Star Raft: China's Encounter with Africa*, Ithaca: Cornell University Press, 1988.

72. For more on the expansionist dynamic inherent in capitalism, see Ernest Mandel, *Late Capitalism*, London: New Left Books, 1975, chapter 2.

73. Paul Cammack, 'The Shape of Capitalism to Come', *Antipode*, Vol. 41, Suppl. 1 (2010), pp. 262–80.

Chapter 3

1. *IAEA International Fact Finding Expert Mission of the Fukushima Dai-Ichi NPP Accident Following the Great East Japan Earthquake and Tsunami*, Vienna: International Atomic Energy Agency, 2011.

2. 'Nuclear power: the dream that failed', *The Economist*, 10 March 2012.
3. Nathalie Bernasconi-Osterwalder and Rhea Tamara Hoffmann, 'Der deutsche Atomausstieg auf dem Prüfstand eines internationalen Investitionsschiedsgerichts? Hintergründe zum neuen Streitfall Vattenfall gegen Deutschland (II)', Berlin: PowerShift, October 2012; Jakob Schlandt, 'Vattenfall fordert Milliarden', *Frankfurter Rundschau*, 21 December 2012.
4. Klaus Stratmann, 'Vattenfall verklagt Deutschland', *Handelsblatt*, 2 November 2011; Nathalie Bernasconi-Osterwalder, 'Background paper on Vattenfall v Germany arbitration', Winnipeg: International Institute for Sustainable Development, 2009.
5. Naomi Klein, *The Shock Doctrine: The Rise of Disaster Capitalism*, London: Penguin, 2007.
6. Chakravarthi Raghavan, *Recolonization: GATT, the Uruguay Round & the Third World*, Penang: Third World Network, 1990; for more on the project to 'complete' the world market, see Paul Cammack, 'The Governance of Global Capitalism: A New Materialist Analysis', *Historical Materialism*, Vol. 11, No. 2 (2003), pp. 37–59.
7. Sophia Murphy, 'Free Trade in Agriculture: A Bad Idea Whose Time is Done', *Monthly Review*, Vol. 61, No. 3 (2009), pp. 78–91.
8. Duncan Matthews, *Globalising Intellectual Property Rights: The TRIPs Agreement*, London: Routledge, 2002.
9. David Hartridge, 'What the General Agreement on Trade in Services Can Do', speech to British Invisibles and Clifford Chance conference, 'Opening Markets for Banking Worldwide: The WTO General Agreement on Trade in Services', London, 8 January 1997. The European Commission was equally candid in its admission that GATS is 'first and foremost an instrument for the benefit of business, and not only for business in general, but for individual service companies wishing to export services or to invest and operate abroad'; European Commission, 'Where Next? The GATS 2000 Negotiations', European Commission 'Info-Point' on World Trade in Services; both cited in John Hilary, *The Wrong Model: GATS, Trade Liberalisation and Children's Right to Health*, London: Save the Children, 2001.
10. In the WTO's categorisation, mode 3 of services trade covers foreign investment, as it governs the conditions under which service companies are permitted to establish a commercial presence in the host economy; John Hilary, 'Foreign Investment in Services: The threat of GATS 2000 negotiations', paper delivered at the WTO Symposium, Geneva, 30 April 2002.
11. For the threat caused by such balance of payment problems, see David Woodward, *The Next Crisis? Direct and Equity Investment in Developing Countries*, London: Zed Books, 2001; more generally, see *Elimination of TRIMs: The Experience of Selected Developing Countries*, New York and Geneva: United Nations Conference on Trade and Development, 2007.
12. Judith L. Goldstein and Richard H. Steinberg, 'Negotiate or Litigate? Effects of WTO Judicial Delegation on US Trade Politics', *Law and Contemporary Problems*, Vol. 71 (2008), pp. 257–82.

13. Christian Deblock and Dorval Brunelle, 'Globalization and New Normative Frameworks: The Multilateral Agreement on Investment', in Guy Lachapelle and John Trent (eds), *Globalization, Governance and Identity: The Emergence of New Partnerships*, Montréal: Les Presses de l'Université de Montréal, 2000, pp. 83–126; for the text of the MAI, see *The Multilateral Agreement on Investment: Draft Consolidated Text*, OECD Document DAFFE/MAI(98)7/REV1, Paris: Organisation for Economic Cooperation and Development, 22 April 1998.

14. A blow-by-blow account of the WTO's Doha ministerial conference, including a unique exposé of the underhand tactics used on developing country representatives, is given in Fatoumata Jawara and Aileen Kwa, *Behind the Scenes at the WTO: The Real World of International Trade Negotiations*, London: Zed Books, 2nd edition, 2004.

15. John Hilary, *Divide and Rule: The EU and US Response to Developing Country Alliances at the WTO*, Johannesburg: ActionAid International, 2004.

16. The website bilaterals.org is an important source of information on all bilateral and regional trade agreements, including the investment dimension increasingly included within them.

17. Bruno Ciccaglione, *Free Trade and Trade Unions of the Americas: Strategies, Practices, Struggles, Achievements*, Vienna: Arbeiterkammer Wien, 2009.

18. For general background on the TPP, see Ian F. Ferguson, William H. Cooper, Remy Jurenas and Brock R. Williams, *The Trans-Pacific Partnership Negotiations and Issues for Congress*, Washington DC: Congressional Research Service, 2013; for critiques, see Jagdish Bhagwati, 'America's Threat to Trans-Pacific Trade', *Project Syndicate*, 30 December 2011; and the analyses collected in the TPP section of the Public Citizen website: citizen.org.

19. John Hilary, 'Challenging Corporate Europe', *Renewal*, Vol. 17, No. 2 (2009), pp. 33–7; Andreas Bieler, 'Globalisation and European Integration: The Internal and External Dimensions of Neo-Liberal Restructuring', in Petros Nousios, Henk Overbeek and Andreas Tsolakls (eds), *Globalisation and European Integration: Critical Approaches to Regional Order and International Relations*, Abingdon: Routledge, 2012, pp. 197–217; Peter Fuchs, '"Global Europe" – die neue Strategie der Europäischen Union zur externen Wettbewerbsfähigkeit', Berlin: Die Linke, 2007.

20. *A New Era for Transatlantic Trade Leadership: A Report from the Transatlantic Task Force on Trade and Investment*, Berlin and Brussels: German Marshall Fund and European Centre for International Political Economy, 2012.

21. *Bilateral Investment Treaties 1959–1999*, New York and Geneva: United Nations Conference on Trade and Development, 2000; *World Investment Report 2012: Towards a New Generation of Investment Policies*, New York and Geneva: United Nations Conference on Trade and Development, 2012.

22. Of a total of 1,185 regulatory changes in those years, 1,121 served to liberalise the investment regime; author's calculation from *World Investment Report 2000: Cross-Border Mergers and Acquisitions and Development*, New York and Geneva: United Nations Conference on Trade and Development, 2000, supplemented by *World Investment Report 2011: Non-Equity Modes of International Production and Development*, New York and Geneva: United Nations Conference on Trade and Development, 2011.

23. Gus Van Harten, 'Private Authority and Transnational Governance: The Contours of the International System of Investor Protection', *Review of International Political Economy*, Vol. 12, No. 4 (2005), pp. 600–23.

24. *Dispute Settlement: Investor-State*, New York and Geneva: United Nations Conference on Trade and Development, 2003. The new ICC arbitration rules, which came into force as of January 2012, are available in *Arbitration and ADR Rules*, Paris: International Chamber of Commerce, 2011. Examples of the Permanent Court's involvement in investor-state cases are available on its website: www.pca-cpa.org.

25. M. Sornarajah, 'The Retreat of Neo-Liberalism in Investment Treaty Arbitration', in Catherine A. Rogers and Roger P. Alford (eds), *The Future of Investment Arbitration*, New York: Oxford University Press, 2009, pp. 273–96; see also Alexandre de Gramont, 'After the Water War: The Battle for Jurisdiction in Aguas del Tunari SA v Republic of Bolivia', *Transnational Dispute Management*, Vol. 3, No. 5 (2006).

26. In his dissenting opinion, the presiding arbitrator noted: 'The ICSID mechanism and remedy are not meant for investments made in a State by its own citizens with domestic capital through the channel of a foreign entity, whether preexistent or created for that purpose ... The object and purpose of the ICSID Convention is not – and its effect, therefore, should not be – to afford domestic, national corporations the means of evading the jurisdiction of their domestic, national tribunals.' Dissenting Opinion of Professor Prosper Weil, President of the ICSID tribunal, Case No. ARB/02/18, 29 April 2004.

27. The characterisation comes from Toby Landau QC, cited in Pia Eberhardt and Cecilia Olivet, *Profiting from Injustice: How Law Firms, Arbitrators and Financiers are Fuelling an Investment Arbitration Boom*, Amsterdam: Corporate Europe Observatory and Transnational Institute, 2012.

28. Gus Van Harten, *Investment Treaty Arbitration and Public Law*, Oxford: Oxford University Press, 2007, p. 171.

29. Ibid., chapter 6.

30. Nicole Yazbek, 'Bilateral Investment Treaties: The Foreclosure of Domestic Policy Space', *South African Journal of International Affairs*, Vol. 17, No. 1 (2010), pp. 103–20; *Bilateral Investment Treaties 1995–2006: Trends in Investment Rulemaking*, New York and Geneva: United Nations Conference on Trade and Development, 2007.

31. Documentation of all NAFTA investor-state cases can be found on the website www.naftaclaims.com. For a summary of early claims, see *NAFTA Chapter 11 Investor-to-State Cases: Bankrupting Democracy*, Washington DC: Public Citizen, 2001; for an updated list, see 'Table of Foreign Investor-State Cases and Claims under NAFTA and Other US Trade Deals', Washington DC: Public Citizen, 2012.

32. Stuart Trew, 'Trade Committee Begins Hearings into AbitibiBowater NAFTA Settlement', Council of Canadians, 8 March 2011.

33. Documentation of ICSID cases is available via the ICSID website: icsid.worldbank.org. All investment treaty awards are conveniently listed, with documentation, on the Investment Treaty Arbitration website: italaw.com. A summary of notable cases is given in Nathalie Bernasconi-Osterwalder and Lise Johnson (eds), *International Investment Law and Sustainable Development:*

Key Cases from 2000–2010, Winnipeg: International Institute for Sustainable Development, 2011.

34. 'Argentina Rejects Azurix Claims on ICSID Award in Letter to Geithner', *Inside US Trade*, 16 September 2011.

35. Luke Eric Peterson, *Human Rights and Bilateral Investment Treaties: Mapping the Role of Human Rights Law within Investor-State Arbitration*, Montréal: Rights & Democracy, 2009.

36. Jim Shultz, 'The Cochabamba Water Revolt and its Aftermath', in Jim Shultz and Melissa Crane Draper (eds), *Dignity and Defiance: Stories from Bolivia's Challenge to Globalization*, Berkeley: University of California Press, 2008, pp. 9–42.

37. See, for example, Susan D. Franck, 'The Legitimacy Crisis in Investment Treaty Arbitration: Privatizing Public International Law through Inconsistent Decisions', *Fordham Law Review*, Vol. 73, No. 4 (2005), pp. 1521–625.

38. 'Public Statement on the Investment Regime', 31 August 2010, available in various languages at www.osgoode.yorku.ca/public_statement.

39. *Investment Policy Framework for Sustainable Development*, New York and Geneva: United Nations Conference on Trade and Development, 2012.

40. The joint decision to withdraw from ICSID was announced at the fifth annual Congress of the Bolivarian Alternative for the Americas (ALBA) in 2007; Cuba and Dominica, also members of ALBA, have never been signatories to the ICSID Convention. For Argentina's decision, see 'Argentina in the process of quitting from World Bank investment disputes centre', *MercoPress*, 31 January 2013.

41. Kyla Tienhaara and Patricia Ranald, 'Australia's Rejection of Investor-State Dispute Settlement: Four Potential Contributing Factors', *Investment Treaty News*, 12 July 2011; the fact that Philip Morris had brought a similar claim against Uruguay under the Switzerland-Uruguay BIT is another example of the ability of TNCs to assume multiple identities when 'forum shopping' for investor-state dispute mechanisms.

42. Subhomoy Bhattacharjee, 'India seeks treaty revisions to deal with corporate suits', *Indian Express*, 4 April 2012.

43. 'Bilateral Investment Treaty Policy Framework Review: Government Position Paper', Department of Trade and Industry, Pretoria, June 2009, section 7.2.

44. Speech delivered by Minister of Trade and Industry Rob Davies at the South African launch of the UNCTAD Investment Policy Framework for Sustainable Development, University of the Witwatersrand, 26 July 2012.

45. *World Investment Report 2011: Non-Equity Modes of International Production and Development*, New York and Geneva: United Nations Conference on Trade and Development, 2011, pp. 94–5.

46. *Cannes B20 Business Summit: Final Report with Appendices*, Paris: MEDEF, 2011, p. 17.

Chapter 4

1. The annual Responsible Business Summit is run by business intelligence consultancy Ethical Corporation; all information on corporate participants is as shown on its website: http://events.ethicalcorp.com/rbs.

2. Jem Bendell, 'Barricades and Boardrooms: A Contemporary History of the Corporate Accountability Movement', Geneva: United Nations Research Institute for Social Development, 2004.

3. This book will retain the familiar terminology of corporate social responsibility (CSR) in preference to other variants such as corporate responsibility (CR), corporate citizenship (CC) or corporate sustainability (CS). It will not engage with the related debate on the rise of philanthrocapitalism, documented in titles such as Matthew Bishop and Michael Green, *Philanthrocapitalism: How Giving Can Save the World*, London: A&C Black, 2008, and Michael Edwards, *Just Another Emperor? The Myths and Realities of Philanthrocapitalism*, London: Demos/Young Foundation, 2008; for a critique, see Slavoj Žižek, *Violence*, London: Profile Books, 2008, chapter 1.

4. See the various definitions cited in Archie B. Carroll, 'A History of Corporate Social Responsibility: Concepts and Practices', in Andrew Crane, Abagail McWilliams, Dirk Matten, Jeremy Moon and Donald S. Siegel (eds), *The Oxford Handbook of Corporate Social Responsibility*, Oxford: Oxford University Press, 2008, pp. 19–46.

5. 'Implementing the Partnership for Growth and Jobs: Making Europe a Pole of Excellence on Corporate Social Responsibility', Brussels: Commission of the European Communities, 2006.

6. David Sadler and Stuart Lloyd, 'Neo-Liberalising Corporate Social Responsibility: A Political Economy of Corporate Citizenship', *Geoforum*, Vol. 40, No. 4 (2009), pp. 613–22; see also James K. Rowe, 'Corporate Social Responsibility as Business Strategy', in Ronnie D. Lipschutz and James K. Rowe, *Globalization, Governmentality and Global Politics: Regulation for the Rest of Us?* Abingdon: Routledge, 2005, pp. 130–70; Peter Utting and José Carlos Marques, 'The Intellectual Crisis of CSR', in Peter Utting and José Carlos Marques (eds), *Corporate Social Responsibility and Regulatory Governance: Towards Inclusive Development?*, Basingstoke: Palgrave Macmillan, 2010, pp. 1–25.

7. Stephen A. Marglin and Juliet B. Schor (eds), *The Golden Age of Capitalism: Reinterpreting the Postwar Experience*, Oxford: Clarendon Press, 1990; 'Programme of Action on the Establishment of a New International Economic Order', Resolution Adopted by the General Assembly, UN document A/RES/S-6/3202, 1 May 1974.

8. An account of the origins and negotiation of the Code is given in the UN Centre on Transnational Corporations publication *The New Code Environment*, New York: United Nations, 1990, while the initial UN study that set the process in motion is *Multinational Corporations in World Development*, New York: United Nations, 1973. The history of the Code in its broader UN context is told in Tagi Sagafi-nejad and John Dunning, *The UN and Transnational Corporations: From Code of Conduct to Global Compact*, Bloomington: Indiana University Press, 2008; see also M. Sornarajah, *The International Law on Foreign Investment*, Cambridge: Cambridge University Press, 3rd edition, 2010, chapter 6.

9. As noted by the editors of the UN Intellectual History Project, it is ironic that the US Senate hearings inspired work on the UN Code, given that the USA was to become one of its greatest opponents; Louis Emmerij and Richard

Jolly, 'The UN and Transnational Corporations', United Nations Intellectual History Project, Briefing Note No. 17, New York: Ralph Bunche Institute for International Studies, July 2009.

10. *Multinational Corporations and United States Foreign Policy: Hearings Before the Subcommittee on Multinational Corporations of the Committee on Foreign Relations, United States Senate, Ninety-Third Congress, on The International Telephone and Telegraph Company and Chile, 1970–1*, Washington DC: US Government Printing Office, 1973; also 'Covert Action in Chile: 1963–1973', Staff Report of the Select Committee to Study Governmental Operations With Respect to Intelligence Activities, Washington DC: United States Senate, 1975; and 'CIA Activities in Chile', Washington DC: Central Intelligence Agency, 2000.

11. For the full story of United Fruit's involvement in Guatemala (and elsewhere in Latin America), see Peter Chapman, *Jungle Capitalists: A Story of Globalisation, Greed and Revolution*, Edinburgh: Canongate, 2007.

12. *Summary of the Hearings Before the Group of Eminent Persons to Study the Impact of Multinational Corporations on Development and on International Relations*, New York: United Nations, 1974; the final report of the Group of Eminent Persons was published by the UN Department of Economic and Social Affairs as *The Impact of Multinational Corporations on Development and on International Relations*, New York: United Nations, 1974.

13. 'The Code: Outstanding Issues', *CTC Reporter* No. 18 (1984), pp. 8–14; Patrick L. Robinson, 'The June 1985 Reconvened Special Session on the Code', *CTC Reporter* No. 20 (1985), pp. 11–14; 'Outstanding Issues in the Draft Code of Conduct on Transnational Corporations', New York: United Nations, 1985.

14. Sagafi-nejad and Dunning, *The UN and Transnational Corporations*, p. 121; the Centre's research agenda was incorporated into the work programme of the UN Conference on Trade and Development (UNCTAD), with a more technical focus attuned to promoting and attracting foreign investment.

15. *OECD Guidelines for Multinational Enterprises: Recommendations for Responsible Business Conduct in a Global Context*, Paris: Organisation for Economic Cooperation and Development, 2011.

16. See, for example, *10 Years On: Assessing the Contribution of the OECD Guidelines for Multinational Enterprises to Responsible Business Conduct*, Amsterdam: OECD Watch, 2010; Jernej Letnar Černič, 'Corporate Responsibility for Human Rights: A Critical Analysis of the OECD Guidelines for Multinational Enterprises', *Hanse Law Review*, Vol. 4, No. 1 (2008), pp. 71–100; *Flagship or Failure? The UK's Implementation of the OECD Guidelines and Approach to Corporate Accountability*, London: Amnesty International, Christian Aid and Friends of the Earth, 2006.

17. Aurora Voiculescu, 'Human Rights and the Normative Ordering of Global Capitalism', in Aurora Voiculescu and Helen Yanacopulos (eds), *The Business of Human Rights: An Evolving Agenda for Corporate Responsibility*, London: Zed Books, 2011, pp. 10–28.

18. For a full account, see Judith Richter, *Holding Corporations Accountable: Corporate Conduct, International Codes, and Citizen Action*, London: Zed

Books, 2001; also Andrew Chetley, *The Baby Killer Scandal*, London: War on Want, 1979.

19. *Agenda 21: The United Nations Programme of Action from Rio*, New York: United Nations, 1993, chapter 30: 'Strengthening the Role of Business & Industry'.

20. Michael Blowfield and Jedrzej George Frynas, 'Setting New Agendas: Critical Perspectives on Corporate Social Responsibility in the Developing World', *International Affairs*, Vol. 81, No. 3 (2005), pp. 499–513; Peter Newell, 'Citizenship, Accountability and Community: The Limits of the CSR Agenda', *International Affairs*, Vol. 81, No. 3 (2005), pp. 541–57.

21. John Sharp, 'Corporate Social Responsibility And Development: An Anthropological Perspective', *Development Southern Africa*, Vol. 23, No. 2 (2006), pp. 213–22.

22. *Catalyzing Change: A Short History of the WBCSD*, Geneva: World Business Council for Sustainable Development, 2006; the Business Council for Sustainable Development merged with the ICC's World Industry Council on the Environment in January 1995 to become the World Business Council for Sustainable Development (WBCSD). See also Kenny Bruno and Joshua Karliner, *earthsummit.biz: The Corporate Takeover of Sustainable Development*, Oakland: Food First Books, 2002, chapter 2; Andrew Rowell, *Green Backlash: Global Subversion of the Environmental Movement*, London: Routledge, 1996, chapter 4.

23. Stephan Schmidheiny, *Changing Course: A Global Business Perspective on Development and the Environment,* Cambridge MA: MIT Press, 1992.

24. For a compendium of national CSR initiatives from both North and South, see Wayne Visser and Nick Tolhurst (eds), *The World Guide to CSR: A Country-by-Country Analysis of Sustainability and Responsibility*, Sheffield: Greenleaf Publishing, 2010.

25. Peter Utting, 'Business Responsibility for Sustainable Development', Geneva: United Nations Research Institute for Social Development, 2000; see also *Self-Regulation of Environmental Management: An Analysis of Guidelines Set by World Industry Associations for their Member Firms*, Geneva: United Nations Conference on Trade and Development, 1996; and *Self-Regulation of Environmental Management: Guidelines Set by World Industry Associations for their Members' Firms: An Update*, Geneva: United Nations Conference on Trade and Development, 2003.

26. E.V.K. Fitzgerald , 'Regulating Large International Firms', Geneva: United Nations Research Institute for Social Development, 2001; Rhys Jenkins, 'Corporate Codes of Conduct: Self-Regulation in a Global Economy', Geneva: United Nations Research Institute for Social Development, 2001.

27. The text of Annan's speech is reproduced in 'Secretary-General Proposes Global Compact on Human Rights, Labour, Environment, in Address to World Economic Forum in Davos', UN press release SG/SM/6881, 1 February 1999.

28. Ann Elizabeth Mayer, 'Human Rights as a Dimension of CSR: The Blurred Lines Between Legal and Non-Legal Categories', *Journal of Business Ethics*, Vol. 88 (2009), pp. 561–77; the Compact's tenth principle, on corruption, was introduced after the nine original principles, in June 2004.

29. Ann Zammit, *Development at Risk: Rethinking UN-Business Partnerships*, Geneva: South Centre and United Nations Research Institute for Social Development, 2003, chapter 4; 'Bluewashed and boilerplated: a breakthrough in international corporate diplomacy', *The Economist*, 17 June 2004; John Hilary, 'In Bed with the UN', *Corporate Watch*, No. 10 (2000), p. 28.

30. Papa Louis Fall and Mohamed Mounir Zahran, 'United Nations Corporate Partnerships: The Role and Functioning of the Global Compact', Geneva: United Nations Joint Inspection Unit, 2010.

31. John Gerard Ruggie, 'Taking Embedded Liberalism Global: The Corporate Connection', in John Gerard Ruggie (ed.) *Embedding Global Markets: An Enduring Challenge*, Aldershot: Ashgate Publishing, 2008, pp. 231–54; Georg Kell and David Levin, 'The Evolution of the Global Compact Network: An Historic Experiment in Learning and Action', paper presented at the Academy of Management Annual Conference 'Building Effective Networks', Denver, 11–14 August 2002. Against this, the internal UN review cited above noted: 'The voluntary nature of the commitment and the "learning" premise on which the initiative is based do not provide adequate safeguards for behaviour.' Fall and Zahran, *United Nations Corporate Partnerships*, p. iv.

32. Four of the participating NGOs – Oxfam, Amnesty International, Lawyers Committee for Human Rights and Human Rights Watch – sent an open letter to UN Deputy Secretary-General Louise Fréchette in April 2003 criticising the Global Compact for its failure to enhance corporate accountability. Oxfam and Human Rights Watch are now no longer participants in the Compact.

33. See the annual progress reports by the UN Secretary-General; for example, *Partnerships for Sustainable Development: Report of the Secretary General*, 24 February 2010, UN document E/CN.17/2010/13.

34. 'Business Welcomes Summit Agreement, But Expresses Some Disappointments', Business Action for Sustainable Development statement, Johannesburg, 4 September 2002.

35. Peter Utting and Ann Zammit, 'Beyond Pragmatism: Appraising UN-Business Partnerships', Geneva: United Nations Research Institute for Social Development, 2006.

36. Charles Clover, '"Junk food" pact with Unicef causes outrage', *Daily Telegraph*, 27 August 2002; Patrick Butler, 'Unicef in McDonald's link row', *Guardian*, 3 August 2002

37. Zammit, *Development at Risk*, pp. xix–xxvii.

38. Upendra Baxi, 'Market Fundamentalisms: Business Ethics at the Altar of Human Rights', *Human Rights Law Review*, Vol. 5, No. 1 (2005), pp. 1–26.

39. David Kinley and Rachel Chambers, 'The UN Human Rights Norms for Corporations: The Private Implications of Public International Law', *Human Rights Law Review*, Vol. 6, No. 3 (2006), pp. 447–97.

40. For more on the legal impact of the Norms, see Larry Catá Backer, 'Multinational Corporations, Transnational Law: The United Nations' Norms on the Responsibilities of Transnational Corporations as a Harbinger of Corporate Social Responsibility in International Law', *Columbia Human Rights Law Review*, Vol. 37 (2005), pp. 101–92.

41. 'Norms on the Responsibilities of Transnational Corporations and Other Business Enterprises with Regard to Human Rights', 26 August 2003, UN

document E/CN.4/Sub.2/2003/12/Rev.2; the Commentary on the Norms provides no more detail on how respect for national sovereignty might entail corporations' 'expanding economic opportunities' in developing and least developed countries, although it does call for businesses to apply intellectual property rights in a manner that might contribute to technology transfer; see commentary to paragraph 10 of the Norms in 'Commentary on the Norms on the responsibilities of transnational corporations and other business enterprises with regard to human rights', 26 August 2003, UN document E/CN.4/Sub.2/2003/38/Rev.2.

42. 'UNHCHR Norms of Responsibilities of Transnational Corporations and Other Business Enterprises with Regard to Human Rights', United States Council for International Business, January 2003; see also the USCIB 'Talking Points' on the draft Norms and Sir Geoffrey Chandler's November 2003 rebuttal of them, both available on the Business and Human Rights website: www.business-humanrights.org.

43. 'Joint Views of the IOE and ICC on the Draft "Norms on the Responsibilities of Transnational Corporations and Other Business Enterprises with Regard to Human Rights" Submitted to Members of the United Nations Commission on Human Rights', International Organisation of Employers and International Chamber of Commerce, 24 November 2003; 'Joint Views of the IOE and ICC on the Draft "Norms on the Responsibilities of Transnational Corporations and Other Business Enterprises with Regard to Human Rights": The Sub-Commission's Draft Norms', International Organisation of Employers and International Chamber of Commerce, March 2004.

44. 'In the Matter of the Draft "Norms of Responsibilities of Transnational Corporations and Other Business Enterprises with Regard to Human Rights": Opinion of Professor Emeritus Maurice Mendelson QC', London: Blackstone Chambers, 4 April 2004; David Gow, 'CBI cries foul over UN human rights code', *Guardian*, 8 March 2004.

45. 'Status Report on the Draft Human Rights Code of Conduct', USCIB Corporate Responsibility Committee, available on the Business and Human Rights website: www.business-humanrights.org.

46. 'Responsibilities of Transnational Corporations and Related Business Enterprises with Regard to Human Rights', 22 April 2004, UN document E/CN.4/Dec/2004/116.

47. The Australian and US submissions are online at www2.ohchr.org/english/issues/globalization/business/docs/australia.pdf and /us.pdf respectively; the full list of all bodies that provided input is given in the report itself: 'Report of the United Nations High Commissioner on Human Rights on the Responsibilities of Transnational Corporations and Related Enterprises with Regard to Human Rights', 15 February 2005, UN document E/CN.4/2005/91.

48. 'Remarks by John G. Ruggie, UN Special Representative for Business and Human Rights', Forum on Corporate Social Responsibility co-sponsored by the Fair Labor Association and the German Network of Business Ethics, Bamberg, Germany, 14 June 2006.

49. Scott Jerbi, 'Business and Human Rights at the UN: What Might Happen Next?', *Human Rights Quarterly*, Vol. 31 (2009), pp. 299–320.

50. 'Business and Human Rights: Mapping International Standards of Responsibility and Accountability for Corporate Acts', Report of the Special Representative of the Secretary-General (SRSG) on the issue of human rights and transnational corporations and other business enterprises, 9 February 2007, UN document A/HRC/4/035; the Human Rights Council had replaced the UN Commission on Human Rights in 2006.

51. 'Protect, Respect and Remedy: A Framework for Business and Human Rights', Report of the Special Representative of the Secretary-General on the issue of human rights and transnational corporations and other business enterprises, John Ruggie, 7 April 2008, UN document A/HRC/8/5.

52. 'Guiding Principles on Business and Human Rights: Implementing the United Nations "Protect, Respect and Remedy" Framework', Report of the Special Representative of the Secretary-General on the issue of human rights and transnational corporations and other business enterprises, John Ruggie, 21 March 2011, UN document A/HRC/17/31.

53. 'Joint IOE-ICC-BIAC Comments on the Draft Guiding Principles on Business and Human Rights', International Organisation of Employers, International Chamber of Commerce and Business and Industry Advisory Committee to the OECD, Geneva, 26 January 2011.

54. 'Joint Statement on Business & Human Rights to the United Nations Human Rights Council', International Organisation of Employers, International Chamber of Commerce and Business and Industry Advisory Committee to the OECD, Geneva, 30 May 2011.

55. See the joint statement from FIAN International, Transnational Institute, La Via Campesina and 25 other organisations to delegations on the Human Rights Council, 30 May 2011, urging them to reject the Guiding Principles; also the joint statement from Amnesty International, ESCR-Net, Human Rights Watch, International Commission of Jurists, FIDH and RAID of 30 May 2011, which noted that the Guiding Principles failed to address core issues such as extraterritorial obligations, regulation, accountability or the right to remedy; and 'UN Human Rights Council: Weak Stance on Business Standards', Human Rights Watch, Geneva, 16 June 2011. The statement of the government delegation of Ecuador to the Human Rights Council on 16 June 2011 likewise condemned the failure of the Guiding Principles to secure accountability for human rights violations by multinational corporations, and the absence of any enforcement mechanism independent of the companies themselves. All the above are available from the Business and Human Rights website: www.business-humanrights.org.

56. For more detailed exploration of the role of corporations in the normative ordering of global capitalism, see Annegret Flohr et al., *The Role of Business in Global Governance: Corporations as Norm-Entrepreneurs*, Basingstoke: Palgrave Macmillan, 2010.

57. Andrew Cumbers, *Reclaiming Public Ownership: Making Space for Economic Democracy*, London: Zed Books, 2012, chapter 2.

58. For example, the conclusion of the comparative study by Antonio Estache, Sergio Perelman and Lourdes Trujillo, 'Infrastructure Performance and Reform in Developing and Transition Economies: Evidence from a Survey of Productivity Measures', Washington DC: World Bank, 2005: 'Most

cross-country papers on utilities find no statistically significant difference in efficiency scores between public and private providers.' See also the study by the IMF Fiscal Affairs Department, 'Public-Private Partnerships', Washington DC: International Monetary Fund, 2004, which concedes on the issue of efficiency: 'While there is an extensive literature on this subject, the theory is ambiguous and the empirical evidence is mixed.' For more detailed discussion and other references, see the research papers published by the Public Services International Research Unit at Greenwich University: www.psiru.org.

59. Dinah Rajak, *In Good Company: An Anatomy of Corporate Social Responsibility*, Stanford: Stanford University Press, 2011, pp. 53–5.

60. *Cannes B20 Business Summit: Final Report with Appendices*, Paris: MEDEF, 2011, pp. A61–74.

61. Milton Friedman, 'The Social Responsibility of Business is to Increase its Profits', *New York Times Magazine*, 13 September 1970.

62. *The State of Responsible Competitiveness: Making Sustainable Development Count in Global Markets*, London: AccountAbility, 2007; despite all evidence to the contrary, the European Commission has also been active in promoting 'responsible competitiveness' as a distinguishing characteristic of European corporations in the global economy.

63. Jedrzej George Frynas, 'The False Developmental Promise of Corporate Social Responsibility: Evidence from Multinational Oil Companies', *International Affairs*, Vol. 81, No. 3 (2005), pp. 581–98; A. Rani Parker, 'The Public-Private Alliances of USAID in Angola: An Assessment of Lessons Learned and Ways Forward', Washington DC: USAID, 2004.

64. Peter Redfield, 'Bioexpectations: Life Technologies as Humanitarian Goods', *Public Culture*, Vol. 24, No. 1 (2012), pp. 157–84.

65. C.K. Prahalad, *The Fortune at the Bottom of the Pyramid: Eradicating Poverty Through Profits*, Upper Saddle River: Prentice Hall, 2006; for a critique, see Aneel Karnani, 'Fortune at the Bottom of the Pyramid: A Mirage', Ann Arbor: University of Michigan Press, 2006.

66. 'The Future We Want', UN document A/RES/66/288, 11 September 2012.

67. 'A Sustainable Path Forward: Business Perspectives on Rio+20', Business Action for Sustainable Development, 4 October 2012.

68. The final two sentences of Book I read: 'The proposal of any new law or regulation of commerce which comes from this order, ought always to be listened to with great precaution, and ought never to be adopted till after having been long and carefully examined, not only with the most scrupulous, but with the most suspicious attention. It comes from an order of men, whose interest is never exactly the same with that of the public, who have generally an interest to deceive and even to oppress the public, and who accordingly have, upon many occasions, both deceived and oppressed it.'

69. Michael Blowfield, 'Corporate Social Responsibility – The Failing Discipline and Why it Matters for International Relations', *International Relations*, Vol. 19, No. 2 (2005), pp. 173–91.

70. Amparo Merino and Carmen Valor, 'The Potential of Corporate Social Responsibility to Eradicate Poverty: An Ongoing Debate', *Development in Practice*, Vol. 21, No. 2 (2011), pp. 157–67; Peter Utting, 'Corporate

Responsibility and the Movement of Business', *Development in Practice*, Vol. 15, Nos 3–4 (2005), pp. 375–88.

71. Gerard Hanlon, 'Rethinking Corporate Social Responsibility and the Role of the Firm – On the Denial of Politics', in Andrew Crane, Abagail McWilliams, Dirk Matten, Jeremy Moon and Donald S. Siegel (eds), *The Oxford Handbook of Corporate Social Responsibility*, Oxford: Oxford University Press, 2008, p. 167.

Chapter 5

1. *Unleashing Africa's Potential as a Pole of Global Growth: Economic Report on Africa 2012*, Addis Ababa: United Nations Economic Commission for Africa, 2012.

2. 'Promotion and Protection of Human Rights', Interim report of the Special Representative of the Secretary-General on the issue of human rights and transnational corporations and other business enterprises, 22 February 2006, UN document E/CN.4/2006/97.

3. *World Investment Report 2007: Transnational Corporations, Extractive Industries and Development*, New York and Geneva: United Nations Conference on Trade and Development, 2007.

4. Andrew Clapham and Scott Jerbi, 'Categories of Corporate Complicity in Human Rights Abuses', *Hastings International and Comparative Law Journal*, No. 24 (2001), pp. 339–49; see also the fuller treatment in Andrew Clapham, *Human Rights Obligations of Non-State Actors*, Oxford: Oxford University Press, 2006.

5. According to the Forbes list's equal weighting of sales, profits, assets and market value; see the World's Biggest Public Companies for 2012 at www.forbes.com.

6. *Mine 2011 – The Game has Changed: Review of Global Trends in the Mining Industry*, London: PricewaterhouseCoopers, 2011; *Mine 2012 – The Growing Disconnect: Review of Global Trends in the Mining Industry*, London: PricewaterhouseCoopers, 2012.

7. Andy Higginbottom, 'Imperialist Rent in Practice and Theory', *Globalizations*, Vol. 11, No. 1 (forthcoming).

8. *Economic Development in Africa: Rethinking the Role of Foreign Direct Investment*, New York and Geneva: United Nations Conference on Trade and Development, 2005.

9. Nick Mathiason, *Piping Profits: The Secret World of Oil, Gas and Mining Giants*, Oslo: Publish What You Pay Norway, 2011; Simon J. Pak, *Lost Billions: Transfer Pricing in the Extractive Industries*, Oslo: Publish What You Pay Norway, 2012.

10. Manuel Riesco, Gustavo Lagos and Marcos Lima, 'The "Pay Your Taxes" Debate: Perspectives on Corporate Taxation and Social Responsibility in the Chilean Mining Industry', Geneva: United Nations Research Institute for Social Development, 2005.

11. Claire Kumar, *Undermining the Poor: Mineral Taxation Reforms in Latin America*, London: Christian Aid, 2009; Kato Lambrechts, *Breaking the Curse:*

How Transparent Taxation and Fair Taxes can Turn Africa's Mineral Wealth into Development, Johannesburg: Open Society Institute of Southern Africa, 2009.

12. Erwin H. Bulte, Richard Damania and Robert T. Deacon, 'Resource Intensity, Institutions, and Development', *World Development*, Vol. 33, No. 7 (2005), pp. 1029–44; countries endowed with mineral wealth tend to do worst of all: Richard M. Auty, 'Natural Resources, Capital Accumulation and the Resource Curse', *Ecological Economics*, No. 61 (2007), pp. 627–34; also Richard M. Auty (ed.), *Resource Abundance and Economic Development*, Oxford: Oxford University Press, 2001, chapter 1; Michael L. Ross, 'The Political Economy of the Resource Curse', *World Politics*, No. 51 (1999), pp. 297–322.

13. This includes both pre- and post-establishment conditions: *World Investment Report 2011: Non-Equity Modes of International Production and Development*, New York and Geneva: United Nations Conference on Trade and Development, 2011, pp. 94–8.

14. Matthew Hill, 'Zambia Says Tax Avoidance Led by Miners Costs $2 Billion a Year', Bloomberg, 25 November 2012.

15. Details of all WTO dispute settlement cases are available on its website: www.wto.org; the Chinese government has argued that it needs to control the export of rare earths on grounds of environmental sustainability: 'China Defends Rare Earths Export Restrictions', *Bridges Weekly Trade News Digest*, Vol. 16, No. 25, 27 June 2012.

16. 'The raw materials initiative – meeting our critical needs for growth and jobs in Europe', EU document COM(2008) 699, Brussels: Commission of the European Communities, 2008; also the accompanying staff working document SEC(2008) 2741, and subsequent updates, especially 'Tackling the Challenges in Commodity Markets and on Raw Materials', EU document COM(2011) 25, Brussels: European Commission, 2011; updated crude oil dependency figures are available from the Eurostat website: epp.eurostat. ec.europa.eu.

17. Greg Muttitt, *Fuel on the Fire: Oil and Politics in Occupied Iraq*, London: Bodley Head, 2011; *Quadrennial Defense Review Report: February 2010*, Washington DC: US Department of Defense, 2010; 'Joint Operational Access Concept (JOAC)', Washington DC: US Department of Defense, 2012.

18. For further reflection on the relationship between coercive force and the global interests of capital, see Ellen Meiksins Wood, *Empire of Capital*, London: Verso, 2003; and Stephen Gill, *Power and Resistance in the New World Order*, Basingstoke: Palgrave Macmillan, 2nd edition, 2008.

19. *Niger Delta Human Development Report*, Abuja: United Nations Development Programme, 2006.

20. According to Shell annual reports for 2010 and 2011, available at www.shell.com.

21. *Peace and Security in the Niger Delta: Conflict Expert Group Baseline Report*, WAC Global Services, 2003.

22. *Environmental Assessment of Ogoniland*, Nairobi: United Nations Environment Programme, 2011; John Vidal, 'Shell accepts liability for two oil spills in Nigeria', *Guardian*, 3 August 2011; John Vidal, 'Shell Nigeria oil spill "60 times bigger than it claimed"', *Guardian*, 23 April 2012. A similar case brought against Shell in the Nigerian courts by Jonah Gbemre and the

Niger Delta's Iwherekan community concluded with a judgment from the Federal High Court in 2005 that Shell's persistent gas flaring had violated the twin rights to life and dignity of the human person enshrined in the country's constitution.

23. Andy Rowell, 'Secret papers "show how Shell targeted Nigeria oil protests"', *Independent on Sunday*, 14 June 2009.

24. Cameron Duodu, 'Shell admits importing guns for the Nigerian police', *Observer*, 28 January 1996; Andy Rowell, 'Shell admits payments to Nigerian military in Ogoniland', *Big Issue*, 15 December 1996.

25. Documentation of the cases is available on the website of the Center for Constitutional Rights, which has supported the plaintiffs in bringing the suits in the USA: ccrjustice.org.

26. Ben Amunwa, *Counting the Cost: Corporations and Human Rights Abuses in the Niger Delta*, London: Platform, 2011.

27. David Smith, 'WikiLeaks cables: Shell's grip on Nigerian state revealed', *Guardian*, 9 December 2010.

28. Olufemi Amao, 'Human Rights, Ethics and International Business: The Case of Nigeria', in Aurora Voiculescu and Helen Yanacopulos (eds), *The Business of Human Rights: An Evolving Agenda for Corporate Responsibility*, London: Zed Books, 2011, pp. 188–213; *Nigeria: Petroleum, Pollution and Poverty in the Niger Delta*, London: Amnesty International, 2009; for a description of how Amnesty International rethought its approach to corporate accountability in light of the 'limited effectiveness of constructive engagement', see Peter Frankental, 'The Reshaping of Amnesty International's Business and Human Rights Work', Institute for Human Rights and Business, 18 May 2011.

29. 'Nigeria oil spills: Shell rejects liability claim', BBC News online, 11 October 2012.

30. Documentation of the Ilaje case, *Bowoto v Chevron*, can be found on the website of the Center for Constitutional Rights: ccrjustice.org; see also 'Oil Giant Admits Aid Policies Helped Fuel Violence', IRIN news service (UN Office for the Coordination of Humanitarian Affairs), 4 May 2005.

31. David Whyte, 'Lethal Regulation: State-Corporate Crime and the United Kingdom Government's New Mercenaries', *Journal of Law and Society*, Vol. 30, No. 4 (2003), pp. 575–600.

32. Adina Matisoff, *Crude Beginnings: An Assessment of China National Petroleum Corporation's Environmental and Social Performance Abroad*, San Francisco: Friends of the Earth, 2012.

33. Al Gedicks, *Resource Rebels: Native Challenges to Mining and Oil Corporations*, Cambridge MA: South End Press, 2001.

34. *UNCTAD Handbook of Statistics 2011*, New York and Geneva: United Nations Conference on Trade and Development, 2011.

35. Data taken from Monterrico's website: www.monterrico.com; Monterrico was acting as a 'junior' company, in that its role was to conduct the preliminary exploration and feasibility studies for the project and then seek outside investment in order to initiate production – hence its sale to the Zijin consortium in 2007.

36. In its report of 14 November 2006 into the legality of Minera Majaz's presence in Río Blanco; *Informe No. 001-2006/ASPMA-MA*, Lima: Defensoría del

Pueblo, 2006; see also the report of the independent delegation from the UK: *Mining and Development in Peru, With Special Reference to the Rio Blanco Project, Piura*, London: Peru Support Group, 2007.

37. The Río Blanco case and the issues raised by the out-of-court settlement formed the subject of a documentary broadcast on Al Jazeera on 2 May 2012: *Peru: Undermining Justice*; the film, which features interviews with local community members, is available online.

38. Tim Webb, 'UK firm's partner "wanted Peru to curb priests in mine conflict areas"', *Guardian*, 31 January 2011; also 'US embassy cables: Mining companies worried about security', *Guardian*, 31 January 2011.

39. For the oil industry, see Michael J. Watts, 'Righteous Oil? Human Rights, the Oil Complex and Corporate Social Responsibility', *Annual Review of Environment and Resources*, Vol. 30 (2005), pp. 373–407.

40. Bennett Freeman, 'The Voluntary Principles on Security and Human Rights', in Virginia Haufler (ed.), *Case Studies of Multistakeholder Partnership: Policy Dialogue on Business in Zones of Conflict*, New York: UN Global Compact, 2002, pp. 7–14.

41. Anna Zalik, 'The Peace of the Graveyard: The Voluntary Principles on Security and Human Rights in the Niger Delta', in Kees van der Pijl, Libby Assassi and Duncan Wigan (eds), *Global Regulation: Managing Crisis after the Imperial Turn*, London: Palgrave Macmillan, 2004, pp. 111–127.

42. Tanja A. Börzel and Jana Hönke, 'From Compliance to Practice: Mining Companies and the Voluntary Principles on Security and Human Rights in the Democratic Republic of Congo', SFB-Governance Working Paper No. 25, Berlin: DFG Research Center, 2011; Thomas H. Hansen, 'Governing the Extractive Industries: The Extractive Industries Transparency Initiative and the Voluntary Principles on Security and Human Rights', paper presented to the 50th annual convention of the International Studies Association, New York, February 2009.

43. S. Prakash Sethi, 'The Effectiveness of Industry-Based Codes in Serving Public Interest: The Case of the International Council on Mining and Metals', *Transnational Corporations*, Vol. 14, No. 3 (2005), pp. 55–100.

44. Jedrzej George Frynas, 'The False Developmental Promise of Corporate Social Responsibility: Evidence from Multinational Oil Companies', *International Affairs*, Vol. 81, No. 3 (2005), pp. 581–98.

45. Paul Skinner, 'Sustainable Development in the Mining Business', London Business School Stockton Lecture, 24 October 2006; Mark Moody-Stuart, speech to Anglo American AGM, 25 April 2006.

46. *Communities in the Platinum Minefields: A Review of Platinum Mining in the Bojanala District of the North West Province*, Johannesburg: Bench Marks Foundation, 2012, p. 81; Alex Lichtenstein, 'What Went Wrong at Marikana?', *Los Angeles Review of Books*, 1 September 2012.

47. For an account of the massacre based on workers' testimonies, see Peter Alexander, Thapelo Lekgowa, Botsang Mmope, Luke Sinwell and Bongani Xezwi, *Marikana: A View from the Mountain and a Case to Answer*, Auckland Park: Jacana, 2012.

48. David Fig, 'Manufacturing Amnesia: Corporate Social Responsibility in South Africa', *International Affairs*, Vol. 81, No. 3 (2005), pp. 599–617;

see also Dinah Rajak, *In Good Company: An Anatomy of Corporate Social Responsibility*, Stanford: Stanford University Press, 2011.

Chapter 6

1. Angela Hale and Jane Wills (eds), *Threads of Labour: Garment Industry Supply Chains from the Workers' Perspective*, Oxford: Blackwell, 2005.
2. Gary Gereffi and Olga Memedovic, *The Global Apparel Value Chain: What Prospects for Upgrading by Developing Countries*, Vienna: United Nations Industrial Development Organisation, 2003.
3. Will Martin, 'China's Textile and Clothing Trade and Global Adjustment', in Ross Garnaut, Ligang Song and Wing Thye Woo (eds), *China's New Place in a World in Crisis: Economic, Geopolitical and Environmental Dimensions*, Canberra: Australian National University Press, 2009, pp. 303–23; Marion Werner and Jennifer Bair, 'After Sweatshops? Apparel Politics in the Circum-Caribbean', *NACLA Report on the Americas*, Vol. 42, No. 4 (2009), pp. 6–10; Maya Forstater, 'Sectoral Coverage of the Global Economic Crisis: Implications of the Global Financial and Economic Crisis on the Textile and Clothing Sector', Geneva: International Labour Organisation, 2009; Raphael Kaplinsky and Mike Morris, 'Do the Asian Drivers Undermine Export-Oriented Industrialization in SSA?', *World Development*, Vol. 36, No. 2 (2008), pp. 254–73.
4. Verena Tandrayen-Ragoobur and Anisha Ayrga, 'Phasing Out of the MFA: Impact on Women Workers in the Mauritian EPZ Sector', paper presented to the International Conference on International Trade and Investment, Pointe Aux Piments, Mauritius, December 2011; Naoko Otobe, 'Global Economic Crisis, Gender And Employment: The Impact and Policy Response', Geneva: International Labour Organisation, 2011.
5. Gladys Lopez Acevedo and Raymond Robertson (eds), *Sewing Success? Employment, Wages, and Poverty following the End of the Multi-fibre Arrangement*, Washington DC: World Bank, 2012.
6. *World Investment Report 2011: Non-Equity Modes of International Production and Development*, New York and Geneva: United Nations Conference on Trade and Development, 2011.
7. The classic account remains Naomi Klein's *No Logo: Taking Aim at the Brand Bullies*, London: Flamingo, 2000.
8. Rhys Jenkins, 'Globalization, Corporate Social Responsibility and Poverty', *International Affairs*, Vol. 81, No. 3 (2005), pp. 525–40.
9. According to UK government and ETI reports, DFID funding to the ETI totals in excess of £6 million for the period 1998–2014.
10. See, for example, the Robert Greenwald film *Wal-Mart: The High Cost of Low Price*; among other labour rights violations in numerous cases from across the USA, Wal-Mart was required to pay over $5 million in May 2012 in damages, penalties and back pay for more than 4,500 Wal-Mart employees who had been denied paid overtime.
11. Nancy Cleeland, Evelyn Iritani and Tyler Marshall, 'Scouring the Globe to Give Shoppers an $8.63 Polo Shirt', *Los Angeles Times*, 24 November 2003.

12. Cited in Doug Miller, 'Towards Sustainable Labour Costing in the Global Apparel Industry: Some Evidence from UK Fashion Retail', paper presented at the Textile Institute Centenary Conference, Manchester, November 2010.

13. Wording used on several job advertisements during 2012 on www.tesco-careers.com; see also Alison Mann, 'It's Tesco that needs help', *Scottish Farmer*, 16 August 2012.

14. Simon Warburton, 'Tesco Vows to Make F&F World's Top Fashion Brand', just-style.com, 4 March 2010.

15. Jeroen Merk, 'Cross-Border Wage Struggles in the Global Garment Industry', in Andreas Bieler and Ingemar Lindberg (eds), *Global Restructuring, Labour and the Challenges for Transnational Solidarity*, Abingdon: Routledge, 2011, pp. 116–30.

16. Lopez-Acevedo and Robertson, *Sewing Success?*

17. Refayet Ullah Mirdha, 'Falling prices cut into RMG makers' profits', *Daily Star* (Dhaka), 26 August 2012.

18. Neal Lawson, *All Consuming: How Shopping Got Us Into This Mess and How We Can Find Our Way Out*, London: Penguin, 2009.

19. Calculated from US Bureau of Labor Statistics consumer price index data: www.bls.gov.

20. Calculated from retail price index data published in 'Focus on Consumer Price Indices: Data for January 2009', London: Office for National Statistics, 2009.

21. Alex Cuadros, 'Spain's Ortega Overtakes Buffet as World's Third-Richest', Bloomberg, 7 August 2012; all statistics taken from company reports.

22. Frederick H. Abernathy, John T. Dunlop, Janice H. Hammond and David Weil, *A Stitch in Time: Lean Retailing and the Transformation of Manufacturing – Lessons from the Apparel and Textile Industries*, Oxford: Oxford University Press, 1999; Liz Barnes and Gaynor Lea-Greenwood, 'Fast Fashioning the Supply Chain: Shaping the Research Agenda', *Journal of Fashion Marketing and Management*, Vol. 10, No. 3 (2006), pp. 259–71; Nebahat Tokatli and Ömür Kızılgün, 'From Manufacturing Garments for Ready-to-Wear to Designing Collections for Fast Fashion: Evidence from Turkey', *Environment and Planning A*, Vol. 41 (2009), pp. 146–62.

23. Doug Miller and Peter Williams, 'What Price a Living Wage? Implementation Issues in the Quest for Decent Wages in the Global Apparel Sector', *Global Social Policy*, Vol. 9, No. 1 (2009), pp. 99–125.

24. See reports in the *Annual Survey of Violations of Trade Union Rights* produced each year by the International Trade Union Confederation.

25. Jeroen Merk, *10 Years of the Better Factories Cambodia Project: A Critical Evaluation*, Amsterdam: Clean Clothes Campaign, 2012; Reiko Harima, *Restricted Rights: Migrant Women Workers in Thailand, Cambodia and Malaysia*, London: War on Want, 2012; Mom Kunthear, 'Bonuses "won't end strikes"', *Phnom Penh Post*, 28 August 2012.

26. *Better Work Vietnam Baseline Report: Worker Perspectives from the Factory and Beyond*, Geneva: International Labour Office, 2012; Ben Bland, 'Vietnam's factories grapple with growing unrest', *Financial Times*, 9 January 2012.

27. Ben Otto and I. Made Sentana, 'Indonesia strikers turn out in force', *Wall Street Journal*, 3 October 2012.

28. 'Myanmar Garment Workers Protest in Yangon', AFP News, 8 September 2012.

29. Momoe Makino, 'Garment Industry in Pakistan in the Post-MFA Period', in Takahiro Fukunishi (ed.), *Dynamics of the Garment Industry in Low-Income Countries: Experience of Asia and Africa (Interim Report)*, Chiba: Institute of Developing Economies, 2012, chapter 4.

30. Declan Walsh, 'Anger rolls across Pakistani city in aftermath of factory fire', *New York Times*, 13 September 2012; the final death toll in Karachi was revised downwards from original reports of 289 workers killed.

31. These results, from the Boston Consulting Group's China Fashion Research Survey 2010, represent the size of the market for men's and women's clothing by consumers aged between 14 and 45 living in urban areas, and do not include sleepwear, hosiery, accessories or children's wear; see Vincent Lui et al., 'Capturing the Dynamic Growth of China's Fashion Market', www.bcg-perspectives.com, 21 July 2011.

32. Rahul Jacob, 'China wage rises bring shift in production', *Financial Times*, 6 September 2011; Ethirajan Anbarasan, 'Chinese factories turn to Bangladesh as labour costs rise', BBC News, 29 August 2012.

33. Marcus Taylor, 'Race you to the Bottom … and Back Again? The Uneven Development of Labour Codes of Conduct', *New Political Economy*, Vol. 16, No. 4 (2011), pp. 445–62.

34. Stephanie Barrientos and Sally Smith, *The ETI Code of Labour Practice: Do Workers Really Benefit?* Brighton: Institute of Development Studies, 2006.

35. Mark Anner, 'Auditing Rights at Work in a Globalizing Economy: The Limits of Corporate Social Responsibility', paper presented to 16th ILERA World Congress, Philadelphia, July 2012.

36. 'Reviewing the MFA Forum: Learning Lessons from the Global Multi-Stakeholder Textile Initiative', draft unpublished report prepared by AccountAbility, May 2011.

37. Tugce Bulut and Christel Lane, 'The Private Regulation of Labour Standards and Rights in the Global Clothing Industry: An Evaluation of Its Effectiveness in Two Developing Countries', *New Political Economy*, Vol. 16, No. 1 (2011), pp. 41–71; 'Codes and Compliance Under Scrutiny: A Final Report of the Joint Initiative for Corporate Accountability and Workers' Rights (JO-IN) Turkey Project', London. Joint Initiative for Corporate Accountability and Workers' Rights, 2008.

38. Sarah Butler, 'Workers can fight for their own rights', *Drapers*, 20 March 2010.

39. *Getting Smarter at Auditing: Tackling the Growing Crisis in Ethical Trade Auditing*, London: Ethical Trading Initiative, 2006; Alan Sadler, 'Where do you stand on SEDEX?' ETI blog, 29 March 2012, www.ethicaltrade.org.

40. Doug Miller, Simon Turner and Don Grinter, 'Back to the Future? A Critical Reflection on Neil Kearney's Mature System of Industrial Relations Perspective on the Governance of Outsourced Apparel Supply Chains', Manchester: Capturing the Gains, 2011.

41. For more examples of 'associational power' in action, see Beverly J. Silver, *Forces of Labor: Workers' Movements and Globalization since 1870*, New York: Cambridge University Press, 2003.

42. Merk, 'Cross-Border Wage Struggles', p. 119.

43. Michael Lebowitz, *The Socialist Alternative: Real Human Development*, New York: Monthly Review Press, 2010, p. 136.
44. Georg Lukács, *History and Class Consciousness*, London: Merlin Press, 1971, p. 76.
45. See the essays in Andreas Bieler, Ingemar Lindberg and Devan Pillay (eds), *Labour and the Challenges of Globalization: What Prospects for Transnational Solidarity?*, London: Pluto Press, 2008; and Andreas Bieler and Ingemar Lindberg (eds), *Global Restructuring, Labour and the Challenges for Transnational Solidarity*, Abingdon: Routledge, 2011.
46. Karl Marx and Friedrich Engels, *Manifesto of the Communist Party*, Moscow: Progress Publishers, 2nd edition, 1977, p. 45.
47. Karl Marx, *Wage Labour and Capital & Wages, Price and Profit*, London: Bookmarks, 1996, p. 119.

Chapter 7

1. Walden Bello, *The Food Wars*, London: Verso, 2009.
2. *The State of Food Insecurity in the World 2009: Economic Crises – Impacts and Lessons Learned*, Rome: Food and Agriculture Organisation, 2012; 'More people than ever are victims of hunger', FAO press briefing, 19 June 2009.
3. *The State of Food Insecurity in the World 2012: Economic Growth is Necessary but not Sufficient to Accelerate Reduction of Hunger and Malnutrition*, Rome: Food and Agriculture Organisation, 2012, especially Annex 2, and the accompanying technical note 'FAO methodology to estimate the prevalence of undernourishment', 9 October 2012; I am grateful to Mark Curtis for highlighting this point.
4. For an application of the food regime concept to the current conjuncture, see Philip McMichael, 'A Food Regime Analysis of the "World Food Crisis"', *Agriculture and Human Values*, No. 26 (2009), pp. 281–95; for the historical development of the concept, see Philip McMichael, 'A Food Regime Genealogy', *Journal of Peasant Studies*, Vol. 36, No. 1 (2009), pp. 139–69.
5. Eduardo Galeano, *Open Veins of Latin America: Five Centuries of the Pillage of a Continent*, New York: Monthly Review Press, 1973, especially chapter 2.
6. Emmanuel Dalle Mulle and Violette Ruppanner, *Exploring the Global Food Supply Chain: Markets, Companies, Systems*, Geneva: 3D, 2010; *Who Will Control the Green Economy?* Ottawa: ETC Group, 2011; Sue Branford, *Food Sovereignty: Reclaiming the Global Food System*, London: War on Want, 2011.
7. *Towards a Green Economy: Pathways to Sustainable Development and Poverty Eradication*, Nairobi: United Nations Environment Programme, 2011.
8. Henry Bernstein, '"The Peasantry" in Global Capitalism: Who, Where and Why?', in Leo Panitch and Colin Leys (eds), *Working Classes, Global Realities: Socialist Register 2001*, London: Merlin Press, 2000, pp. 25–51.
9. Vandana Shiva, *Biopiracy: The Plunder of Nature and Knowledge*, Dartington: Green Books, 1998.
10. Andy Beer, 'Developing Agchem Markets Dominate in 2010', agrow.com, 10 March 2011.
11. Frances Moore Lappé, Joseph Collins and Peter Rosset, *World Hunger: 12 Myths*, London: Earthscan, 2nd edition, 1998, chapter 5.

12. Prabhu L. Pingali and Mark W. Rosengrant, *Confronting the Environmental Consequences of the Green Revolution in Asia*, Washington DC: International Food Policy Research Institute, 1994; 'Fertilizer Use Responsible for Increase in Nitrous Oxide in Atmosphere', University of California, Berkeley, 2 April 2012.

13. Donald K. Freebairn, 'Did the Green Revolution Concentrate Incomes? A Quantitative Study of Research Reports', *World Development*, Vol. 23, No. 2 (1995), pp. 265–79.

14. P. Sainath, 'In 16 years, farm suicides cross a quarter million', *The Hindu*, 29 October 2011; Ritambhara Hebbar, 'Framing the Development Debate: The Case of Farmers' Suicide in India', in Chandan Sengupta and Stuart Corbridge (eds), *Democracy, Development and Decentralisation in India: Continuing Debates*, New Delhi: Routledge, 2010, pp. 84–110.

15. Raj Patel, *Stuffed & Starved: Markets, Power and the Hidden Battle for the World Food System*, London: Portobello Books, 2007; Sanjay Suri, 'Environment: Indian Farmers Win Battle against GM Cotton', Inter Press Service, 25 May 2005.

16. Raj Patel, 'The Long Green Revolution', *Journal of Peasant Studies*, Vol. 40, No. 1 (2013), pp. 1–63.

17. Elenita C. Daño, *Unmasking the New Green Revolution in Africa: Motives, Players and Dynamics*, Penang: Third World Network, 2007.

18. For a good overview of the political strategy behind the various pro-corporate initiatives designed to transform African agriculture, see Eric Holt-Giménez and Raj Patel, *Food Rebellions: Crisis and the Hunger for Justice*, Cape Town: Pambazuka Press, 2009.

19. Miguel A. Altieri, *Small Farms as a Planetary Ecological Asset: Five Key Reasons Why We Should Support the Revitalisation of Small Farms in the Global South*, Penang: Third World Network, 2008.

20. Mark Curtis and John Hilary, *The Hunger Games: How DFID Support for Agribusiness is Fuelling Poverty in Africa*, London: War on Want, 2012.

21. Helena Paul and Ricarda Steinbrecher, *African Agricultural Growth Corridors: Who Benefits, Who Loses?* London: EcoNexus, 2012.

22. Carol B. Thompson, 'Alliance for a Green Revolution in Africa (AGRA): Advancing the Theft of African Genetic Wealth', *Review of African Political Economy*, Vol. 39, No. 132 (2012), pp. 345–50.

23. Mariam Mayet, 'The New Green Revolution in Africa: Trojan Horse for GMOs?', in Aksel Naerstad (ed.), *Africa Can Feed Itself*, Oslo: Development Fund, 2007, pp. 158–65.

24. For more on the AATF, see its annual reports and other information at www.aatf-africa.org; also Curtis and Hilary, *The Hunger Games*.

25. 'Africa's Wealth of Seed Diversity and Farmer Knowledge – Under Threat from the Gates/Rockefeller "Green Revolution" Initiative', Statement of African civil society organisations at the World Social Forum, Nairobi, 25 January 2007.

26. African Centre for Biosafety, *Alliance for a Green Revolution in Africa (AGRA): Laying the Groundwork for the Commercialisation of African Agriculture*, Melville: African Centre for Biosafety, 2012; see also Eric Holt-Giménez,

'Out of AGRA: The Green Revolution returns to Africa', *Development*, Vol. 51, No. 4 (2008), pp. 464–71.

27. 'Letter from African Civil Society Critical of Foreign Investment in African Agriculture at G8 Summit', 15 May 2012; available on foodfirst.org.

28. For an introduction to some of these, see Curtis and Hilary, *The Hunger Games*.

29. Ben White et al., 'The New Enclosures: Critical Perspectives on Corporate Land Deals', *Journal of Peasant Studies*, Vol. 39, Nos 3–4 (2012), pp. 619–47; unhelpfully for our purposes, the German word '*Landdiebstahl*', rendered as 'land grabbing' in the original English translation of *Capital*, becomes 'thefts of land' in the modern Penguin translation; Karl Marx, *Capital: Volume 1*, London: Penguin, 1976, p. 556.

30. Ward Anseeuw et al., *Transnational Land Deals for Agriculture in the Global South: Analytical Report based on the Land Matrix Database*, Bern/Montpellier/Hamburg: CDE/CIRAD/GIGA, 2012; though far from complete, the Land Matrix database is a publicly available resource on the larger transnational agricultural land deals: landportal.info/landmatrix; news pieces on individual cases are collected on the dedicated GRAIN website: farmlandgrab.org, while GRAIN also publishes important data sets on many aspects of land grabbing on its own website: www.grain.org.

31. For details based on research from Cambodian rights group Licadho, see the special *Cambodia Daily* supplement, 'Carving up Cambodia', 10–11 March 2012.

32. Ben White and Anirban Dasgupta, 'Agrofuels Capitalism: A View from Political Economy', *Journal of Peasant Studies*, Vol. 37, No. 4 (2010), pp. 593–607.

33. Abbi Buxton, Mark Campanale and Lorenzo Cotula, 'Farms and Funds: Investment Funds in the Global Land Rush', London: International Institute for Environment and Development, 2012.

34. 'New Research Predicts Rising Trend in India's Violent Land Conflicts; 130 Districts Struggle', Rights and Resources press release, 17 December 2012; Shankar Gopalakrishnan, *Undemocratic and Arbitrary: Control, Regulation and Expropriation of India's Forest and Common Lands*, New Delhi: Society for Promotion of Wastelands Development, 2012; John Vidal, 'Indian investors are forcing Ethiopians off their land', *Guardian*, 7 February 2013.

35. Lorenzo Cotula, 'The International Political Economy of the Global Land Rush: A Critical Appraisal of Trends, Scale, Geography and Drivers', *Journal of Peasant Studies*, Vol. 39, Nos 3–4 (2012), pp. 649–80.

36. Mark Tran, 'Cambodian soldiers accused of land rights abuse in Prey Trolach forest', *Guardian*, 3 August 2012.

37. Gemma Houldey, *Fuelling Fear: The Human Cost of Biofuels in Colombia*, London: War on Want, 2008; Comisión Intereclesial de Justicia y Paz, *Colombia: Banacol, a company implicated in paramilitarism, and land grabbing in Curvaradó and Jiguamiandó*, Berlin: FDCL, 2012.

38. Bertram Zagema, 'Land and Power: The Growing Scandal Surrounding the New Wave of Investments in Land', Oxford: Oxfam International, 2011.

39. 'Report of the Special Rapporteur on the Right to Food', 11 August 2010, UN document A/65/281.

40. 'Farmers' Militant Actions Victoriously Shut Down the Bioethanol Plant', Asian Peasant Coalition news release, 30 August 2012.

41. Sandra Evers, Perrine Burnod, Rivo Andrianirina Ratsialonana and André Teyssier, 'Foreign Land Acquisitions in Madagascar: Competing Jurisdictions of Access Claims', in Ton Dietz, Kjell Havnevik, Mayke Kaag and Terje Oestigaard (eds), *African Engagements: Africa Negotiating an Emerging Multipolar World*, Leiden: Brill, 2011, pp. 110–32.

42. For these and other examples, see the essays in Saturnino M. Borras Jr, Marc Edelman and Cristóbal Kay (eds), *Transnational Agrarian Movements Confronting Globalization*, Chichester: Wiley-Blackwell, 2008.

43. Sue Branford and Jan Rocha, *Cutting the Wire: The Story of the Landless Movement in Brazil*, London: Latin America Bureau, 2002; also the interview with João Pedro Stedile, 'Landless Battalions: The Sem Terra Movement of Brazil', *New Left Review*, No. 15 (2002), pp. 77–104.

44. Neil Harvey, *The Chiapas Rebellion: The Struggle for Land and Democracy*, Durban: Duke University Press, 1998; also the interview with Subcomandante Marcos, 'The Punch Card and the Hour Glass', *New Left Review*, No. 9 (2001), pp. 68–79; and Ioan Grillo, 'Return of the Zapatistas: Are Mexico's Rebels Still Relevant?', *Time Magazine*, 8 January 2013.

45. For historical accounts, see Annette Aurélie Desmarais, *La Vía Campesina: Globalization and the Power of Peasants*, Nova Scotia: Fernwood, 2007, and María Elena Martínez-Torres and Peter M. Rosset, 'La Vía Campesina: The Birth and Evolution of a Transnational Social Movement', *Journal of Peasant Studies*, Vol. 37, No. 1 (2010), pp. 149–75; for a more detailed political treatment, see Saturnino M. Borras Jr, 'La Vía Campesina and its Global Campaign for Agrarian Reform', in Saturnino M. Borras Jr, Marc Edelman and Cristóbal Kay (eds), *Transnational Agrarian Movements Confronting Globalization*, Chichester: Wiley-Blackwell, 2008, pp. 91–122.

46. The full definition is included within the Declaration of Nyéléni, available at www.nyeleni.org; for further elaboration of the concept of food sovereignty, see Hannah Wittman, Annette Aurélie Desmarais and Nettie Wiebe (eds), *Food Sovereignty: Reconnecting Food, Nature and Community*, Oakland: Food First Books, 2010; Michael Windfuhr and Jennie Jonsén, *Food Sovereignty: Towards Democracy in Localised Food Systems*, Rugby: ITDG Publishing, 2005.

47. 'Food Sovereignty in Europe Now!', Final declaration of the European Forum for Food Sovereignty 2011, Krems, Austria, 21 August 2011.

48. Michel Pimbert, *Towards Food Sovereignty*, London: International Institute for Environment and Development, 2009.

49. Hugh Campbell, 'Breaking New Ground in Food Regime Theory: Corporate Environmentalism, Ecological Feedbacks and the "Food from Somewhere" Regime?', *Agriculture and Human Values*, No. 26 (2009), pp. 309–19.

50. The primary cause of species extinction is confirmed to be habitat loss due to industrial agriculture and unsustainable forest management in the UN's *Global Biodiversity Outlook 3*, Montréal: Secretariat of the Convention on Biological Diversity, 2010.

51. Miguel A. Altieri and Victor Manuel Toledo, 'The Agroecological Revolution in Latin America: Rescuing Nature, Ensuring Food Sovereignty And Empowering Peasants', *Journal of Peasant Studies*, Vol. 38, No. 3 (2011), pp.

587–612; Steve Gliessman, 'Agroecology: Growing the Roots of Resistance', *Agroecology and Sustainable Food Systems*, Vol. 37, No. 1 (2013), pp. 19–31.

52. 'Report Submitted by the Special Rapporteur on the Right to Food, Olivier De Schutter', 20 December 2010, UN document A/HRC/16/49.

53. Jules Pretty et al., 'Resource-Conserving Agriculture Increases Yields In Developing Countries', *Environmental Science & Technology*, Vol. 40, No. 4 (2006), pp. 1114–19.

54. Tim LaSalle and Paul Hepperly, 'Regenerative Organic Farming: A Solution to Global Warming', Kutztown: Rodale Institute, 2008; 'Earth Matters: Tackling the Climate Crisis from the Ground Up', *Seedling*, October 2009, pp. 9–16.

55. *Agriculture at a Crossroads: Global Report of the International Assessment of Agricultural Knowledge, Science and Technology for Development*, Washington DC: Island Press, 2009; *Organic Agriculture and Food Security in Africa*, Report of the UNEP-UNCTAD Capacity Building Task Force on Trade, Environment and Development, New York and Geneva: United Nations, 2008; UNEP, *Towards a Green Economy*.

56. Shepard Daniel and Anuradha Mittal, *(Mis)investment in Agriculture: The Role of the International Finance Corporation in Global Land Grabs*, Oakland: Oakland Institute, 2010; Birgit Zimmerle, *When Development Cooperation becomes Land Grabbing: The Role of Development Finance Institutions*, Bern: Brot für Alle, 2012; Kate Geary, '"Our Land, Our Lives": Time Out on the Global Land Rush', Oxford: Oxfam International, 2012.

57. See, for example, the rejection of the Principles for Responsible Agricultural Investment in the international statement 'Stop Land Grabbing Now! Say NO to the Principles of "Responsible" Agro-Enterprise Investment Promoted by the World Bank', 22 April 2010; in the declaration of the International Conference of Peasants and Farmers held in Nyéléni, Mali, in November 2011; and in the Dakar Appeal against land grabbing from the World Social Forum held in Dakar, Senegal, in February 2011; for the Bank's own admission, see Klaus Deininger and Derek Byerlee, *Rising Global Interest in Farmland: Can it Yield Sustainable and Equitable Benefits?* Washington DC: World Bank, 2012, p. 3; also Saturnino Borras Jr and Jennifer Franco, 'From Threat to Opportunity? Problems with the Idea of a "Code of Conduct" for Land-Grabbing', *Yale Human Rights and Development Law Journal*, Vol. 13, No. 2 (2010), pp. 507–23.

58. Nora McKeon, '"One Does Not Sell the Land Upon Which the People Walk": Land Grabbing, Transnational Rural Social Movements, and Global Governance', *Globalizations*, Vol. 10, No. 1 (2013), pp. 105–22.

59. 'Responsible Farmland Investing? Current Efforts to Regulate Land Grabs Will Make Things Worse', GRAIN, 22 August 2012; Saturnino Borras Jr, Jennifer Franco and Chunyu Wang, 'The Challenge of Global Governance of Land Grabbing: Changing International Agricultural Context and Competing Political Views and Strategies', *Globalizations*, Vol. 10, No. 1 (2013), pp. 161–79.

60. The text of the Voluntary Guidelines is reproduced in *The Right to Food Guidelines: Information Papers and Case Studies*, Rome: Food and Agriculture Organisation, 2006.

61. Julian Germann, 'The Human Right to Food: "Voluntary Guidelines" Negotiations', in Yildiz Atasoy (ed.), *Hegemonic Transitions, the State and Crisis in Neoliberal Capitalism*, Abingdon: Routledge, 2009, pp. 126–43; also his fuller treatment in 'Hegemony, Discursive Struggle, and Voluntary Guidelines on the "Right to Food": A Study in the Negotiation of Meaning', Linköping: Linköpings Universitet, 2006.
62. Hannah Miller, 'From "Rights-Based" to "Rights-Framed" Approaches: A Social Constructionist View of Human Rights Practice', *International Journal of Human Rights*, Vol. 14, No. 6 (2010), pp. 915–31; for a discussion of the various forms of political power wielded by transnational corporations over the governance of the global food regime, see Jennifer Clapp and Doris Fuchs, 'Agrifood Corporations, Global Governance, and Sustainability: A Framework for Analysis', in Jennifer Clapp and Doris Fuchs (eds), *Corporate Power in Global Agrifood Governance*, Cambridge MA: MIT Press, 2009, pp. 1–26.
63. Eric Holt-Giménez and Miguel A. Altieri, 'Agroecology, Food Sovereignty, and the New Green Revolution', *Agroecology and Sustainable Food Systems*, Vol. 37, No. 1 (2013), pp. 90–102.
64. See also the interview with Paul Nicholson of La Vía Campesina in Paul Nicholson, Xavier Montagut and Javiera Rulli, *Terre et liberté! A la conquête de la souveraineté alimentaire*, Geneva: CETIM, 2012; the interview has been translated as 'Food sovereignty, a basis for transforming the dominant economic and social model'.

Chapter 8

1. For instance, Walden Bello, *Deglobalization: Ideas for a New World Economy*, London: Zed Books, 2004; Kavaljit Singh, *Questioning Globalization*, New Delhi: Madhyam Books, 2005, Martin Khor, *Rethinking Globalization: Critical Issues and Policy Choices*, London: Zed Books, 2001; Colin Hines, *Localization: A Global Manifesto*, London: Earthscan, 2000; Amory Starr, *Naming the Enemy: Anti-Corporate Movements Confront Globalization*, London: Zed Books, 2000, William F. Fisher and Thomas Ponniah (eds), *Another World is Possible: Popular Alternatives to Globalization at the World Social Forum*, Nova Scotia: Fernwood, 2003.
2. For more on anti-systemic movements, see Giovanni Arrighi, Terence K. Hopkins and Immanuel Wallerstein, *Anti-Systemic Movements*, London: Verso, 1989; and for a later update, Immanuel Wallerstein, 'New Revolts Against the System', *New Left Review*, No. 18 (2002), pp. 29–39.
3. 'This containment of social change is perhaps the most singular achievement of advanced industrial society', Herbert Marcuse, *One Dimensional Man*, London: Abacus, 1972, p. 11; see also John Kenneth Galbraith, *The Culture of Contentment*, London: Penguin, 1992.
4. Doreen Massey, 'Learning from Latin America', *Soundings*, No. 50 (2012), pp. 131–41.
5. Beatriz Stolowicz, *The Latin American Left: Between Governability and Change*, Amsterdam: Transnational Institute, 2004.

6. Atilio A. Boron, 'Strategy and Tactics in Popular Struggles in Latin America', in Leo Panitch, Greg Albo and Vivek Chibber (eds), *The Question of Strategy: Socialist Register 2013*, Pontypool: Merlin Press, 2012, pp. 241–54.

7. For recent overviews in English, see Marta Harnecker, 'Latin America and Twenty-First Century Socialism: Inventing to Avoid Mistakes', *Monthly Review*, Vol. 62, No. 3 (2010), pp. 1–86; Claudio Katz, 'The Singularities of Latin America', in Leo Panitch, Greg Albo and Vivek Chibber (eds), *The Crisis and the Left: Socialist Register 2012*, Pontypool: Merlin Press, 2011, pp. 200–16; Roger Burbach, Michael Fox and Federico Fuentes, *Latin America's Turbulent Transitions: The Future of Twenty-First Century Socialism*, London: Zed Books, 2013; Benjamin Dangl, *Dancing with Dynamite: Social Movements and States in Latin America*, Oakland: AK Press, 2010; Jeffery R. Webber and Barry Carr (eds), *The New Latin American Left: Cracks in the Empire*, Lanham: Rowman & Littlefield, 2013.

8. For the political and economic background, see Lecio Morais and Alfredo Saad-Filho, 'Lula and the Continuity of Neoliberalism in Brazil: Strategic Choice, Economic Imperative or Political Schizophrenia?', *Historical Materialism*, Vol. 13, No. 1 (2005), pp. 3–32; also Richard Bourne, *Lula of Brazil: The Story So Far*, London: Zed Books, 2008.

9. Emilia Castorina, 'Crisis and Recomposition in Argentina', in Jeffery R. Webber and Barry Carr (eds), *The New Latin American Left: Cracks in the Empire*, Lanham: Rowman & Littlefield, 2013, pp. 233–54.

10. Burbach, Fox and Fuentes, *Latin America's Turbulent Transitions*, chapter 5; Benjamin Kohl and Linda Farthing, 'Material Constraints to Popular Imaginaries: The Extractive Economy and Resource Nationalism in Bolivia', *Political Geography*, No. 31 (2012), pp. 225-235; 'Bolivia: Results of a New Economic Model', La Paz: Ministry of Economy and Public Finance, 22 November 2012.

11. Mark Weisbrot, Jake Johnston and Stephan Lefebvre, 'Ecuador's New Deal: Reforming and Regulating the Financial Sector', Washington DC: Center for Economic and Policy Research, 2013; see also the wide-ranging interview with Rafael Correa, 'Ecuador's Path', *New Left Review*, No. 77 (2012), pp. 88–104.

12. Eduardo Gudynas, 'Buen Vivir: Today's Tomorrow', *Development*, Vol. 54, No. 4 (2011), pp. 441–47.

13. The new constitution had granted communities the right to consultation over resource extraction on their lands, but not a veto; see Marc Becker, 'Correa, Indigenous Movements, and the Writing of a New Constitution in Ecuador', *Latin American Perspectives*, Vol. 38, No. 1 (2011), pp. 47–62.

14. Francisco Domínguez, 'Understanding Venezuela', *Soundings*, No. 37 (2007), pp. 92–104; Sarah Wagner, 'The Bolivarian Response to the Feminization of Poverty in Venezuela', Venezuelanalysis.com, 5 February 2005.

15. Burbach, Fox and Fuentes, *Latin America's Turbulent Transitions*, chapter 4; Chris Carlson, 'Venezuelan Government Accelerates Land Expropriations', Venezuelanalysis.com, 20 November 2012.

16. ALBA originally stood for the Alternativa Bolivariana (in direct opposition to ALCA, Spanish for FTAA), but was changed to the Alianza Bolivariana in 2009 in recognition of the fact that the threat of an FTAA had disappeared.

By 2013, ALBA comprised eight member states: Venezuela, Cuba, Bolivia, Nicaragua, Dominica, Ecuador, St Vincent & the Grenadines and Antigua & Barbuda, with Suriname and St Lucia as honorary members and Haiti holding observer status; Honduras, which had joined in 2008, withdrew from ALBA following the 2009 coup.

17. The arrangement was subsequently cancelled by Conservative mayor Boris Johnson; see Doreen Massey, 'A Counterhegemonic Relationality of Place', in Eugene McCann and Kevin Ward (eds), *Mobile Urbanism: Cities and Policymaking in the Global Age*, Minneapolis: University of Minnesota Press, 2011, pp. 1–14.

18. Jeffery R. Webber and Barry Carr, 'The Latin American Left in Theory and Practice', in Jeffery R. Webber and Barry Carr (eds), *The New Latin American Left: Cracks in the Empire*, Lanham: Rowman & Littlefield, 2013, pp. 1–27.

19. Roger Merino Acuña, 'What is "Post" in Post-Neoliberal Political Economy? Indigenous Land Rights and the Extractive Industry in Peru, Bolivia and Ecuador', paper presented at Postgraduates in Latin American Studies conference, Oxford, June 2012; Carmen Martínez Novo, 'The Backlash against Indigenous Rights in Ecuador's Citizen's Revolution', in Todd A. Eisenstadt, Michael S. Danielson, Moisés Jaime Bailón Corres and Carlos Sorroza Polo (eds), *Latin America's Multicultural Movements: The Struggle Between Communitarianism, Autonomy and Human Rights*, New York: Oxford University Press, 2013, pp. 111–33.

20. Álvaro García Linera, 'Geopolitics of the Amazon: Landed-Hereditary Power and Capitalist Accumulation', September 2012; available in both Spanish original and English translation at climatcandcapitalism.com.

21. Ryan Haddad, 'An Un-Conventional Approach: Ecuador's Yasuní-ITT Initiative is in Discord with the UNFCCC', *Sustainable Development Law & Policy*, Vol. 12, No. 2 (2012), pp. 15–18; 'Ecuador approves Yasuni park oil drilling in Amazon rainforest', BBC News, 16 August 2013.

22. Harnecker, 'Latin America and Twenty-First Century Socialism', p. 78.

23. Compare, in this context, Erik Olin Wright, 'Compass Points: Towards a Socialist Alternative', *New Left Review*, No. 41 (2006), pp. 93–124.

24. See, for example, *The Least Developed Countries Report 2009: The State and Development Governance*, New York and Geneva: United Nations Conference on Trade and Development, 2009.

25. Ali Abdel Gadir Ali, 'Development Planning in Africa: Key Issues, Challenges and Prospects', background paper for the Meeting of the Committee of Experts of the 4th Joint Annual Meetings of the African Union and UN Economic Commission for Africa, Addis Ababa, 16 March 2011, UN document E/ECA/COE/30/8.

26. Anthony Baah, 'History of African Development Initiatives', paper presented to the Africa Labour Research Network Workshop, Johannesburg, 22–23 May 2003.

27. Vivek Chibber, 'Reviving the Developmental State? The Myth of the "National Bourgeoisie"', in Leo Panitch and Colin Leys (eds), *The Empire Reloaded: Socialist Register 2005*, London: Merlin Press, 2004, pp. 144–65.

28. Étienne Balibar, *We, the People of Europe? Reflections on Transnational Citizenship*, Princeton: Princeton University Press, 2004, p. 160; emphasis in original.
29. Robert Latham, 'Social Sovereignty', *Theory, Culture & Society*, Vol. 17, No. 4 (2000), pp. 1–18.
30. Harnecker, 'Latin America and Twenty-First Century Socialism', p. 40.
31. Frédéric Viale, *L'Horreur Européenne*, Vincennes: Tatamis, 2010; Susan George, *We the Peoples of Europe*, London: Pluto Press, 2008; David Cronin, *Corporate Europe: How Big Business Sets Policies on Food, Climate and War*, London: Pluto Press, 2013.
32. For interesting case studies from Brazil and the UK, see Hilary Wainwright, *Reclaim the State: Experiments in Popular Democracy*, London: Verso, 2003. For more reflections on relations between the state and social movements from the Bolivian context, see Raúl Zibechi, *Dispersing Power: Social Movements as Anti-State Forces*, Oakland: AK Press, 2010; also Dangl, *Dancing with Dynamite*.
33. The call for development of a more coordinated political programme has been made on a number of occasions, notably in the Porto Alegre Manifesto of 2005 and the Bamako Appeal of 2006; see also the proposal from founding luminary Chico Whitaker to the 2013 World Social Forum in Tunis that the Forum should in future be developed into a global movement rather than just an open space: 'World Social Forum: Space or Movement?', 6 December 2012 at chichowhitaker.net.
34. Michael Hardt and Antonio Negri, *Multitude: War and Democracy in the Age of Empire*, London: Penguin, 2005, p. 217.
35. Samir Amin, *Ending the Crisis of Capitalism or Ending Capitalism?*, Cape Town: Pambazuka Press, 2011, p. 186.
36. Costas Lapavitsas, 'Financialised Capitalism: Crisis and Financial Expropriation', *Historical Materialism*, Vol. 17, No. 2 (2009), pp. 114–48.
37. David U. Himmelstein, Deborah Thorne, Elizabeth Warren and Steffie Woolhandler, 'Medical Bankruptcy in the United States, 2007: Results of a National Study', *American Journal of Medicine*, Vol. 122. No. 8 (2009), pp. 741–6; Jens Holst and Assia Brandrup-Lukanow, *Extending Social Protection in Health: Developing Countries' Experiences, Lessons Learnt and Recommendations*, Frankfurt: Verlag für Akademische Schriften, 2007.
38. Maude Barlow, *Our Right to Water: A People's Guide to Implementing the United Nations' Recognition of the Right to Water and Sanitation*, Ottawa: Council of Canadians, 2011.
39. Michael Hardt, 'The Common in Communism', in Costas Douzinas and Slavoj Žižek (eds), *The Idea of Communism*, London: Verso, 2010, pp. 131–44.
40. Vandana Shiva, Ruchi Shroff and Caroline Lockhart (eds), *Seed Freedom: A Global Citizen's Report*, New Delhi: Navdanya, 2012.
41. David M. Berry and Giles Moss, *Libre Culture: Meditations on Free Culture*, Winnipeg: Pygmalion Books, 2008.
42. Derek Wall, 'Open Source Anti-Capitalism', in David Ransom and Vanessa Baird (eds), *People First Economics*, Oxford: New Internationalist, 2009, pp. 181–91.

43. Cliff Mills and Will Davies, *Blueprint for a Cooperative Decade*, Geneva: International Cooperative Alliance, 2013; also Bruno Roelants, Diana Dovgan, Hyungsik Eum and Elisa Terrasi, *The Resilience of the Cooperative Model: How Worker Cooperatives, Social Cooperatives and Other Worker-Owned Enterprises Respond to the Crisis and its Consequences*, Brussels: Confédération Européenne des Coopératives de Production, 2012; Vishwas Satgar and Michelle Williams, *The Passion of the People: Successful Cooperative Experiences in Africa*, Geneva: Committee for the Promotion and Advancement of Cooperatives, 2008.

44. J.K. Gibson-Graham, *A Postcapitalist Politics*, Minneapolis: University of Minnesota Press, 2006, chapter 5.

45. Furthermore, the Cooperative Group announced in 2012 that it would no longer engage with any supplier known to be sourcing from Israeli settlements in the Occupied Palestinian Territories, extending the boycott beyond simply produce from the settlements themselves.

46. Jacques Defourny, Patrick Develtere and Bénédicte Fonteneau (eds), *Social Economy: North and South*, Leuven: K.U. Leuven, 2000; Bénédicte Fonteneau et al., *Social and Solidarity Economy: Building a Common Understanding*, Turin: ILO International Training Centre, 2010.

47. Ethan Miller, 'Solidarity Economy: Key Concepts and Issues', in Emily Kawano, Thomas Neal Masterson and Jonathan Teller-Elsberg (eds), *Solidarity Economy I: Building Alternatives for People and Planet*, Amherst: Center for Popular Economics, 2010; Jean-Louis Laville, 'The Solidarity Economy: An International Movement', *RCCS Review*, No. 2 (2010), pp. 3–41.

48. Gar Alperovitz, 'Wall Street is too big to regulate', *New York Times*, 22 July 2012; see also the earlier blog by the former member of the Bank of England's Monetary Policy Committee, now Chief Economist of Citigroup, Willem Buiter: 'Time to take the banks into full public ownership', *Financial Times*, 16 January 2009.

49. George Parker, 'Lawson urges full nationalisation of RBS', *Financial Times*, 31 January 2013; Tim Castle, 'UK's RBS "in limbo", should have been nationalised – Cable', Reuters, 5 February 2013.

50. Greg Albo, Sam Gindin and Leo Panitch, *In and Out of Crisis: The Global Financial Meltdown and Left Alternatives*, Oakland: PM Press, 2010, p. 110.

51. Michael Lebowitz, *The Socialist Alternative: Real Human Development*, New York: Monthly Review Press, 2010.

52. Dennis Soron and Gordon Laxer, 'Decommodification, Democracy, and the Battle for the Commons', in Gordon Laxer and Dennis Soron (eds), *Not for Sale: Decommodifying Public Life*, Peterborough: Broadview Press, 2006, pp. 15–38; emphasis in original.

53. David McNally, 'The Commodity Status of Labour: The Secret of Commodified Life', in Laxer and Soron (eds), *Not for Sale*, pp. 39–54; also Theo Papadopoulos, 'The Recommodification of European Labour: Theoretical and Empirical Explorations', Bath: European Research Institute, 2005.

54. John Vail, 'Decommodification and Egalitarian Political Economy', *Politics & Society*, Vol. 38, No. 3 (2010), pp. 310–46.

55. For fuller exploration of these themes in the context of globalisation, see the essays in Isabella Bakker and Stephen Gill (eds), *Power, Production and Social Reproduction: Human In/security in the Global Political Economy*, Basingstoke: Palgrave Macmillan, 2003.

56. Gøsta Esping-Andersen, *The Three Worlds of Welfare Capitalism*, Cambridge: Polity, 1990, pp. 21–2.

57. The double impossibility known as 'Wollstonecraft's dilemma' after the formulation of Carole Pateman, *The Disorder of Women: Democracy, Feminism and Political Theory*, Cambridge: Polity, 1989, p. 196; for an early feminist critique of Esping-Andersen's original model of decommodification, see Ann Shola Orloff, 'Gender and the Social Rights of Citizenship: The Comparative Analysis of Gender Relations and Welfare States', *American Sociological Review*, Vol. 58, No. 3 (1993), pp. 303–28.

58. For a reflection in this context on second-wave feminism's 'disturbing convergence' with neoliberalism, see Nancy Fraser, 'Feminism, Capitalism and the Cunning of History', *New Left Review*, No. 56 (2009), pp. 97–117; a similar point is made by David Harvey in relation to the convergence of neoliberalism with the anti-state individualism of the post-1968 protest generation, in *A Brief History of Neoliberalism*, Oxford: Oxford University Press, 2005, chapter 2.

59. *SIPRI Yearbook 2012: Armaments, Disarmament and National Security*, Stockholm: Stockholm International Peace Research Institute, 2012.

60. Vijay Mehta, *The Economics of Killing: How the West Fuels War and Poverty in the Developing World*, London: Pluto Press, 2012; Michael Brzoska, Kees Kingma and Herbert Wulf, 'Demilitarization and Conversion', Bonn: Bonn International Center for Conversion, 1995.

61. Serge Latouche, 'Degrowth', *Journal of Cleaner Production*, Vol. 18, No. 6 (2010), pp. 519–22; for a fuller statement, in which degrowth is posited as a form of ecosocialism, see his *Farewell to Growth*, Cambridge: Polity, 2009, especially pp. 88–92; also Mauro Bonaiuti, 'Degrowth: Tools for a Complex Analysis of the Multidimensional Crisis', *Capitalism, Nature, Socialism*, Vol. 23, No. 1 (2012), pp. 30–50.

62. See the similar conclusion in Andrew Cumbers, *Reclaiming Public Ownership: Making Space for Economic Democracy*, London: Zed Books, 2012.

63. For the 'local production of the global', see Doreen Massey, 'Geographies of Responsibility', *Geografiska Annaler: Series B, Human Geography*, Vol. 86, No. 1 (2004), pp. 5–18; also Gibson-Graham, *A Postcapitalist Politics*.

64. See the useful compendium of legal cases brought together by FIDH in *Corporate Accountability for Human Rights Abuses: A Guide for Victims and NGOs on Recourse Mechanisms*, Paris: International Federation for Human Rights, 2010; on limited liability, see Stephanie Blankenburg, Dan Plesch and Frank Wilkinson, 'Limited Liability and the Modern Corporation in Theory and in Practice', *Cambridge Journal of Economics*, Vol. 34, No. 5 (2010), pp. 821–36, and the other articles in that issue; also Joel Bakan, *The Corporation: The Pathological Pursuit of Profit and Power*, New York: Free Press, 2004.

65. See also Georg Lukács, 'Class Consciousness', in *History and Class Consciousness*, London: Merlin Press, 1971, pp. 46–82.

Bibliography

The bibliography given here lists the main books, reports and articles mentioned in the text and notes; references to media articles and other more ephemeral publications are provided in the notes only.

Abernathy, Frederick H., John T. Dunlop, Janice H. Hammond and David Weil (1999) *A Stitch in Time: Lean Retailing and the Transformation of Manufacturing – Lessons from the Apparel and Textile Industries* (Oxford: Oxford University Press).

AccountAbility (2007) *The State of Responsible Competitiveness: Making Sustainable Development Count in Global Markets* (London: AccountAbility).

African Centre for Biosafety (2012) *Alliance for a Green Revolution in Africa (AGRA): Laying the Groundwork for the Commercialisation of African Agriculture* (Melville: African Centre for Biosafety).

Akyüz, Yılmaz (2005) *Trade, Growth and Industrialisation: Issues, Experiences and Policy Challenges* (Penang: Third World Network).

Albo, Greg, Sam Gindin and Leo Panitch (2010) *In and Out of Crisis: The Global Financial Meltdown and Left Alternatives* (Oakland: PM Press).

Alexander, Peter, Thapelo Lekgowa, Botsang Mmope, Luke Sinwell and Bongani Xezwi (2012) *Marikana: A View from the Mountain and a Case to Answer* (Auckland Park: Jacana).

Ali, Ali Abdel Gadir (2011) 'Development Planning in Africa: Key Issues, Challenges and Prospects', background paper for the Meeting of the Committee of Experts of the 4th Joint Annual Meetings of the African Union and UN Economic Commission for Africa, Addis Ababa, 16 March 2011, UN document E/ECA/COE/30/8.

Altieri, Miguel A. (2008) *Small Farms as a Planetary Ecological Asset: Five Key Reasons Why We Should Support the Revitalisation of Small Farms in the Global South* (Penang: Third World Network).

Altieri, Miguel A. and Victor Manuel Toledo (2011) 'The Agroecological Revolution in Latin America: Rescuing Nature, Ensuring Food Sovereignty and Empowering Peasants', *Journal of Peasant Studies*, Vol. 38, No. 3, pp. 587–612.

Amao, Olufemi (2011) 'Human Rights, Ethics and International Business: The Case of Nigeria', in Aurora Voiculescu and Helen Yanacopulos (eds), *The Business of Human Rights: An Evolving Agenda for Corporate Responsibility* (London: Zed Books), pp. 188–213.

Amin, Samir (1997) *Capitalism in the Age of Globalization: The Management of Contemporary Society* (London: Zed Books).

Amin, Samir (2003) 'The Destructive Dimension of the Accumulation of Capital', in Gernot Köhler and Emilio José Chaves (eds), *Globalization: Critical Perspectives* (New York: Nova Science Publishers), pp. 1–15.

Amin, Samir (2011) *Ending the Crisis of Capitalism or Ending Capitalism?* (Cape Town: Pambazuka Press).

Amunwa, Ben (2011) *Counting the Cost: Corporations and human rights abuses in the Niger Delta* (London: Platform).

Anner, Mark (2012) 'Auditing Rights at Work in a Globalizing Economy: The Limits of Corporate Social Responsibility', paper presented to 16th ILERA World Congress, Philadelphia, July 2012.

Anseeuw, Ward et al. (2012) *Transnational Land Deals for Agriculture in the Global South: Analytical Report Based on the Land Matrix Database* (Bern/ Montpellier/Hamburg: CDE/CIRAD/GIGA).

Arrighi, Giovanni (2007) *Adam Smith in Beijing: Lineages of the Twenty-First Century* (London: Verso).

Arrighi, Giovanni (2010) *The Long Twentieth Century: Money, Power and the Origins of Our Time* (London: Verso).

Arrighi, Giovanni and Jessica Drangel (1986) 'The Stratification of the World-Economy: An Exploration of the Semiperipheral Zone', *Review*, Vol. 10, No. 1, pp. 9–74.

Arrighi, Giovanni, Terence K. Hopkins and Immanuel Wallerstein (1989) *Anti-Systemic Movements* (London: Verso).

Arrighi, Giovanni, Beverly J. Silver and Benjamin D. Brewer (2003) 'Industrial Convergence, Globalization and the Persistence of the North-South Divide', *Studies in Comparative International Development*, Vol. 38, No. 1, pp. 3–31.

Auty, Richard M. (2001) *Resource Abundance and Economic Development* (Oxford: Oxford University Press).

Auty, Richard M. (2007) 'Natural Resources, Capital Accumulation and the Resource Curse', *Ecological Economics*, No. 61, pp. 627–34.

Baah, Anthony (2003) 'History of African Development Initiatives', paper presented to the Africa Labour Research Network Workshop, Johannesburg, May 2003.

Backer, Larry Catá (2005) 'Multinational Corporations, Transnational Law: The United Nations' Norms on the Responsibilities of Transnational Corporations as a Harbinger of Corporate Social Responsibility in International Law', *Columbia Human Rights Law Review*, Vol. 37, pp. 101–92.

Bagchi, Amiya Kumar (2006) *Perilous Passage: Mankind and the Global Ascendancy of Capital* (New Delhi: Oxford University Press).

Bahgat, Gawdat (2010) 'The USA's Policy on Sovereign Wealth Funds' Investments', in Xu Yi-chong and Gawdat Bahgat (eds), *The Political Economy of Sovereign Wealth Funds* (Basingstoke: Palgrave Macmillan), pp. 228–44.

Bakan, Joel (2004) *The Corporation: The Pathological Pursuit of Profit and Power* (New York: Free Press).

Bakker, Isabella and Stephen Gill (2003) *Power, Production and Social Reproduction: Human In/security in the Global Political Economy* (Basingstoke: Palgrave Macmillan).

Balanyá, Belén, Ann Doherty, Olivier Hoedeman, Adam Ma'anit and Erik Wesselius (2003) *Europe, Inc: Regional and Global Restructuring and the Rise of Corporate Power* (London: Pluto Press).

Balibar, Étienne (2004) *We, the People of Europe? Reflections on Transnational Citizenship* (Princeton: Princeton University Press).

Barlow, Maude (2011) *Our Right to Water: A People's Guide to Implementing the United Nations' Recognition of the Right to Water and Sanitation* (Ottawa: Council of Canadians).

Barnes, Liz and Gaynor Lea-Greenwood (2006) 'Fast Fashioning the Supply Chain: Shaping the Research Agenda', *Journal of Fashion Marketing and Management*, Vol. 10, No. 3, pp. 259–71.

Barrientos, Stephanie and Sally Smith (2006) *The ETI Code of Labour Practice: Do Workers Really Benefit?* (Brighton: Institute of Development Studies).

Baxi, Upendra (2005) 'Market Fundamentalisms: Business Ethics at the Altar of Human Rights', *Human Rights Law Review*, Vol. 5, No. 1, pp. 1–26.

Becker, Marc (2011) 'Correa, Indigenous Movements, and the Writing of a New Constitution in Ecuador', *Latin American Perspectives*, Vol. 38, No. 1, pp. 47–62

Bello, Walden (2004) *Deglobalization: Ideas for a New World Economy* (London: Zed Books).

Bello, Walden (2006) 'The Capitalist Conjuncture: Over-Accumulation, Financial Crises, and the Retreat from Globalisation', *Third World Quarterly*, Vol. 27, No. 8, pp. 1345–67.

Bello, Walden (2009) *The Food Wars* (London: Verso).

Bench Marks (2012) *Communities in the Platinum Minefields: A Review of Platinum Mining in the Bojanala District of the North West Province* (Johannesburg: Bench Marks Foundation).

Bendell, Jem (2004) 'Barricades and Boardrooms: A Contemporary History of the Corporate Accountability Movement' (Geneva: United Nations Research Institute for Social Development)

Bernasconi-Osterwalder, Nathalie (2009) 'Background paper on Vattenfall v Germany arbitration' (Winnipeg, International Institute for Sustainable Development).

Bernasconi-Osterwalder, Nathalie and Rhea Tamara Hoffmann (2012) 'Der deutsche Atomausstieg auf dem Prüfstand eines internationalen Investitionsschiedsgerichts? Hintergründe zum neuen Streitfall Vattenfall gegen Deutschland (II)' (Berlin: PowerShift).

Bernasconi-Osterwalder, Nathalie and Lise Johnson (2011) *International Investment Law and Sustainable Development: Key Cases from 2000–2010* (Winnipeg: International Institute for Sustainable Development).

Bernstein, Henry (2000) '"The Peasantry" in Global Capitalism: Who, Where and Why?', in Leo Panitch and Colin Leys (eds), *Working Classes, Global Realities: Socialist Register 2001* (London: Merlin Press), pp. 25–51.

Berry, David M. and Giles Moss (2008) *Libre Culture: Meditations on Free Culture* (Winnipeg: Pygmalion Books).

Bieler, Andreas (2012) 'Globalisation and European Integration: The Internal and External Dimensions of Neo-Liberal Restructuring', in Petros Nousios, Henk Overbeek and Andreas Tsolakis (eds), *Globalisation and European Integration: Critical Approaches to Regional Order and International Relations* (Abingdon: Routledge), pp. 197–217.

Bieler, Andreas and Ingemar Lindberg (2011) *Global Restructuring, Labour and the Challenges for Transnational Solidarity* (Abingdon: Routledge).

Bieler, Andreas, Ingemar Lindberg and Devan Pillay (2008) *Labour and the Challenges of Globalization: What Prospects for Transnational Solidarity?* (London: Pluto Press).

Bishop, Matthew and Michael Green (2008) *Philanthrocapitalism: How Giving Can Save the World* (London: A&C Black).

Blankenburg, Stephanie, Dan Plesch and Frank Wilkinson (2010) 'Limited Liability and the Modern Corporation in Theory and in Practice', *Cambridge Journal of Economics*, Vol. 34, No. 5, pp. 821–36.

Blowfield, Michael (2005) 'Corporate Social Responsibility – The Failing Discipline and Why it Matters for International Relations', *International Relations*, Vol. 19, No. 2, pp. 173–91.

Blowfield, Michael and Jedrzej George Frynas (2005) 'Setting New Agendas: Critical Perspectives on Corporate Social Responsibility in the Developing World', *International Affairs*, Vol. 81, No. 3, pp. 499–513.

Bonaiuti, Mauro (2012) 'Degrowth: Tools for a Complex Analysis of the Multi-dimensional Crisis', *Capitalism, Nature, Socialism*, Vol. 23, No. 1, pp. 30–50.

Bond, Patrick (2004) 'US Empire and South African Subimperialism', in Leo Panitch and Colin Leys (eds), *The Empire Reloaded: Socialist Register 2005* (London: Merlin Press), pp. 218–38.

Boron, Atilio A. (2012) 'Strategy and Tactics in Popular Struggles in Latin America', in Leo Panitch, Greg Albo and Vivek Chibber (eds), *The Question of Strategy: Socialist Register 2013* (Pontypool: Merlin Press), pp. 241–54.

Borras, Saturnino M. Jr (2008) 'La Vía Campesina and its Global Campaign for Agrarian Reform', in Saturnino M. Borras Jr, Marc Edelman and Cristóbal Kay (eds), *Transnational Agrarian Movements Confronting Globalization* (Chichester: Wiley-Blackwell), pp. 91–122.

Borras, Saturnino M. Jr and Jennifer Franco (2010) 'From Threat to Opportunity? Problems with the Idea of a "Code of Conduct" for Land-Grabbing', *Yale Human Rights and Development Law Journal*, Vol. 13, No. 2, pp. 507–23.

Borras, Saturnino M. Jr, Jennifer Franco and Chunyu Wang (2013) 'The Challenge of Global Governance of Land Grabbing: Changing International Agricultural Context and Competing Political Views and Strategies', *Globalizations*, Vol. 10, No. 1, pp. 161–79.

Börzel, Tanja A. and Jana Hönke (2011) 'From Compliance to Practice: Mining Companies and the Voluntary Principles on Security and Human Rights in the Democratic Republic of Congo' (Berlin: DFG Research Center).

Bourne, Richard (2008) *Lula of Brazil: The Story So Far* (London: Zed Books).

Brandt, Willy (1980) *North-South: A Programme for Survival; Report of the International Commission on International Development Issues under the Chairmanship of Willy Brandt* (London: Pan Books).

Branford, Sue (2011) *Food Sovereignty: Reclaiming the Global Food System* (London: War on Want).

Branford, Sue and Jan Rocha (2002) *Cutting the Wire: The Story of the Landless Movement in Brazil* (London: Latin America Bureau).

Brautigam, Deborah (2009) *The Dragon's Gift: The Real Story of China in Africa* (Oxford: Oxford University Press).

BRICS (2012) *The BRICS Report: A Study of Brazil, Russia, India, China and South Africa with Special Focus on Synergies and Complementarities* (New Delhi: Oxford University Press).

Bruno, Kenny and Joshua Karliner (2002) *earthsummit.biz: The Corporate Takeover of Sustainable Development* (New York and San Francisco: Institute for Food and Development Policy and CorpWatch).

Brzoska, Michael, Kees Kingma and Herbert Wulf (1995) 'Demilitarization and Conversion' (Bonn: Bonn International Center for Conversion).

Bulte, Erwin H., Richard Damania and Robert T. Deacon (2005) 'Resource Intensity, Institutions, and Development', *World Development*, Vol. 33, No. 7, pp. 1029–44.

Bulut, Tugce and Christel Lane (2011) 'The Private Regulation of Labour Standards and Rights in the Global Clothing Industry: An Evaluation of Its Effectiveness in Two Developing Countries', *New Political Economy*, Vol. 16, No. 1, pp. 41–71.

Burbach, Roger, Michael Fox and Federico Fuentes (2013) *Latin America's Turbulent Transitions: The Future of Twenty-First Century Socialism* (London: Zed Books).

Burk, Kathleen and Alec Cairncross (1992) '*Goodbye, Great Britain': The 1976 IMF Crisis* (New Haven: Yale University Press).

Buxton, Abbi, Mark Campanale and Lorenzo Cotula (2012) 'Farms and Funds: Investment Funds in the Global Land Rush' (London: International Institute for Environment and Development).

Cabral, Amilcar (1966) 'The Weapon of Theory', speech delivered to the first Tricontinental Conference of the Peoples of Asia, Africa and Latin America, Havana.

Callinicos, Alex (2009) *Imperialism and Global Political Economy* (Cambridge: Polity).

Cammack, Paul (2003) 'The Governance of Global Capitalism: A New Materialist Analysis', *Historical Materialism*, Vol. 11, No. 2, pp. 37–59.

Cammack, Paul (2004) 'What the World Bank Means by Poverty Reduction, and Why it Matters', *New Political Economy*, Vol. 9, No. 2, pp. 189–211.

Cammack, Paul (2010) 'The Shape of Capitalism to Come', *Antipode*, Vol. 41, Suppl. 1, pp. 262–80.

Campbell, Hugh (2009) 'Breaking New Ground in Food Regime Theory: Corporate Environmentalism, Ecological Feedbacks and the "Food from Somewhere" Regime?', *Agriculture and Human Values*, No. 26, pp. 309–19.

Carroll, Archie B. (2008) 'A History of Corporate Social Responsibility: Concepts and Practices', in Andrew Crane, Abagail McWilliams, Dirk Matten, Jeremy Moon and Donald S. Siegel (eds), *The Oxford Handbook of Corporate Social Responsibility* (Oxford: Oxford University Press), pp. 19–46.

Carroll, William K. (2010) *The Making of a Transnational Capitalist Class: Corporate Power in the 21st century* (London: Zed Books).

Castorina, Emilia (2013) 'Crisis and Recomposition in Argentina', in Jeffery R. Webber and Barry Carr (eds), *The New Latin American Left: Cracks in the Empire* (Lanham: Rowman & Littlefield), pp. 233–54.

Chapman, Peter (2007) *Jungle Capitalists: A Story of Globalisation, Greed and Revolution* (Edinburgh: Canongate).

Chase-Dunn, Christopher (1988) 'Comparing World-Systems: Toward a Theory of Semiperipheral Development', *Comparative Civilizations Review*, No. 19, pp. 29–66.

Chen, Shaohua and Martin Ravallion (2008) 'The Developing World is Poorer than We Thought, but No Less Successful in the Fight against Poverty' (Washington DC: World Bank).

Chetley, Andrew (1979) *The Baby Killer Scandal* (London: War on Want).

Chibber, Vivek (2004) 'Reviving the Developmental State? The Myth of the "National Bourgeoisie"', in Leo Panitch and Colin Leys (eds), *The Empire Reloaded: Socialist Register 2005* (London: Merlin Press), pp. 144–65.

Chin, Gregory (2010) 'The Emerging Countries and China in the G20: Reshaping Global Economic Governance', *Studia Diplomatica*, Vol. 63, No. 2, pp. 105–24.

Chorev, Nitsan and Sarah Babb (2009) 'The Crisis of Neoliberalism and the Future of International Institutions: A Comparison of the IMF and the WTO', *Theory and Society*, Vol. 38, No. 5, pp. 459–84.

Chossudovsky, Michel (1997) *The Globalization of Poverty: Impacts of IMF and World Bank Reforms* (London: Zed Books).

Church Committee (1973) *Multinational Corporations and United States Foreign Policy: Hearings Before the Subcommittee on Multinational Corporations of the Committee on Foreign Relations, United States Senate, Ninety-Third Congress, on The International Telephone and Telegraph Company and Chile, 1970–1*, (Washington DC: US Government Printing Office).

Church Committee (1975) 'Covert Action in Chile: 1963–1973', Staff Report of the Select Committee to Study Governmental Operations With Respect to Intelligence Activities (Washington DC: United States Senate).

CIA (2000) 'CIA Activities in Chile' (Washington DC: Central Intelligence Agency).

Ciccaglione, Bruno (2009) *Free Trade and Trade Unions of the Americas: Strategies, Practices, Struggles, Achievements* (Vienna: Arbeiterkammer Wien).

Clapham, Andrew (2006) *Human Rights Obligations of Non-State Actors* (Oxford: Oxford University Press).

Clapham, Andrew and Scott Jerbi (2001) 'Categories of Corporate Complicity in Human Rights Abuses', *Hastings International and Comparative Law Journal*, No. 24, pp. 339–49.

Clapp, Jennifer and Doris Fuchs (2009) 'Agrifood Corporations, Global Governance, and Sustainability: A Framework for Analysis', in Jennifer Clapp and Doris Fuchs (eds), *Corporate Power in Global Agrifood Governance* (Cambridge MA: MIT Press), pp. 1–26.

Clegg, Jenny (2009) *China's Global Strategy: Towards a Multipolar World* (London: Pluto Press).

Collier, Paul (2007) *The Bottom Billion: Why the Poorest Countries are Failing and What Can be Done About It* (Oxford: Oxford University Press).

Comisión Intereclesial de Justicia y Paz (2012) *Colombia: Banacol, a Company Implicated in Paramilitarism, and Land Grabbing in Curvaradó and Jiguamiandó* (Berlin: FDCL).

Correa, Rafael (2012) 'Ecuador's Path', *New Left Review*, No. 77, pp. 88–104.

Cotula, Lorenzo (2012) 'The International Political Economy of the Global Land Rush: A Critical Appraisal of Trends, Scale, Geography and Drivers', *Journal of Peasant Studies*, Vol. 39, Nos 3–4, pp. 649–80.

Cronin, David (2013) *Corporate Europe: How Big Business Sets Policies on Food, Climate and War* (London: Pluto Press).

Cumbers, Andrew (2012) *Reclaiming Public Ownership: Making Space for Economic Democracy* (London: Zed Books).

Curtis, Mark (1995) *The Ambiguities of Power: British Foreign Policy since 1945* (London: Zed Books).

Curtis, Mark and John Hilary (2012) *The Hunger Games: How DFID Support for Agribusiness is Fuelling Poverty in Africa* (London: War on Want).

Dalle Mulle, Emmanuel and Violette Ruppanner (2010) *Exploring the Global Food Supply Chain: Markets, Companies, Systems* (Geneva: 3D).

Dangl, Benjamin (2010) *Dancing with Dynamite: Social Movements and States in Latin America* (Oakland: AK Press).

Daniel, Shepard and Anuradha Mittal (2010) *(Mis)investment in Agriculture: The Role of the International Finance Corporation in Global Land Grabs* (Oakland: Oakland Institute).

Daño, Elenita C. (2007) *Unmasking the New Green Revolution in Africa: Motives, Players and Dynamics* (Penang: Third World Network).

Davies, James B., Susanna Sandström, Anthony Shorrocks and Edward N. Wolff (2008) 'The World Distribution of Household Wealth' (Helsinki: United Nations University World Institute for Development Economics Research).

Davies, Ken (2010) 'Outward FDI from China and its Policy Context' (New York: Vale Columbia Center on Sustainable International Investment).

Deblock, Christian and Dorval Brunelle (2000) 'Globalization and New Normative Frameworks: The Multilateral Agreement on Investment', in Guy Lachapelle and John Trent (eds), *Globalization, Governance and Identity: The Emergence of New Partnerships* (Montréal: Les Presses de l'Université de Montréal), pp. 03–126.

Defourny, Jacques, Patrick Develtere and Bénédicte Fonteneau (2000) *Social Economy: North and South* (Leuven: K.U. Leuven).

de Gramont, Alexandre (2006), 'After the Water War: The Battle for Jurisdiction in Aguas del Tunari SA v Republic of Bolivia', *Transnational Dispute Management*, Vol. 3, No. 5.

Deininger, Klaus and Derek Byerlee (2012) *Rising Global Interest in Farmland: Can It Yield Sustainable and Equitable Benefits?* (Washington DC: World Bank).

Department of Defense (2010) *Quadrennial Defense Review Report: February 2010* (Washington DC: US Department of Defense).

Department of Defense (2012) 'Joint Operational Access Concept (JOAC)' (Washington DC: US Department of Defense).

De Schutter, Olivier (2010) 'Report of the Special Rapporteur on the Right to Food', 11 August 2010, UN document A/65/281.

De Schutter, Olivier (2010) 'Report submitted by the Special Rapporteur on the Right to Food, Olivier De Schutter', 20 December 2010, UN document A/HRC/16/49.

Desmarais, Annette Aurélie (2007) *La Vía Campesina: Globalization and the Power of Peasants* (Nova Scotia: Fernwood).

Domínguez, Francisco (2007) 'Understanding Venezuela', *Soundings*, No. 37, pp. 92–104.

Dorling, Daniel et al. (2007) *Poverty, Wealth and Place in Britain, 1968 to 2005* (Bristol: The Policy Press).

Dutt, Srikant (1984) *India and the Third World: Altruism or Hegemony?* (London: Zed Books).

Eberhardt, Pia and Cecilia Olivet (2012) *Profiting from Injustice: How Law Firms, Arbitrators and Financiers are Fuelling an Investment Arbitration Boom* (Amsterdam: Corporate Europe Observatory and Transnational Institute).

Edwards, Michael (2008) *Just Another Emperor? The Myths and Realities of Philanthrocapitalism* (London: Demos and Young Foundation).

Ellis, Lucy and Kathryn Smith (2007) 'The Global Upward Trend in the Profit Share' (Basel: Bank for International Settlements).

Emmerij, Louis and Richard Jolly (2009) 'The UN and Transnational Corporations', United Nations Intellectual History Project, Briefing Note No. 17 (New York: Ralph Bunche Institute for International Studies).

Esping-Andersen, Gøsta (1990) *The Three Worlds of Welfare Capitalism* (Cambridge: Polity).

Estache, Antonio, Sergio Perelman and Lourdes Trujillo (2005) 'Infrastructure Performance and Reform in Developing and Transition Economies: Evidence from a Survey of Productivity Measures' (Washington DC: World Bank).

ETC (2011) *Who Will Control the Green Economy?* (Ottawa: ETC Group).

ETI (2006) *Getting Smarter at Auditing: Tackling the Growing Crisis in Ethical Trade Auditing* (London: Ethical Trading Initiative).

European Commission (2006) 'Implementing the Partnership for Growth and Jobs: Making Europe a Pole of Excellence on Corporate Social Responsibility' (Brussels: Commission of the European Communities).

European Commission (2008) 'The Raw Materials Initiative – Meeting Our Critical Needs for Growth and Jobs in Europe' (Brussels: Commission of the European Communities).

Evers, Sandra, Perrine Burnod, Rivo Andrianirina Ratsialonana and André Teyssier (2011) 'Foreign Land Acquisitions in Madagascar: Competing Jurisdictions of Access Claims', in Ton Dietz, Kjell Havnevik, Mayke Kaag and Terje Oestigaard (eds), *African Engagements: Africa Negotiating an Emerging Multipolar World* (Leiden: Brill), pp. 110–32.

Fall, Papa Louis and Mohamed Mounir Zahran (2010) 'United Nations Corporate Partnerships: The Role and Functioning of the Global Compact' (Geneva: United Nations Joint Inspection Unit).

Fanon, Frantz (2004) *The Wretched of the Earth* (New York: Grove Press).

FAO (various years) *The State of Food Insecurity in the World* (Rome: Food and Agriculture Organisation).

FAO (2006) *The Right to Food Guidelines: Information Papers and Case Studies* (Rome: Food and Agriculture Organisation).

Ferguson, Ian F., William H. Cooper, Remy Jurenas and Brock R. Williams (2013) *The Trans-Pacific Partnership Negotiations and Issues for Congress* (Washington DC: Congressional Research Service).

Ferreira, Francisco H.G. and Martin Ravallion (2008) 'Global Poverty and Inequality: A Review of the Evidence' (Washington DC: World Bank).

FIDH (2010) *Corporate Accountability for Human Rights Abuses: A Guide for Victims and NGOs on Recourse Mechanisms* (Paris: International Federation for Human Rights).

Fig, David (2005) 'Manufacturing Amnesia: Corporate Social Responsibility in South Africa', *International Affairs*, Vol. 81, No. 3, pp. 599–617.

Fisher, William F. and Thomas Ponniah (2003) *Another World is Possible: Popular Alternatives to Globalization at the World Social Forum* (Nova Scotia: Fernwood).

Fitzgerald, E.V.K. (2001) 'Regulating Large International Firms' (Geneva: United Nations Research Institute for Social Development).

Flohr, Annegret et al. (2010) *The Role of Business in Global Governance: Corporations as Norm-Entrepreneurs* (Basingstoke: Palgrave Macmillan).

Flynn, Matthew (2007) 'Between Subimperialism and Globalization: A Case Study in the Internationalization of Brazilian Capital', *Latin American Perspectives*, Vol. 34, No. 6, pp. 9–27.

Fonteneau, Bénédicte et al. (2010) *Social and Solidarity Economy: Building a Common Understanding* (Turin: ILO International Training Centre).

Forstater, Maya (2009) 'Sectoral Coverage of the Global Economic Crisis: Implications of the Global Financial and Economic Crisis on the Textile and Clothing Sector' (Geneva: International Labour Organisation).

Foster, John Bellamy, Brett Clark and Richard York (2010) *The Ecological Rift: Capitalism's War on the Earth* (New York: Monthly Review Press).

Foster, John Bellamy and Fred Magdoff (2009) *The Great Financial Crisis: Causes and Consequences* (New York: Monthly Review Press).

Franck, Susan D. (2005) 'The Legitimacy Crisis in Investment Treaty Arbitration: Privatizing Public International Law through Inconsistent Decisions', *Fordham Law Review*, Vol. 73, No. 4, pp. 1521–625.

Fraser, Nancy (2009) 'Feminism, Capitalism and the Cunning of History', *New Left Review*, No. 56, pp. 97–117.

Freebairn, Donald K. (1995) 'Did the Green Revolution Concentrate Incomes? A Quantitative Study of Research Reports', *World Development*, Vol. 23, No. 2, pp. 265–79.

Freeland, Chrystia (2012) *Plutocrats: The Rise of the New Global Super-Rich and the Fall of Everyone Else* (London: Allen Lane).

Freeman, Bennett (2002) 'The Voluntary Principles on Security and Human Rights', in Virginia Haufler (ed.), *Case Studies of Multistakeholder Partnership: Policy Dialogue on Business in Zones of Conflict* (New York: UN Global Compact), pp. 7–14.

Friedman, Milton (1970) 'The Social Responsibility of Business is to Increase its Profits', *New York Times Magazine*, 13 September 1970.

Frynas, Jedrzej George (2005) 'The False Developmental Promise of Corporate Social Responsibility: Evidence from Multinational Oil Companies', *International Affairs*, Vol. 81, No. 3, pp. 581–98.

Fuchs, Peter (2007) '"Global Europe" – die neue Strategie der Europäischen Union zur externen Wettbewerbsfähigkeit' (Berlin: Die Linke).

Gabor, Daniela (2010) 'The International Monetary Fund and its New Economics', *Development and Change*, Vol. 41, No. 5, pp. 805–30.

Galbraith, James K., Deepshikha RoyChowdhury and Sanjeev Shrivastava (2004) 'Pay Inequality in the Indian Manufacturing Sector, 1979–1998' (Austin: University of Texas Inequality Project).

Galbraith, John Kenneth (1992) *The Culture of Contentment* (London: Penguin)

Galeano, Eduardo (1973) *Open Veins of Latin America: Five Centuries of the Pillage of a Continent* (New York: Monthly Review Press).

García Linera, Álvaro (2012) 'Geopolitics of the Amazon: Landed-Hereditary Power and Capitalist Accumulation', at climateandcapitalism.com.

Geary, Kate (2012) '"Our Land, Our Lives": Time Out on the Global Land Rush' (Oxford: Oxfam International).

Gedicks, Al (2001) *Resource Rebels: Native Challenges to Mining and Oil Corporations* (Cambridge MA: South End Press).

George, Susan (2008) *We the Peoples of Europe* (London: Pluto Press).

Gereffi, Gary and Olga Memedovic (2003) *The Global Apparel Value Chain: What Prospects for Upgrading by Developing Countries* (Vienna: United Nations Industrial Development Organisation).

Germann, Julian (2006) 'Hegemony, Discursive Struggle, and Voluntary Guidelines on the "Right to Food": A Study in the Negotiation of Meaning' (Linköping: Linköpings Universitet).

Germann, Julian (2009) 'The Human Right to Food: "Voluntary Guidelines" Negotiations', in Yildiz Atasoy (ed.), *Hegemonic Transitions, the State and Crisis in Neoliberal Capitalism* (Abingdon: Routledge), pp. 126–43.

Gibson-Graham, J.K. (2006) *A Postcapitalist Politics* (Minneapolis: University of Minnesota Press).

Gill, Stephen (2008) *Power and Resistance in the New World Order* (Basingstoke: Palgrave Macmillan).

Gills, Barry K. (2010) 'Globalization, Crisis and Transformation: World Systemic Crisis and the Historical Dialectics of Capital', *Globalizations*, Vol. 7, Nos 1–2, pp. 273–86.

Giovannoni, Olivier (2008) 'Functional Distribution of Income, Inequality and the Incidence of Poverty: Stylized Facts and the Role of Macroeconomic Policy' (Geneva: United Nations Research Institute for Social Development).

Gliessman, Steve (2013) 'Agroecology: Growing the Roots of Resistance', *Agroecology and Sustainable Food Systems*, Vol. 37, No. 1, pp. 19–31.

Goldstein, Judith L. and Richard H. Steinberg (2008) 'Negotiate or Litigate? Effects of WTO Judicial Delegation on US Trade Politics', *Law and Contemporary Problems*, Vol. 71, pp. 257–82.

Gopalakrishnan, Shankar (2012) *Undemocratic and Arbitrary: Control, Regulation and Expropriation of India's Forest and Common Lands* (New Delhi: Society for Promotion of Wastelands Development).

Gudynas, Eduardo (2011) 'Buen Vivir: Today's tomorrow', *Development*, Vol. 54, No. 4, pp. 441–7.

Haddad, Ryan (2012) 'An Un-Conventional Approach: Ecuador's Yasuní-ITT Initiative is in Discord with the UNFCCC', *Sustainable Development Law & Policy*, Vol. 12, No. 2, pp. 15–18.

Hale, Angela and Jane Wills (2005) *Threads of Labour: Garment Industry Supply Chains from the Workers' Perspective* (Oxford: Blackwell).

Hanlon, Gerard (2008) 'Rethinking Corporate Social Responsibility and the Role of the Firm – On the Denial of Politics', in Andrew Crane, Abagail McWilliams, Dirk Matten, Jeremy Moon and Donald S. Siegel (eds), *The Oxford Handbook of Corporate Social Responsibility* (Oxford: Oxford University Press), pp. 156–72.

Hansen, Thomas H. (2009) 'Governing the Extractive Industries: The Extractive Industries Transparency Initiative and the Voluntary Principles on Security and Human Rights', paper presented to the 50th annual convention of the International Studies Association, New York, February 2009.

Hardt, Michael (2010) 'The Common in Communism', in Costas Douzinas and Slavoj Žižek (eds), *The Idea of Communism* (London: Verso), pp. 131–44.

Hardt, Michael and Antonio Negri (2005) *Multitude: War and Democracy in the Age of Empire* (London: Penguin).

Harima, Reiko (2012) *Restricted Rights: Migrant women workers in Thailand, Cambodia and Malaysia* (London: War on Want).

Harnecker, Marta (2010) 'Latin America and Twenty-First Century Socialism: Inventing to Avoid Mistakes', *Monthly Review*, Vol. 62, No. 3, pp. 1–86.

Harris, Nigel (1986) *The End of the Third World: Newly Industrializing Countries and the Decline of an Ideology* (London: I.B. Tauris).

Hart-Landsberg, Martin (2010) 'The US Economy and China: Capitalism, Class, and Crisis', *Monthly Review*, Vol. 61, No. 9, pp. 14–31.

Harvey, David (2003) *The New Imperialism* (Oxford: Oxford University Press).

Harvey, David (2005) *A Brief History of Neoliberalism* (Oxford: Oxford University Press).

Harvey, David (2006) *Spaces of Global Capitalism: Towards a Theory of Uneven Geographical Development* (London: Verso).

Harvey, David (2010) *The Enigma of Capital and the Crises of Capitalism* (Oxford: Oxford University Press).

Harvey, Neil (1998) *The Chiapas Rebellion: The Struggle for Land and Democracy* (Durban: Duke University Press).

Hebbar, Ritambhara (2010) 'Framing the Development Debate: The Case of Farmers' Suicide in India', in Chandan Sengupta and Stuart Corbridge (eds), *Democracy, Development and Decentralisation in India: Continuing Debates* (New Delhi: Routledge), pp. 84–110.

Hickson, Kevin (2005) *The IMF Crisis of 1976 and British Politics* (London: I.B. Tauris)

Higginbottom, Andy (forthcoming) 'Imperialist Rent in Practice and Theory', *Globalizations*, Vol. 11, No. 1.

Hilary, John (2002) 'Foreign Investment in Services: The Threat of GATS 2000 Negotiations', paper delivered at the WTO Symposium, Geneva, April 2002.

Hilary, John (2004) *Divide and Rule: The EU and US response to developing country alliances at the WTO* (Johannesburg: ActionAid International).

Hilary, John (2004) 'Trade Liberalization, Poverty and the WTO: Assessing the Realities', in Homi Katrak and Roger Strange (eds), *The WTO and Developing Countries* (London: Palgrave Macmillan), pp. 38–62.

Hilary, John (2009) 'Challenging Corporate Europe', *Renewal*, Vol. 17, No. 2, pp. 33–7.

Himmelstein, David U., Deborah Thorne, Elizabeth Warren and Steffie Woolhandler (2009) 'Medical Bankruptcy in the United States, 2007: Results of a National Study', *American Journal of Medicine*, Vol. 122. No. 8, pp. 741–6.

Hines, Colin (2000) *Localization: A Global Manifesto* (London: Earthscan).

Holt-Giménez, Eric (2008) 'Out of AGRA: The Green Revolution Returns to Africa', *Development*, Vol. 51, No. 4, pp. 464–71.

Holt-Giménez, Eric and Miguel A. Altieri (2013) 'Agroecology, Food Sovereignty, and the New Green Revolution', *Agroecology and Sustainable Food Systems*, Vol. 37, No. 1, pp. 90–102.

Holt-Giménez, Eric and Raj Patel (2009) *Food Rebellions: Crisis and the Hunger for Justice* (Cape Town: Pambazuka Press).

Holst, Jens and Assia Brandrup-Lukanow (2007) *Extending Social Protection in Health: Developing Countries' Experiences, Lessons Learnt and Recommendations* (Frankfurt: Verlag für Akademische Schriften).

Houldey, Gemma (2008) *Fuelling Fear: The Human Cost of Biofuels in Colombia* (London: War on Want).

Hung, Ho-fung (2011) 'Sinomania: Global Crisis, China's Crisis?', in Leo Panitch, Greg Albo and Vivek Chibbers (eds), *The Crisis and the Left: Socialist Register 2012*, Pontypool: Merlin Press, pp. 217–34.

IAASTD (2009) *Agriculture at a Crossroads: Global Report of the International Assessment of Agricultural Knowledge, Science and Technology for Development* (Washington DC: Island Press).

IAEA (2011) *IAEA International Fact Finding Expert Mission of the Fukushima Dai-Ichi NPP Accident Following the Great East Japan Earthquake and Tsunami* (Vienna: International Atomic Energy Agency).

ICC (2011) *Arbitration and ADR Rules* (Paris: International Chamber of Commerce).

ILO (2008) *World of Work Report 2008: Income Inequalities in the Age of Financial Globalization* (Geneva: International Labour Organisation).

ILO (2010) *Global Wage Report 2010/11: Wage Policies in Times of Crisis* (Geneva: International Labour Organisation).

ILO (2012) *Better Work Vietnam Baseline Report: Worker Perspectives from the Factory and Beyond* (Geneva: International Labour Organisation).

IMF (2004) 'Public-Private Partnerships' (Washington DC: International Monetary Fund).

IMF (2005) *The IMF's Approach to Capital Account Liberalization: Evaluation Report* (Washington DC: International Monetary Fund).

IMF (2007) *Structural Conditionality in IMF-Supported Programs* (Washington DC: International Monetary Fund).

ITUC (various years) *Annual Survey of Violations of Trade Union Rights* (Brussels: International Trade Union Confederation).

Jawara, Fatoumata and Aileen Kwa (2004) *Behind the Scenes at the WTO: The Real World of International Trade Negotiations* (London: Zed Books).

Jenkins, Rhys (2001) 'Corporate Codes of Conduct: Self-Regulation in a Global Economy' (Geneva: United Nations Research Institute for Social Development).

Jenkins, Rhys (2005) 'Globalization, Corporate Social Responsibility and Poverty', *International Affairs*, Vol. 81, No. 3, pp. 525–40.

Jerbi, Scott (2009) 'Business and Human Rights at the UN: What Might Happen Next?', *Human Rights Quarterly*, Vol. 31, pp. 299–320.

Kaplinksy, Raphael (2005) *Globalization, Poverty and Inequality: Between a Rock and a Hard Place* (Cambridge: Polity).

Kaplinsky, Raphael and Mike Morris (2008), 'Do the Asian Drivers Undermine Export-Oriented Industrialization in SSA?', *World Development*, Vol. 36, No. 2, pp. 254–73.

Karnani, Aneel (2006) 'Fortune at the Bottom of the Pyramid: A Mirage' (Ann Arbor: University of Michigan Press).

Katz, Claudio (2011) 'The Singularities of Latin America', in Leo Panitch, Greg Albo and Vivek Chibber (eds), *The Crisis and the Left: Socialist Register 2012*, Pontypool: Merlin Press, pp. 200–16.

Kell, Georg and David Levin (2002) 'The Evolution of the Global Compact Network: An Historic Experiment in Learning and Action', paper presented at the Academy of Management Annual Conference 'Building Effective Networks', Denver, August 2002.

Khor, Martin (2001) *Rethinking Globalization: Critical Issues and Policy Choices* (London: Zed Books).

Kinley, David and Rachel Chambers (2006) 'The UN Human Rights Norms for Corporations: The Private Implications of Public International Law', *Human Rights Law Review*, Vol. 6, No. 3, pp. 447–97.

Kinley, David, Justine Nolan and Natalie Zerial (2007) 'The Politics of Corporate Social Responsibility: Reflections on the United Nations Human Rights Norms for Corporations', *Company and Securities Law Journal*, Vol. 25, No. 1, pp. 30–42.

Klein, Naomi (2000) *No Logo: Taking Aim at the Brand Bullies* (London: Flamingo).

Klein, Naomi (2007) *The Shock Doctrine: The Rise of Disaster Capitalism* (London: Penguin).

Kohl, Benjamin and Linda Farthing (2012) 'Material Constraints to Popular Imaginaries: The Extractive Economy and Resource Nationalism in Bolivia', *Political Geography*, No. 31, pp. 225–35.

Krepinevich, Andrew F. (2009) 'The Pentagon's Wasting Assets: The Eroding Foundations of American Power', *Foreign Affairs*, Vol. 88, No. 4, pp. 18–33.

Krugman, Paul (2007) *The Conscience of a Liberal: Reclaiming America from the Right* (London: Allen Lane).

Kumar, Claire (2009) *Undermining the Poor: Mineral Taxation Reforms in Latin America* (London: Christian Aid).

Lambrechts, Kato (2009) *Breaking the Curse: How Transparent Taxation and Fair Taxes can Turn Africa's Mineral Wealth into Development* (Johannesburg: Open Society Institute of Southern Africa).

Lansley, Stewart (2009) *Unfair to Middling: How Middle Income Britain's Shrinking Wages Fuelled the Crash and Threaten Recovery* (London: Trades Union Congress).

Lapavitsas, Costas (2009) 'Financialised Capitalism: Crisis and Financial Expropriation', *Historical Materialism*, Vol. 17, No. 2, pp. 114–48.

Lappé, Frances Moore, Joseph Collins and Peter Rosset (1998) *World Hunger: 12 Myths* (London: Earthscan).

LaSalle, Tim and Paul Hepperly (2008) 'Regenerative Organic Farming: A Solution to Global Warming' (Kutztown: Rodale Institute).

Latham, Robert (2000) 'Social Sovereignty', *Theory, Culture & Society*, Vol. 17, No. 4, pp. 1–18.

Latouche, Serge (2009) *Farewell to Growth* (Cambridge: Polity).

Latouche, Serge (2010) 'Degrowth', *Journal of Cleaner Production*, Vol. 18, No. 6, pp. 519–22.

Laville, Jean-Louis (2010) 'The Solidarity Economy: An International Movement', *RCCS Review*, No. 2, pp. 3–41.

Lawson, Neal (2009) *All Consuming: How Shopping Got Us Into This Mess and How We Can Find Our Way Out* (London: Penguin).

Lebowitz, Michael (2010) *The Socialist Alternative: Real Human Development* (New York: Monthly Review Press).

Letnar Černič, Jernej (2008) 'Corporate Responsibility for Human Rights: A Critical Analysis of the OECD Guidelines for Multinational Enterprises', *Hanse Law Review,* Vol. 4, No. 1, pp. 71–100.

Li Mingqi (2005) 'The Rise of China and the Demise of the Capitalist World-Economy: Exploring Historical Possibilities in the 21st Century', *Science & Society*, Vol. 69, No. 3, pp. 420–48.

Lopez-Acevedo, Gladys and Raymond Robertson (2012) *Sewing Success? Employment, Wages, and Poverty following the End of the Multi-fibre Arrangement* (Washington DC: World Bank)

Lukács, Georg (1971) *History and Class Consciousness* (London: Merlin Press).

Makino, Momoe (2012) 'Garment Industry in Pakistan in the Post-MFA Period', in Takahiro Fukunishi (ed.) *Dynamics of the Garment Industry in Low-Income Countries: Experience of Asia and Africa (Interim Report)* (Chiba: Institute of Developing Economies).

Mandel, Ernest (1975) *Late Capitalism* (London: New Left Books).

Manji, Firoze and Stephen Marks (2007) *African Perspectives on China in Africa* (Nairobi and Oxford: Fahamu).

Marcos, Subcomandante (2001) 'The Punch Card and the Hour Glass', *New Left Review*, No. 9, pp. 68–79.

Marcuse, Herbert (1972) *One Dimensional Man* (London: Abacus).

Marglin, Stephen A. and Juliet B. Schor (1990) *The Golden Age of Capitalism: Reinterpreting the Postwar Experience* (Oxford: Clarendon Press).

Marini, Ruy Mauro (1972) 'Brazilian Subimperialism', *Monthly Review*, Vol. 23, No. 9, pp. 14–24.

Martin, Will (2009) 'China's Textile and Clothing Trade and Global Adjustment', in Ross Garnaut, Ligang Song and Wing Thye Woo (eds), *China's New Place in a World in Crisis: Economic, Geopolitical and Environmental Dimensions* (Canberra: Australian National University Press), pp. 303–23.

Martínez Novo, Carmen (2013) 'The Backlash against Indigenous Rights in Ecuador's Citizen's Revolution', in Todd A. Eisenstadt, Michael S. Danielson, Moisés Jaime Bailón Corres and Carlos Sorroza Polo (eds), *Latin America's Multicultural Movements: The Struggle Between Communitarianism, Autonomy and Human Rights* (New York: Oxford University Press), pp. 111–33.

Martínez-Torres, María Elena and Peter M. Rosset (2010) 'La Vía Campesina: The Birth and Evolution of a Transnational Social Movement', *Journal of Peasant Studies*, Vol. 37, No. 1, pp. 149–75.

Marx, Karl (1976) *Capital: Volume 1* (London: Penguin).

Marx, Karl (1996) *Wage Labour and Capital & Wages, Price and Profit* (London: Bookmarks).

Marx, Karl and Friedrich Engels (1977) *Manifesto of the Communist Party* (Moscow: Progress Publishers).

Massey, Doreen (2004) 'Geographies of Responsibility', *Geografiska Annaler: Series B, Human Geography*, Vol. 86, No. 1, pp. 5–18.

Massey, Doreen (2011) 'A Counterhegemonic Relationality of Place', in Eugene McCann and Kevin Ward (eds), *Mobile Urbanism: Cities and Policymaking in the Global Age* (Minneapolis: University of Minnesota Press), pp. 1–14.

Massey, Doreen (2012) 'Learning from Latin America', *Soundings*, No. 50, pp. 131–41.

Mathiason, Nick (2011) *Piping Profits: The Secret World of Oil, Gas and Mining Giants* (Oslo: Publish What You Pay Norway)

Matisoff, Adina (2012) *Crude Beginnings: An Assessment of China National Petroleum Corporation's Environmental and Social Performance Abroad* (San Francisco: Friends of the Earth).

Matthews, Duncan (2002) *Globalising Intellectual Property Rights: The TRIPs Agreement* (London: Routledge).

Mayer, Ann Elizabeth (2009) 'Human Rights as a Dimension of CSR: The Blurred Lines Between Legal and Non-Legal Categories', *Journal of Business Ethics*, Vol. 88, pp. 561–77.

Mayet, Mariam (2007) 'The New Green Revolution in Africa: Trojan Horse for GMOs?', in Aksel Naerstad (ed.), *Africa Can Feed Itself* (Oslo: Development Fund), pp. 158–65.

McKeon, Nora (2013) '"One Does Not Sell the Land Upon Which the People Walk": Land Grabbing, Transnational Rural Social Movements, and Global Governance', *Globalizations*, Vol. 10, No. 1, pp. 105–22.

McMichael, Philip (2009) 'A Food Regime Genealogy', *Journal of Peasant Studies*, Vol. 36, No. 1, pp. 139–69.

McMichael, Philip (2009) 'A Food Regime Analysis of the "World Food Crisis"', *Agriculture and Human Values*, No. 26, pp. 281–95.

McNally, David (2006) 'The Commodity Status of Labour: The Secret of Commodified Life', in Gordon Laxer and Dennis Soron (eds), *Not for Sale: Decommodifying Public Life* (Peterborough: Broadview Press), pp. 39–54.

Mehta, Vijay (2012) *The Economics of Killing: How the West Fuels War and Poverty in the Developing World* (London: Pluto Press).

Merino, Amparo and Carmen Valor (2011) 'The Potential of Corporate Social Responsibility to Eradicate Poverty: An Ongoing Debate', *Development in Practice*, Vol. 21, No. 2, pp. 157–67.

Merino Acuña, Roger (2012) 'What is "Post" in Post-Neoliberal Political Economy? Indigenous Land Rights and the Extractive Industry in Peru, Bolivia and Ecuador', paper presented at Postgraduates in Latin American Studies conference, Oxford, June 2012.

Merk, Jeroen (2011) 'Cross-Border Wage Struggles in the Global Garment Industry', in Andreas Bieler and Ingemar Lindberg (eds), *Global Restructuring, Labour and the Challenges for Transnational Solidarity* (Abingdon: Routledge), pp. 116–30.

Merk, Jeroen (2012) *10 Years of the Better Factories Cambodia Project: A Critical Evaluation* (Amsterdam: Clean Clothes Campaign).

Milanovic, Branko (2005) *Worlds Apart: Measuring International and Global Inequality* (Princeton: Princeton University Press).

Milanovic, Branko (2011) *The Haves and the Have-Nots: A Brief and Idiosyncratic History of Global Inequality* (New York: Basic Books).

Miliband, Ralph (1969) *The State in Capitalist Society: The Analysis of the Western System of Power* (London: Weidenfeld & Nicholson).

Miliband, Ralph (1983) 'State Power and Class Interests', *New Left Review,* No. 138, pp. 157–68.

Miller, Doug (2010) 'Towards Sustainable Labour Costing in the Global Apparel Industry: Some Evidence from UK Fashion Retail', paper presented at the Textile Institute Centenary Conference, Manchester, November 2010.

Miller, Doug, Simon Turner and Don Grinter (2011) 'Back to the Future? A Critical Reflection on Neil Kearney's Mature System of Industrial Relations Perspective on the Governance of Outsourced Apparel Supply Chains' (Manchester: Capturing the Gains).

Miller, Doug and Peter Williams (2009) 'What Price a Living Wage? Implementation Issues in the Quest for Decent Wages in the Global Apparel Sector', *Global Social Policy*, Vol. 9, No. 1, pp. 99–125.

Miller, Ethan (2010) 'Solidarity Economy: Key Concepts and Issues', in Emily Kawano, Thomas Neal Masterson and Jonathan Teller-Elsberg (eds), *Solidarity Economy I: Building Alternatives for People and Planet* (Amherst: Center for Popular Economics).

Miller, Hannah (2010) 'From "Rights-Based" to "Rights-Framed" Approaches: A Social Constructionist View of Human Rights Practice', *International Journal of Human Rights*, Vol. 14, No. 6, pp. 915–31.

Mills, Cliff and Will Davies (2013) *Blueprint for a Cooperative Decade* (Geneva: International Cooperative Alliance).

Molero Simarro, Ricardo (2011) 'Functional Distribution of Income and Economic Growth in the Chinese Economy, 1978–2007' (London: School of Oriental and African Studies).

Morais, Lecio and Alfredo Saad-Filho (2005) 'Lula and the Continuity of Neoliberalism in Brazil: Strategic Choice, Economic Imperative or Political Schizophrenia?', *Historical Materialism*, Vol. 13, No. 1, pp. 3–32.

Murphy, Sophia (2009) 'Free Trade in Agriculture: A Bad Idea Whose Time is Done', *Monthly Review*, Vol. 61, No. 3, pp. 78–91.

Muttitt, Greg (2011) *Fuel on the Fire: Oil and Politics in Occupied Iraq* (London: Bodley Head).

Nagaraj, R. (2010) *Country Study: India* (Geneva: United Nations Research Institute for Social Development).

Newcombe, Andrew and Lluís Paradell (2009) *Law and Practice of Investment Treaties: Standards of Practice* (Alphen aan den Rijn: Kluwer).

Newell, Peter (2005) 'Citizenship, Accountability and Community: The Limits of the CSR Agenda', *International Affairs*, Vol. 81, No. 3, pp. 541–57.

Nicholson, Paul, Xavier Montagut and Javiera Rulli (2012) *Terre et liberté! A la conquête de la souveraineté alimentaire* (Geneva: CETIM).

Nolan, Peter (2012) *Is China Buying the World?* (Cambridge: Polity).

OECD (1998) *The Multilateral Agreement on Investment: Draft Consolidated Text* (Paris: Organisation for Economic Cooperation and Development).

OECD (2011) *OECD Guidelines for Multinational Enterprises: Recommendations for Responsible Business Conduct in a Global Context* (Paris: Organisation for Economic Cooperation and Development).

OECD Watch (2010) *10 Years On: Assessing the Contribution of the OECD Guidelines for Multinational Enterprises to Responsible Business Conduct* (Amsterdam: OECD Watch).

Oi, Jean C. (2010) 'Development Strategies, Welfare Regime and Poverty Reduction in China' (Geneva: United Nations Research Institute for Social Development).

Orloff, Ann Shola (1993) 'Gender and the Social Rights of Citizenship: The Comparative Analysis of Gender Relations and Welfare States', *American Sociological Review*, Vol. 58, No. 3, pp. 303–28.

Otobe, Naoko (2011) 'Global Economic Crisis, Gender and Employment: The Impact and Policy Response' (Geneva: International Labour Organisation).

Pak, Simon J. (2012) *Lost Billions: Transfer Pricing in the Extractive Industries* (Oslo: Publish What You Pay Norway).

Palma, José Gabriel (2005) 'The Seven Main "Stylized Facts" of the Mexican Economy since Trade Liberalization and NAFTA', *Industrial and Corporate Change*, Vol. 14, No. 6, pp. 941–91.

Papadopoulos, Theo (2005) 'The Recommodification of European Labour: Theoretical and Empirical Explorations' (Bath: European Research Institute).

Parker, A. Rani (2004) 'The Public-Private Alliances of USAID in Angola: An Assessment of Lessons Learned and Ways Forward' (Washington DC: USAID).

Patel, Raj (2007) *Stuffed & Starved: Markets, Power and the Hidden Battle for the World Food System* (London: Portobello Books).

Patel, Raj (2013) 'The Long Green Revolution', *Journal of Peasant Studies*, Vol. 40, No. 1, pp. 1–63.

Pateman, Carole (1989) *The Disorder of Women: Democracy, Feminism and Political Theory* (Cambridge: Polity).

Paul, Helena and Ricarda Steinbrecher (2012) *African Agricultural Growth Corridors: Who Benefits, Who Loses?* (London: EcoNexus).

Pedersen, Jørgen Dige (2008) 'The Second Wave of Indian Investments Abroad', *Journal of Contemporary Asia*, Vol. 38, No. 4, pp. 613–37.

Peru Support Group (2007) *Mining and Development in Peru, With Special Reference to the Rio Blanco Project, Piura* (London: Peru Support Group)

Peterson, Luke Eric (2009) *Human Rights and Bilateral Investment Treaties: Mapping the Role of Human Rights Law within Investor-State Arbitration* (Montréal: Rights & Democracy).

Piketty, Thomas and Emmanuel Saez (2003) 'Income Inequality in the United States, 1913–1998', *Quarterly Journal of Economics*, Vol. 118, No. 1, pp. 1–39.

Pimbert, Michel (2009) *Towards Food Sovereignty* (London: International Institute for Environment and Development).

Pingali, Prabhu L. and Mark W. Rosengrant (1994) *Confronting the Environmental Consequences of the Green Revolution in Asia* (Washington DC: International Food Policy Research Institute).

Polanyi, Karl (1944) *The Great Transformation: The Political and Economic Origins of Our Time* (Boston: Beacon Press).

Prahalad, C.K. (2006) *The Fortune at the Bottom of the Pyramid: Eradicating Poverty Through Profits* (Upper Saddle River: Prentice Hall).

Pretty, Jules et al. (2006) 'Resource-Conserving Agriculture Increases Yields in Developing Countries', *Environmental Science & Technology*, Vol. 40, No. 4, pp. 1114–19.

Public Citizen (2001) *NAFTA Chapter 11 Investor-to-State Cases: Bankrupting Democracy* (Washington DC: Public Citizen).

Public Citizen (2012) 'Table of Foreign Investor-State Cases and Claims under NAFTA and Other US Trade Deals' (Washington DC: Public Citizen).

Raghavan, Chakravarthi (1990) *Recolonization: GATT, the Uruguay Round & the Third World* (Penang: Third World Network).

Rajak, Dinah (2011) *In Good Company: An Anatomy of Corporate Social Responsibility* (Stanford: Stanford University Press).

Razmi, Arslan and Robert A. Blecker (2008) 'Developing Country Exports of Manufactures: Moving Up the Ladder to Escape the Fallacy of Composition?', *Journal of Development Studies*, Vol. 44, No. 1, pp. 21–48.

Redfield, Peter (2012) 'Bioexpectations: Life Technologies as Humanitarian Goods', *Public Culture*, Vol. 24, No. 1, pp. 157–84.

Richardson, Ian, Andrew Kakabadse and Nada Kakabadse (2011) *Bilderberg People: Elite Power and Consensus in World Affairs* (London: Routledge).

Richter, Judith (2001) *Holding Corporations Accountable: Corporate Conduct, International Codes, and Citizen Action* (London: Zed Books).

Riesco, Manuel, Gustavo Lagos and Marcos Lima (2005) 'The "Pay Your Taxes" Debate: Perspectives on Corporate Taxation and Social Responsibility in the

Chilean Mining Industry' (Geneva: United Nations Research Institute for Social Development).

Robinson, Patrick L. (1985) 'The June 1985 Reconvened Special Session on the Code', *CTC Reporter*, No. 20, pp. 11–14.

Robinson, William I. (2004) *A Theory of Global Capitalism: Production, Class, and State in a Transnational World* (Baltimore: Johns Hopkins University Press).

Roelants, Bruno, Diana Dovgan, Hyungsik Eum and Elisa Terrasi (2012) *The Resilience of the Cooperative Model: How Worker Cooperatives, Social Cooperatives and Other Worker-Owned Enterprises Respond to the Crisis and its Consequences* (Brussels: Confédération Européenne des Coopératives de Production).

Ross, Michael L. (1999) 'The Political Economy of the Resource Curse', *World Politics*, No. 51, pp. 297–322.

Rowe, James K. (2005) 'Corporate Social Responsibility as Business Strategy', in Ronnie D. Lipschutz and James K. Rowe, *Globalization, Governmentality and Global Politics: Regulation for the Rest of Us?* (Abingdon: Routledge), pp. 130–70.

Rowell, Andrew (1996) *Green Backlash: Global Subversion of the Environmental Movement* (London: Routledge).

Ruggie, John (2006) 'Promotion and Protection of Human Rights', Interim report of the Special Representative of the Secretary-General on the issue of human rights and transnational corporations and other business enterprises, 22 February 2006, UN document E/CN.4/2006/97.

Ruggie, John (2007) 'Business and Human Rights: Mapping International Standards of Responsibility and Accountability for Corporate Acts', Report of the Special Representative of the Secretary-General (SRSG) on the issue of human rights and transnational corporations and other business enterprises, 9 February 2007, UN document A/HRC/4/035.

Ruggie, John (2008) 'Protect, Respect and Remedy: A Framework for Business and Human Rights', Report of the Special Representative of the Secretary-General on the issue of human rights and transnational corporations and other business enterprises, 7 April 2008, UN document A/HRC/8/5.

Ruggie, John (2008) 'Taking Embedded Liberalism Global: The Corporate Connection', in John Gerard Ruggie (ed.) *Embedding Global Markets: An Enduring Challenge* (Aldershot: Ashgate Publishing), pp. 231–54.

Ruggie, John (2011) 'Guiding Principles on Business and Human Rights: Implementing the United Nations "Protect, Respect and Remedy" Framework', Report of the Special Representative of the Secretary-General on the issue of human rights and transnational corporations and other business enterprises, 21 March 2011, UN document A/HRC/17/31.

Sadler, David and Stuart Lloyd (2009) 'Neo-Liberalising Corporate Social Responsibility: A Political Economy of Corporate Citizenship', *Geoforum*, Vol. 40, No. 4, pp. 613–22.

Sagafi-nejad, Tagi and John Dunning (2008) *The UN and Transnational Corporations: From Code of Conduct to Global Compact* (Bloomington: Indiana University Press).

SAPRIN (2004) *Structural Adjustment: The Policy Roots of Economic Crisis, Poverty and Inequality* (London: Zed Books).

Satgar, Vishwas and Michelle Williams (2008) *The Passion of the People: Successful Cooperative Experiences in Africa* (Geneva: Committee for the Promotion and Advancement of Cooperatives).

Schmidheiny, Stephan (1992) *Changing Course: A Global Business Perspective on Development and the Environment* (Cambridge MA: MIT Press).

Sethi, S. Prakash (2005) 'The Effectiveness of Industry-Based Codes in Serving Public Interest: The Case of the International Council on Mining and Metals', *Transnational Corporations*, Vol. 14, No. 3, pp. 55–100.

Sharp, John (2006) 'Corporate Social Responsibility and Development: An Anthropological Perspective', *Development Southern Africa*, Vol. 23, No. 2, pp. 213–22.

Shaxson, Nicholas (2011) *Treasure Islands: Tax Havens and the Men Who Stole the World* (London: Bodley Head).

Shiva, Vandana (1998) *Biopiracy: The Plunder of Nature and Knowledge* (Dartington: Green Books).

Shiva, Vandana, Ruchi Shroff and Caroline Lockhart (2012) *Seed Freedom: A Global Citizen's Report* (New Delhi: Navdanya).

Shorrocks, Anthony, James B. Davies and Rodrigo Lluberas (2012) *Global Wealth Report 2012* (Zurich: Credit Suisse Research Institute).

Shultz, Jim (2008) 'The Cochabamba Water Revolt and its Aftermath', in Jim Shultz and Melissa Crane Draper (eds), *Dignity and Defiance: Stories from Bolivia's Challenge to Globalization* (Berkeley: University of California Press), pp. 9–42.

Silk, Mitchell and Richard Malish (2006) 'Are Chinese Companies Taking Over the World?' *Chicago Journal of International Law*, Vol. 7, No. 1, pp. 105–31.

Silver, Beverly J. (2003) *Forces of Labor: Workers' Movements and Globalization since 1870* (New York: Cambridge University Press).

Singh, Kavaljit (2005) *Questioning Globalization* (New Delhi: Madhyam Books).

SIPRI (2012) *SIPRI Yearbook 2012: Armaments, Disarmament and National Security* (Stockholm: Stockholm International Peace Research Institute).

Sklair, Leslie (2001) *The Transnational Capitalist Class* (Oxford: Blackwell).

Sklair, Leslie (2002) *Globalization: Capitalism & its Alternatives* (Oxford: Oxford University Press).

Sklair, Leslie and Peter T. Robbins (2002) 'Global Capitalism and Major Corporations from the Third World', *Third World Quarterly*, Vol. 23, No. 1, pp. 81–100.

Snow, Philip (1988) *The Star Raft: China's Encounter with Africa* (Ithaca: Cornell University Press).

Sornarajah, M. (2009) 'The Retreat of Neo-Liberalism in Investment Treaty Arbitration', in Catherine A. Rogers and Roger P. Alford (eds), *The Future of Investment Arbitration*, New York: Oxford University Press, pp. 273–96.

Sornarajah, M. (2010) *The International Law on Foreign Investment* (Cambridge: Cambridge University Press).

Soron, Dennis and Gordon Laxer (2006) 'Decommodification, Democracy, and the Battle for the Commons', in Gordon Laxer and Dennis Soron (eds),

Not for Sale: Decommodifying Public Life (Peterborough: Broadview Press), pp. 15–38.

Starr, Amory (2000) *Naming the Enemy: Anti-Corporate Movements Confront Globalization* (London: Zed Books)

Stedile, João Pedro (2002) 'Landless Battalions: The Sem Terra Movement of Brazil', *New Left Review*, No. 15, pp. 77–104.

Stolowicz, Beatriz (2004) *The Latin American Left: Between Governability and Change* (Amsterdam: Transnational Institute).

Tandrayen-Ragoobur, Verena and Anisha Ayrga (2011) 'Phasing Out of the MFA: Impact on Women Workers in the Mauritian EPZ Sector', paper presented to the International Conference on International Trade and Investment, Pointe Aux Piments, Mauritius, December 2011.

Taylor, Marcus (2011) 'Race you to the Bottom... and Back Again? The Uneven Development of Labour Codes of Conduct', *New Political Economy*, Vol. 16, No. 4, pp. 445–62.

Thompson, Carol B. (2012) 'Alliance for a Green Revolution in Africa (AGRA): Advancing the Theft of African Genetic Wealth', *Review of African Political Economy*, Vol. 39, No. 132, pp. 345–50.

Tokatli, Nebahat and Ömür Kızılgün (2009) 'From Manufacturing Garments for Ready-to-Wear to Designing Collections for Fast Fashion: Evidence from Turkey', *Environment and Planning A*, Vol. 41, pp. 146–62.

Turner, Graham (2008) *The Credit Crunch: Housing Bubbles, Globalisation and the Worldwide Economic Crisis* (London: Pluto Press).

UN Centre on Transnational Corporations (1990) *The New Code Environment* (New York: United Nations).

UNCTAD (various years) *UNCTAD Handbook of Statistics* (New York and Geneva: United Nations Conference on Trade and Development).

UNCTAD (various years) *World Investment Report* (New York and Geneva: United Nations Conference on Trade and Development).

UNCTAD (1996) *Self-Regulation of Environmental Management: An Analysis of Guidelines Set by World Industry Associations for their Member Firms* (Geneva: United Nations Conference on Trade and Development).

UNCTAD (2000) *Bilateral Investment Treaties 1959–1999* (New York and Geneva: United Nations Conference on Trade and Development).

UNCTAD (2003) *Dispute Settlement: Investor-State* (New York and Geneva: United Nations Conference on Trade and Development).

UNCTAD (2003) *Self-Regulation of Environmental Management: Guidelines Set by World Industry Associations for their Members' Firms: An Update* (Geneva: United Nations Conference on Trade and Development).

UNCTAD (2005) *Economic Development in Africa: Rethinking the Role of Foreign Direct Investment* (New York and Geneva: United Nations Conference on Trade and Development).

UNCTAD (2007) *Bilateral Investment Treaties 1995–2006: Trends in Investment Rulemaking* (New York and Geneva: United Nations Conference on Trade and Development).

UNCTAD (2007) *Elimination of TRIMs: The Experience of Selected Developing Countries* (New York and Geneva: United Nations Conference on Trade and Development).

UNCTAD (2009) *The Global Economic Crisis: Systemic Failures and Multilateral Remedies* (New York and Geneva: United Nations Conference on Trade and Development).

UNCTAD (2009) *The Least Developed Countries Report 2009: The State and Development Governance* (New York and Geneva: United Nations Conference on Trade and Development).

UNCTAD (2012) *Investment Policy Framework for Sustainable Development* (New York and Geneva: United Nations Conference on Trade and Development).

UN Department of Economic and Social Affairs (1973) *Multinational Corporations in World Development* (New York: United Nations).

UN Department of Economic and Social Affairs (1974) *Summary of the Hearings Before the Group of Eminent Persons to Study the Impact of Multinational Corporations on Development and on International Relations* (New York: United Nations).

UN Department of Economic and Social Affairs (1974) *The Impact of Multinational Corporations on Development and on International Relations* (New York: United Nations).

UNDP (2006) *Niger Delta Human Development Report* (Abuja: United Nations Development Programme).

UNECA (2012) *Unleashing Africa's Potential as a Pole of Global Growth: Economic Report on Africa 2012* (Addis Ababa: United Nations Economic Commission for Africa).

UNEP (2011) *Environmental Assessment of Ogoniland* (Nairobi: United Nations Environment Programme).

UNEP (2011) *Towards a Green Economy: Pathways to Sustainable Development and Poverty Eradication* (Nairobi: United Nations Environment Programme).

UNEP-UNCTAD (2008) *Organic Agriculture and Food Security in Africa* (New York and Geneva: United Nations).

UNRISD (2010) *Combating Poverty and Inequality: Structural Change, Social Policy and Politics* (Geneva: United Nations Research Institute for Social Development).

Utting, Peter (2000) 'Business Responsibility for Sustainable Development' (Geneva: United Nations Research Institute for Social Development).

Utting, Peter (2005) 'Corporate Responsibility and the Movement of Business', *Development in Practice*, Vol. 15, Nos 3–4, pp. 375–88.

Utting, Peter and José Carlos Marques (2010) 'The Intellectual Crisis of CSR', in Peter Utting Peter and José Carlos Marques (eds), *Corporate Social Responsibility and Regulatory Governance: Towards Inclusive Development?* (Basingstoke: Palgrave Macmillan), pp. 1–25.

Utting, Peter and Ann Zammit (2006) 'Beyond Pragmatism: Appraising UN-Business Partnerships' (Geneva: United Nations Research Institute for Social Development).

Vail, John (2010) 'Decommodification and Egalitarian Political Economy', *Politics & Society*, Vol. 38, No. 3, pp. 310–46.

Van Harten, Gus (2005) 'Private Authority and Transnational Governance: The Contours of the International System of Investor Protection', *Review of International Political Economy*, Vol. 12, No. 4, pp. 600–23.

Van Harten, Gus (2007) *Investment Treaty Arbitration and Public Law* (Oxford: Oxford University Press)

Viale, Frédéric (2010) *L'Horreur Européenne* (Vincennes: Tatamis).

Visser, Wayne and Nick Tolhurst (2010) *The World Guide to CSR: A Country-by-Country Analysis of Sustainability and Responsibility* (Sheffield: Greenleaf Publishing).

Voiculescu, Aurora (2011) 'Human Rights and the Normative Ordering of Global Capitalism', in Aurora Voiculescu and Helen Yanacopulos (eds), *The Business of Human Rights: An Evolving Agenda for Corporate Responsibility* (London: Zed Books), pp. 10–28.

Wainwright, Hilary (2003) *Reclaim the State: Experiments in Popular Democracy* (London: Verso).

Wall, Derek (2009) 'Open Source Anti-Capitalism', in David Ransom and Vanessa Baird (eds), *People First Economics* (Oxford: New Internationalist), pp. 181–91.

Wallerstein, Immanuel (1979) *The Capitalist World-Economy* (Cambridge: Cambridge University Press).

Wallerstein, Immanuel (2002) 'New Revolts against the System', *New Left Review*, No. 18, pp. 29–39.

Watts, Michael J. (2005) 'Righteous Oil? Human Rights, the Oil Complex and Corporate Social Responsibility', *Annual Review of Environment and Resources*, Vol. 30, pp. 373–407.

WBCSD (2006) *Catalyzing Change: A Short History of the WBCSD* (Geneva: World Business Council for Sustainable Development).

Webber, Jeffery R. and Barry Carr (2013) *The New Latin American Left: Cracks in the Empire* (Lanham: Rowman & Littlefield).

Weisbrot, Mark, Jake Johnston and Stephan Lefebvre (2013) 'Ecuador's New Deal: Reforming and Regulating the Financial Sector' (Washington DC: Center for Economic and Policy Research).

Werner, Marion and Jennifer Bair (2009) 'After Sweatshops? Apparel Politics in the Circum-Caribbean', *NACLA Report on the Americas*, Vol. 42, No. 4, pp. 6–10.

White, Ben and Anirban Dasgupta (2010) 'Agrofuels Capitalism: A View from Political Economy', *Journal of Peasant Studies*, Vol. 37, No. 4, pp. 593–607.

White, Ben et al. (2012) 'The New Enclosures: Critical Perspectives on Corporate Land Deals', *Journal of Peasant Studies*, Vol. 39, Nos. 3-4, pp. 619–47.

Whittaker, Matthew and Lee Savage (2011) *Missing Out: Why Ordinary Workers are Experiencing Growth without Gain* (London: Resolution Foundation).

Whyte, David (2003) 'Lethal Regulation: State-Corporate Crime and the United Kingdom Government's New Mercenaries', *Journal of Law and Society*, Vol. 30, No. 4, pp. 575–600.

Windfuhr, Michael and Jennie Jonsén (2005) *Food Sovereignty: Towards Democracy in Localised Food Systems* (Rugby: ITDG Publishing).

Wittman, Hannah, Annette Aurélie Desmarais and Nettie Wiebe (2010) *Food Sovereignty: Reconnecting Food, Nature and Community* (Oakland: Food First Books)

Wood, Ellen Meiksins (2003) *Empire of Capital* (London: Verso).

Woodward, David (2001) *The Next Crisis? Direct and Equity Investment in Developing Countries* (London: Zed Books).

Worth, Owen and Phoebe Moore (2009) *Globalization and the 'New' Semi-Peripheries* (Basingstoke: Palgrave Macmillan).

Wright, Erik Olin (2006) 'Compass Points: Towards a Socialist Alternative', *New Left Review*, No. 41, pp. 93–124.

Yazbek, Nicole (2010) 'Bilateral Investment Treaties: The Foreclosure of Domestic Policy Space', *South African Journal of International Affairs*, Vol. 17, No. 1, pp. 103–20.

Zagema, Bertram (2011) 'Land and Power: The Growing Scandal Surrounding the New Wave of Investments in Land' (Oxford: Oxfam International).

Zalik, Anna (2004) 'The Peace of the Graveyard: The Voluntary Principles on Security and Human Rights in the Niger Delta', in Kees van der Pijl, Libby Assassi and Duncan Wigan (eds), *Global Regulation: Managing Crisis after the Imperial Turn* (London: Palgrave Macmillan), pp. 111–27.

Zammit, Ann (2003) *Development at Risk: Rethinking UN-Business Partnerships* (Geneva: South Centre and United Nations Research Institute for Social Development).

Zibechi, Raúl (2010) *Dispersing Power: Social Movements as Anti-State Forces* (Oakland: AK Press).

Zimmerle, Birgit (2012) *When Development Cooperation becomes Land Grabbing: The Role of Development Finance Institutions* (Bern: Brot für alle).

Žižek, Slavoj (2008) *Violence* (London: Profile Books).

Index

AbitibiBowater (Canada), 47, 51
ABN Amro (Netherlands), 155
ABP pension fund (Netherlands), 92
Abu Dhabi Investment Authority
   (ADIA), 20
accumulation by dispossession, 7,
   26, 151, 167; see also primitive
   accumulation
Addax Petroleum (Switzerland), 21
Adidas (Germany), 112
ADM (USA), 50, 120-1
Afghanistan, 28, 42, 87
Africa, 8, 15-17, 21, 32, 35, 45, 151,
   153-4; golden decade, 148-9;
   extractives, 80, 83-4; garments,
   102-3; food, 118-28; North
   Africa, 103; West Africa, 20, 126
African Agricultural Technology
   Foundation (AATF), 126, 189
African Centre for Biosafety, 126
African Union, 85, 126
Agenda 21, see Earth Summit
Agip (Italy), 87
agriculture, 8, 18, 84, 118-37, 145,
   154; industrial, 8, 119-21, 124,
   134-5, 191; extractive, 119-20;
   agricultural trade, 15-16, 39;
   regulatory changes, 56; see
   also food sovereignty, Green
   Revolution
agroecology, 118, 130, 133-5
ALBA (Alianza Bolivariana para los
   Pueblos de Nuestra América),
   see Bolivarian Alliance for the
   Americas
Algeria, 20
Ali Enterprises disaster, see Pakistan
Alien Tort Statute, see United States
   of America
Allende, Salvador, 61
Alliance for a Green Revolution in
   Africa (AGRA), 124-6
Althusser, Louis, 6

American Express (USA), 40
Amnesty International, 68, 90, 177,
   179, 183
Amstutz, Dan, 39
Anglo American (UK), 84, 92-3, 98
Angola, 15, 77
Angus, Ray, 94
Annan, Kofi, 67-8, 73, 176
Anti-Privatisation Forum, 152
Antigua & Barbuda, 195
Arbenz, Jacobo, 61
Argentina, 28, 34, 43, 45, 85, 92,
   127, 140-1, 145-6, 153, 173; BIT
   arbitrations, 51-6
Armenia, 45
ArmorGroup (UK), formerly Defence
   Systems Limited, 91
Arrighi, Giovanni, 13
Asia, 12, 17, 44, 77, 102-3, 110,
   115, 121 2, 127, 146, 151; East
   Asia, 31-2, 148; East Asian
   financial crisis, 27-8; North
   Asia, 103; South Asia, 15, 103;
   South-East Asia, 103, 110; see also
   Association of South-East Asian
   Nations
Asia Floor Wage, 8, 115-16
Association of South-East Asian
   Nations (ASEAN), 44-5
austerity, 4, 27, 35, 139
Australia, 21, 25, 44, 55, 72-3, 93,
   95, 152, 178
Austria, 131
Aventis CropScience (France), 126
Azerbaijan, 20
Azurix (USA), 53

B20 Business Summit, 34, 57, 77
BAE Systems (UK), 58
Balibar, Étienne, 150
Banco del Sur, 146
Bandung conference, 151

Bangladesh, 92, 100, 103–13; Rana Plaza disaster, 109
Barclays (UK), 20, 58
Barrick (Canada), 84, 92
Bayer (Germany), 121
Bear Creek (Canada), 95
Bechtel (USA), 47, 54
Belgium, 107
Berlusconi, Silvio, 32
BG Group (UK), *formerly* British Gas, 54
Bharti Airtel (India), 21
Bhopal, 71
BHP Billiton (Australia), 84, 92–3
bilateral investment treaty (BIT), 45–8, 51–7
Bilderberg, 30–3, 168–9
Biwater (UK), 53–4
Blair, Tony, 32, 97
Bolivarian Alliance for the Americas (ALBA), *formerly* Bolivarian Alternative for the Americas, 146, 173, 194–5
Bolivarian revolution, 144–5
Bolivia, 9, 47–8, 55, 85, 139–43, 146–7, 150, 152, 195, 196; Cochabamba water privatisation, 47, 54
Borse Dubai, 24
Botswana, 149
BP (UK), *formerly* British Petroleum, 33, 58, 71, 82–4, 91–2
Brandt Report, 6, 26
Braudel, Fernand, 163
Brazil, 14, 20–1, 27, 28, 34, 43, 45, 93, 97, 120, 127–8, 130, 140–1, 145–6, 149, 164, 196; *see also* BRICS
BRICS (Brazil, Russia, India, China, South Africa), 6, 13–14, 26, 34, 82
British American Tobacco (UK), 58
British Virgin Islands, 15
Brown, Gordon, 3
Brunei Darussalam, 44
Brzezinski, Zbigniew, 31
buen vivir, 143–4
Bunge, 21, 120–1
Burkina Faso, 125
Burma (Myanmar), 20, 92, 111

Burston-Marsteller, 65
Business Action for Sustainable Development (BASD), 69, 78
Business Council for Sustainable Development, *see* World Business Council for Sustainable Development

Cable, Vince, 155
Cambodia, 100, 103–6, 109–10, 112, 127–9; Better Factories Cambodia, *see* International Labour Organisation
Cameroon, 21, 129
Canada, 20–1, 25, 43–4, 49–51, 65, 93, 95, 141, 152
capitalism, 2–9, 35, 38, 78, 100–1; 115–17, 118–20, 125–6, 128–31, 136–7, 141; alternatives to, 79, 137, 138–61; finance capitalism, 12–13, 139; Golden Age of, 61; networked capitalism, 8, 101, 114–16, 125; transitions from, 9, 140–2, 147, 150–61; *see also* world system, capitalist
Cargill (USA), 39, 50, 120–1, 124
Caribbean, 15, 17, 45, 103, 120, 140–1, 146
Carrefour (France), 108
Cayman Islands, 15
Central America Free Trade Agreement (CAFTA), 43–4, 146
Central Intelligence Agency (CIA), *see* United States of America
Chad, 2, 20
Chandler, Geoffrey, 90, 178
Chávez, Hugo, 140, 144–5
Chernobyl disaster, 36
Chevron Texaco (USA), 77, 82, 84, 90–2
Chicago School, 155
Chile, 44, 61, 84, 140, 146
China, 10–15, 18–25, 27, 30, 32, 34, 35, 85, 92–3, 122–3, 127–9, 139, 149, 163; garments industry, 102–8, 111–14; cooperatives in, 153; Xinhua news agency, 10–11; *see also* BRICS
China Investment Corporation (CIC), 20

China Minmetals, 21, 25
China Mobile, 19
China National Offshore Oil
    Corporation (CNOOC), 21, 24
China National Petroleum
    Corporation (CNPC), 20, 92, 97
Chinalco (China), 25
Chiquita, see United Fruit Company
Church Committee, 61
Cissokho, Mamadou, 126
Citigroup (USA), formerly Citicorp,
    20, 40
climate change, 2, 127, 159; carbon
    capture, 134–5
Clinton, Bill, 32, 104–5
CMS Gas Transmission Company
    (USA), 51–2
Coca-Cola, 58
Collier, Paul, 16
Colloque, The (France-UK), 30
Colombia, 44, 71, 91–2, 96, 129,
    141, 146, 152
colonialism, 2, 26, 35, 60, 87, 119,
    149, 160; decolonisation, 2, 142,
    144, 149, 160; neocolonialism,
    128; post-colonial, 60, 86, 162
common ownership, 9, 148, 151–6,
    160
Community of Latin American and
    Caribbean States (CELAC), 141
Compagnie Générale des Eaux, see
    Vivendi
Confederation of British Industry
    (CBI), 72
Confederation of German
    Employers' Associations, 72
Congo, 15, 149
Congo, Democratic Republic of, 15,
    85, 127
ConocoPhillips (USA), 82, 84
cooperatives, 5, 9, 130, 143–5,
    153–6
Corn Products International (USA),
    50
corporate complicity, 8, 61, 73, 81–2,
    89–96
corporate social responsibility (CSR),
    6–8, 58–79, 174; extractive
    industries, 90, 96–9; garments

industry, 104, 112–14; food
    industry, 135–7
Correa, Rafael, 140, 143–4, 194
Costa Rica, 102, 159
Cuba, 139–41, 144, 146, 173
Czech Republic, 48, 55

da Silva, Luiz Inácio (Lula), 141
Daewoo (Korea), 130
Dana Petroleum (UK), 20
Davos, see World Economic Forum
Daylight Energy (Canada), 21
De Schutter, Olivier, 129, 134–5
debt, 1, 4, 12, 28, 51, 76; US debt,
    10–12; farmers, 123; debt audit,
    Ecuador, 143
decommodification, 156–8
Defence Systems Limited, see
    ArmorGroup
degrowth (décroissance), 159
Dell (USA), 21
demilitarisation, 158–9
Denmark, 124
Department for International
    Development (DFID), see United
    Kingdom
developmental state, 148–9
Diageo (UK), 124
Disney (USA), 104
DKNY (USA), 112
Doha Round, see World Trade
    Organisation
Dominica, 173, 195
Dominican Republic, 44, 102, 106
Dow (USA), 121, 126
Dubai Ports World, 25
DuPont (USA), 120, 124

Earth Summit (United Nations
    Conference on Environment and
    Development), 64–6, 69, 78
ecology, 2–3, 8–9, 77–8, 87, 98,
    123, 129–37, 147, 159; see also
    agroecology
Economic Partnership Agreement
    (EPA), 45
Economist, The, 37
Ecuador, 9, 20, 55, 85, 92, 98,
    140–4, 146–7, 150, 179, 195
Egypt, 20, 45, 106, 125, 138

El Salvador, 106, 140, 152
Energy Charter Treaty, 37–8
Enron (USA), 54
Equatorial Guinea, 20
Esping-Andersen, Gøsping, 158, 198
ethical auditing, 114
Ethical Corporation, 58
Ethical Trading Initiative (ETI), 66, 104–5, 113–14
Ethiopia, 2, 32, 124, 127–9
Ethyl Corporation (USA), 49–50
European Central Bank, 139
European Commission, 59, 157, 170, 180
European Round Table of Industrialists (ERT), 30–1
European Union (EU), 28, 31, 41–5, 59, 84–6, 102, 146, 150; Global Europe trade strategy, 44–5; Raw Materials Initiative, 86
extractive industries, 7–8, 15, 20, 80–99, 129, 144, 147; regulatory changes, 56, 85; extractivism, 147; *see also* resource curse
Extractive Industries Transparency Initiative (EITI), 66, 97–8
ExxonMobil (USA), 19, 61–2, 82–4, 92

Fair Labor Association (FLA), 66, 104–5, 113
fair trade movement, 157–8
Fair Wear Foundation, 105
fallacy of composition, 16
Federation of German Industry, 72
Felix Resources (Australia), 21
feminisation of labour, 101–2, 158
Fiat (Italy), 62
flex crops, 128
Food and Agriculture Organisation of the United Nations (FAO), 118–19, 124, 135–6; FAO Committee on World Food Security, 135–6
food sovereignty, 9, 118, 130–7, 152, 191; seven principles of, 132–3; seed sovereignty, 152, 160
Ford (USA), 24
Ford Foundation, 124

foreign direct investment (FDI), 3, 13–15, 21, 24, 41, 42, 45, 84
France, 3, 30, 53, 153–4
free culture movement, 153
free trade agreement (FTA), 7, 38, 43–5, 146, 160
Free Trade Area of the Americas (FTAA), 43, 145–6, 194
Freeman, Bennett, 96
Friedman, Milton, 77
Fu Ying, 30
Fukushima nuclear disaster, 36–7

G4S (UK), 91
G8, 4, 13, 27, 34, 59, 86, 124–6, 138
G20, 3–4, 13, 26–9, 34, 56, 77
Gabon, 21, 128, 149
Galeano, Eduardo, 119–20
Gant (USA), 112
Gap (USA), 103–4, 107, 109
García, Alan, 93
García Gonzales, Melanio, 94
García Linera, Álvaro, 147
garments industry, 8, 100–17, 125
Gates Foundation, Bill & Melinda, 124–5
Gauff (Germany), 53–4
Gazprom (Russia), 82
General Agreement on Tariffs and Trade (GATT), 28, 33, 39–40
General Agreement on Trade in Services (GATS), 40, 170
General Electric (USA), 19
genetically modified (GM) crops, 123, 125–6
Genoa, 59; Genoese empire, 13
Georgia, 45
Germany, 14, 15, 30, 45, 53, 72, 107, 164; Vattenfall case, 36–8
Ghana, 15, 124, 149
Gibson-Graham, J.K., 153
GlaxoSmithKline (UK), 58
Glencore (Switzerland), 84
Global Compact, 67–74, 78, 82, 177
globalisation, 1–7, 15–19, 27–9, 34, 38–9, 57, 60, 70, 79, 100–1, 108, 116–17, 120, 131, 138, 148–9, 158–60; alter-globalisation movement, 43, 139
Goldman Sachs (USA), 32–3

Government of Singapore
 Investment Corporation (GIC), 20
Great Depression, 18, 155
Great Recession, 1, 18
Greece, 138, 152
Green Revolution, 8, 121–6
Green, Terry, 106
Grenada, 159
Guatemala, 61, 102, 106, 129, 140,
 146, 175
Gulf Oil (USA), 61
Guinea, Gulf of, 88

H&M (Sweden), 108–9
Haiti, 106, 195
Hardt, Michael, 151
Harnecker, Marta, 147–8
Harper, Stephen, 141
Harrods (UK), 24
Hartridge, David, 39–40
Harvest Energy (Canada), 20–1
hegemony, 13, 131, 141, 157;
 'hegemonic duty', 76
Hewlett Packard (USA), 21
Honduras, 102, 106, 129, 140, 195
Horsch, Robert, 125
Huang Yiping, 30
Huawei (China), 25
Humala, Ollanta, 93, 95
human rights, 7–8, 62, 67, 70–5,
 80–2, 89–97, 128; to food, 132,
 136; to water, 152
Human Rights Watch, 68, 177, 179
Hutchison Whampoa (Hong Kong),
 24

IBM (USA), 21, 62
Iceland, 150, 159
Illston, Susan, 90
imperialism, 2, 4, 6, 11, 34–5, 86,
 92, 146, 148, 151, 160; see also
 subimperialism
Inco (Canada), 21
India, 14, 18, 20–1, 24, 27, 32,
 34, 42, 44, 55, 92, 102–3, 106,
 112, 128, 129–30, 149; farmer
 suicides, 123; see also BRICS
Inditex (Spain), 107, 109, 112

Indonesia, 20, 21, 27–8, 34;
 extractives, 92, 96–7; garments,
 110–11; land grabs, 127–8
inequality, 6, 11–12, 16–19, 119,
 123, 141, 145, 164–5
ING (Netherlands), 155
international arbitration, 7, 46–57
International Assessment of
 Agricultural Knowledge, Science
 and Technology for Development
 (IAASTD), 135
International Business Leaders
 Forum, 70
International Centre for Settlement
 of Investment Disputes (ICSID),
 37, 47–55, 172–3
International Chamber of Commerce
 (ICC), 34, 47–8, 62–78
International Code of Marketing
 of Breast-Milk Substitutes, 64,
 175–6
International Cooperative Alliance
 (ICA), 153
International Council on Mining and
 Metals (ICMM), 97–8
International Finance Corporation,
 98
International Fund for Agricultural
 Development (IFAD), 135
International Labour Organisation
 (ILO), 64, 116; Better Factories
 Cambodia, 105, 110
International Monetary Fund
 (IMF), 2, 4, 27–9, 32, 38, 46,
 52, 76, 83, 133, 138, 142, 146,
 149, 164, 168, 180; trade policy,
 15–16; capital controls, 27, 168;
 East Asian financial crisis, 27–8;
 see also structural adjustment
 programmes
International Organisation of
 Employers (IOE), 71–2
International Telephone and
 Telegraph (ITT), 61
Iran, 20, 139
Iraq, 20, 21, 87, 152
Ireland, 107
Islam, Aminul, 109
Israel, 154, 197
Italy, 30, 32, 36

Japan, 14, 19, 30–1, 36, 39, 44–5, 112, 130
jatropha, 128
Joint Initiative for Corporate Accountability and Workers' Rights (JO-IN), 105, 113
Joint Operational Access Concept (JOAC), 86–7
Jordan, 45

Karnataka State Farmers' Association (KRRS; India), 130
Kathie Lee Gifford (USA), 104
Kazakhstan, 20, 97, 127
Kell, Georg, 67
Kenya, 102, 106
Kiobel, Barinem, 89
Kirchner, Cristina, 141
Kirchner, Néstor, 141
Knight, Phil, 104
Königswinter conference (UK-Germany), 30
Korea National Oil Corporation (KNOC), 20–1
Korea, South, 19, 20, 27, 34, 44, 128, 130, 149, 152
Kraft Foods (USA), 120
Kyrgyzstan, 98

Lagarde, Christine, 32
Lamy, Pascal, 42
land grabbing, 126–9, 135–6, 160, 190–2
Landless Rural Workers' Movement (MST; Brazil), 130
Lao People's Democratic Republic, 127–8
Latin America, 9, 12, 15, 17, 32, 84–5, 103, 120–2, 127–8, 154–6, 175; pink tide, 139–50
Latouche, Serge, 159
Lawson, Nigel, 155
Laxer, Gordon, 157
Lehman Brothers (USA), 2–3
Lenovo (China), 21
Lesotho, 102
Levi-Strauss (USA), 104
Li & Fung (Hong Kong), 103
Li Ka-shing, 24
Liberia, 128

Libya, 20
Liechtenstein, 159
Lithuania, 47
Livingstone, Ken, 146
Lockheed Martin (USA), 58, 61
Lombardi, Renato, 62
London Stock Exchange, 24, 139
Lonmin (South Africa), 98–9
Los Angeles Times, The, 105
Louis Dreyfus (France), 120
Lugo, Fernando, 146

Madagascar, 127–8, 130
Malawi, 125
Malaysia, 20, 27, 44, 128
Mali, 2, 131, 192
Manhattan Minerals (Canada), 94
Marikana massacre, see South Africa
Marks & Spencer (UK), 108, 112
Marx, Karl, 117, 127; Capital, 190; Communist Manifesto, 116; Poverty of Philosophy, 6, 161
Massimo Dutti, see Inditex
Mauritania, 20
Mauritius, 102, 159
McDonald's (USA), 58, 69
Mercosur, 45
Merk, Jeroen, 115
Merrill Lynch (USA), 20
Metalclad (USA), 50
Mexico, 18, 31–2, 34, 43–4, 49–50, 83, 102, 106, 130, 139, 146
Middle East, 12, 15, 32, 103
Miliband, Ralph, 34
military power, 12, 86–7
Millennium Development Goals (MDGs), 76–7
Moldova, 45
Mondragón (Spain), 153
Mongolia, 20
Monsanto (USA), 120–6
Monterrico Metals (UK), 93–5, 183
Monti, Mario, 32
Moody-Stuart, Mark, 69, 98
Morales, Evo, 139, 142–4, 147
Morgan Stanley (USA), 20
Morocco, 45, 154
Mother Earth, see Pachamama
Movement for Socialism (MAS) (Bolivia), 139

Mozambique, 124–5, 127, 130
MST (Movimento dos Trabalhadores
    Rurais Sem Terra), see Landless
    Rural Workers' Movement
MTN Group (South Africa), 24
Multi-Fibre Arrangement (MFA),
    101–6, 110–13; MFA Forum,
    105, 113
Multilateral Agreement on
    Investment (MAI), 41–2, 46
multinational corporation (MNC),
    61, 132–3, 174–9, 200; see also
    transnational corporation
Myanmar, see Burma

Nasdaq (USA), 24
national champions, 6, 24, 149
national treatment, 41, 51, 62–3
National Grid (UK), 52
National Union of Peasant Farmers
    (UNAC; Mozambique), 130
Negri, Antonio, 151
neoliberalism, 1–6, 28, 35, 38, 44,
    57, 60, 76, 79, 136, 138–41,
    148–51, 158–60
Nestlé (Switzerland), 58, 120
Netherlands, 47–8, 90, 92, 105, 107,
    127, 155; Dutch empire, 13, 120
New Alliance for Food Security and
    Nutrition, 124–6
New International Economic Order,
    38, 60
New Zealand, 44, 152
Newmont Mining Corporation
    (USA), 95
Nexen (Canada), 21
Nicaragua, 106, 139, 140, 195
Niger, 20
Nigeria, 15, 20–1, 96; Niger Delta,
    71, 87–91, 182–3; Ogoniland,
    88–91
Nigerian National Petroleum
    Corporation, 87
Nike (USA), 103–7, 112
Non-Aligned Movement, 60, 151
non-governmental organisation
    (NGO), 5, 66–8, 70, 76, 79,
    95–6, 104, 177
Noranda (Canada), 25

North American Free Trade
    Agreement (NAFTA), 43,
    145, 172; NAFTA Chapter 11
    disputes, 49–51
Northrop (USA), 61
Norway, 55, 92
Nyéléni Forum for Food Sovereignty,
    131, 191

Obama, Barack, 3, 10
Occidental (USA), 92
Occupy movement, 139
Ogoniland, see Nigeria
Oil and Natural Gas Corporation
    (ONGC; India), 20
Oman, 20
OMX AB (Nordic), 24
OPTI Canada, 21
Organisation for Economic
    Cooperation and Development
    (OECD), 41–6, 62–3, 67; OECD
    Guidelines for Multinational
    Enterprises, 63–4, 74
Organisation of American States
    (OAS), 140–1
Ortega, Amancio, 107
Oxfam, 68, 177

P&O (UK), 25
Pachamama, 144
Pakistan, 45, 103, 106; Ali
    Enterprises disaster, 111–12
Palestinian Territories, Occupied,
    154, 197
Panama, 159
Papua New Guinea, 92
Paraguay, 45, 140, 146
patriarchy, 158–60
PepsiCo (USA), 120
Permanent Court of Arbitration, The
    Hague, 47
Peru, 20, 44, 93–6, 106, 140, 146,
    152
Petrobras (Brazil), 20, 82
PetroChina, 19, 20, 82, 92
Petróleos de Venezuela SA, 144
Petronas (Malaysia), 20, 25
Pfizer (USA), 58, 62
philanthrocapitalism, 124, 174
Philip Morris (USA), 55, 173

Philippines, 44, 92, 127, 130
Pickard, Ann, 89
Pimbert, Michel, 133
Pinochet, Augusto, 61
Pioneer Hi-Bred (USA), 126
Poland, 130
Pontignano conference (UK-Italy),
    30
Porsche (Germany), 24
Portugal, 107, 120, 138
PotashCorp (Canada), 25
poverty, 2–3, 16, 18, 35, 87, 119,
    135, 152, 159, 162; poverty
    reduction, 77, 121, 141–5
Primark, 107–8
primitive accumulation, 118, 151
privatisation, 1–3, 60, 70, 76, 79,
    125–6, 139, 151–2, 156, 160;
    Bolivia, 47, 54; Argentina, 51–2;
    Tanzania, 53–4; Ecuador, 143
Progress Energy (Canada), 25
Proudhon, Pierre-Joseph, 6
public-private partnership,
    60, 65–70, 75–9, 105, 124;
    Partnering Initiative, 70;
    Partnering Toolbook, 70;
    Partnership Brokers Association,
    70
Puma (Germany), 103
purchasing power parity (PPP), 115,
    162, 164

Qatar Investment Authority (QIA),
    24
Québec, 145, 154

Rabobank (Netherlands), 155
Rajak, Dinah, 76
Rana Plaza disaster, see Bangladesh
Reagan, Ronald, 76
recession, 3–4, 83, 107; see also Great
    Recession
resource curse, 80, 84–5, 87
Responsible Business Summit, 58
responsible competitiveness, 7, 75–8,
    180
Rio Group, 140
Rio Tinto (UK), 25, 58, 62, 84, 92–3,
    98
Robinson, Mary, 71

Rockefeller, David, 31
Rockefeller Foundation, 124–6
Rodale Institute, 134
round-tripping, see tax avoidance
Rousseff, Dilma, 141
Royal Bank of Scotland (RBS; UK),
    58, 155
Ruggie, John, 67, 73–5, 80–1
Ruggiero, Renato, 28
Russia, 14, 20, 27, 55, 127, 139, 164;
    see also BRICS

SABMiller (South Africa), 124
Sainsbury's (UK), 24
Samoa, 159
Santander (Spain), 145
Sarkozy, Nicolas, 3
Saro-Wiwa, Ken, 89
Saudi Arabia, 27, 34, 128
Save the Children, 68
Schmidheiny, Stephan, 65–6
Sempra Energy (USA), 54
Senegal, 192
Shell (UK/Netherlands), 19, 58,
    62, 69, 71, 82–4; in Niger Delta,
    87–90
Shenhua (China), 93
Siemens (Germany), 62
Sierra Leone, 129
Singapore, 20, 27, 41, 44, 149;
    Singapore issues, see World Trade
    Organisation
Sinopec (China), 19, 21
Sistema (Russia), 54
Skinner, Paul, 98
Smith, Adam, 78, 180
SNS Reaal (Netherlands), 155
social auditing, see ethical auditing
social economy, 153–4
social production, 9, 148, 156–9
social reproduction, 158
Solomon Islands, 159
Soron, Dennis, 157
South Africa, 15, 24, 34, 85, 92, 102,
    125, 128, 152; review of BITs,
    55–6; Marikana massacre, 98–9;
    see also BRICS
South Centre, 70
sovereign wealth fund, 14, 20, 118,
    128

sovereignty, 1, 39–41, 48, 62, 71, 131, 142, 145, 178; natural resource, 9, 56, 63, 85–6; popular, 9, 138, 148–51, 156; social, 150–1; *see also* food sovereignty

Spain, 30, 107, 120, 138, 145, 152

Spanish Civil War, 154

Sri Lanka, 103, 106, 111

St Lucia, 159

Standard & Poor's, 10

Stockholm Chamber of Commerce, 48

Strong, Maurice, 65–6

Struble, Curt, 95–6

structural adjustment programmes, 2–4, 15, 29, 83, 149, 164

subimperialism, 34, 169

Sudan, 20, 92, 97, 127–8

Sundanese Peasants Union (SPP; West Java), 130

Suriname, 195

Sutherland, Peter, 33

Swaziland, 102

Sweden, 37, 124

Switzerland, 36, 65, 95, 105, 173

Syngenta (Switzerland), 120–1, 124

Syria, 20

Taiwan, 130, 149

Talisman (Canada), 92

Tanganyika Oil (Canada), 21

Tanzania, 53–4, 85, 92, 124–5, 127

tar sands, Alberta, 21

Tate & Lyle (UK), 50

tax avoidance, 15, 62, 83–5, 97, 143; round-tripping, 15, 164; transfer pricing, 62, 84

Telenor (Norway), 54

Temasek Holdings (Singapore), 20

Tertulias conference (UK-Spain), 30

Tesco, 58, 106, 108, 186

Texaco, *see* Chevron Texaco

Thailand, 20, 27, 32, 44

Thatcher, Margaret, 32, 76

Thompson, E.P., 6

Tokios Tokelès (Ukraine), 47–8

Total (France), 82, 87, 92

trade, 3–4, 7, 12–13, 15–16, 27–9, 31, 38–45, 67, 102, 120–1, 131–2, 136, 148; arms trade, 158–9; *see also* free trade agreement, World Trade Organisation

Trade-Related Aspects of Intellectual Property Rights (TRIPs), 39, 122

Trade-Related Investment Measures (TRIMs), 39–40

trade unions, 8, 100, 104–15, 139, 149, 151

TransAtlantic Business Dialogue (TABD), 30–1

Transatlantic Economic Council, 31

TransAtlantic Trade and Investment Partnership, 31, 45

transfer pricing, *see* tax avoidance

transnational capitalist class, 6, 29–34

transnational corporation (TNC), 4, 6–7

Trans-Pacific Partnership (TPP), 44, 146, 171

Trilateral Commission, 30–3

Tunisia, 20, 45, 138, 150, 196

Turkey, 30, 32, 34, 105–6, 113–14, 139, 149

Turkmenistan, 20

UBS (Switzerland), 20

Uganda, 129

Ukraine, 44, 47, 127

UNAC (União Nacional de Camponeses), *see* National Union of Peasant Farmers

Unilever (UK), 62, 124

Union Carbide (USA), 71; *see also* Bhopal

Union of South American Nations (UNASUR), 146

Uniqlo (Japan), 112

United Arab Emirates, 128

United Fruit Company (USA), *now* Chiquita, 61, 175

United Kingdom (UK), 3, 18, 30, 52–5, 72, 76, 87, 94–7, 104, 106–7, 124, 127, 136, 152, 155, 163; Department for International Development (DFID), 53, 104, 124–6, 185; IMF loans to, 29, 168

United Nations (UN), 7, 68, 133, 135; UN General Assembly, 61, 63, 152; UN Code of Conduct on

Transnational Corporations, 60–4, 71, 174–5; UN Centre on Transnational Corporations, 61–3; UN Commission on Transnational Corporations, 61–3; UN Trade and Development Board, 63; UN Norms on the Responsibilities of Transnational Corporations and Other Business Enterprises with Regard to Human Rights, 70–3, 177–8; UN Guiding Principles on Business and Human Rights, 73–5, 179

United Nations Children's Fund (UNICEF), 69

United Nations Commission on Human Rights, 71–3, 179

United Nations Commission on International Trade Law (UNCITRAL), 47–55

United Nations Commission on Sustainable Development, 69

United Nations Conference on Environment and Development (UNCED), see Earth Summit

United Nations Conference on Trade and Development (UNCTAD), 14, 23, 46, 55, 81, 83, 175

United Nations Development Programme (UNDP), 69, 77

United Nations Environment Programme (UNEP), 69

United Nations Human Rights Council, 73–5, 134, 179

United Nations Research Institute for Social Development (UNRISD), 66–7, 70

United Nations Rio+20 Conference on Sustainable Development, 78

United Nations Sub-Commission on the Promotion and Protection of Human Rights, 71–2

United States of America (USA), 10–15, 17–20, 24–5, 28, 31, 39, 43–5, 49–51, 72, 76, 84–5, 92, 120, 134, 136, 140–1, 146, 152, 174, 185; Alien Tort Statute, 89, 92; Central Intelligence Agency (CIA), 61; Department of Defense (Pentagon), 86–7; garments, 102–7, 113

United States Council for International Business (USCIB), 71–2, 178

Unocal (USA), 24, 91

Uruguay, 45, 140, 146, 173; Uruguay Round, see World Trade Organisation

USAID, 77, 124–6

US Business Roundtable, 30–1

US Securities and Exchange Commission, 61

Utting, Peter, 66–7

Uzbekistan, 20, 92

Valdivia, Eduardo, 54

Vale (Brazil), 21, 93, 97

value chain, 5, 8, 26, 101, 107, 112–17

Vattenfall (Sweden), 37–8

Vedanta (UK), 92

Venezuela, 9, 20, 43, 45, 55, 85, 140–1, 144–6, 150, 195

Vía Campesina, La, 130–7, 179

Vietnam, 44, 103, 106, 110, 112, 127, 139

Vivendi (France), formerly Compagnie Générale des Eaux, 52–3

Vodafone (UK), 24, 55

Volkswagen (Germany), 24

voluntarism, 59, 63–70

Voluntary Principles on Security and Human Rights, 66, 96–7

Voltaire, 87

Volvo (Sweden), 24

wages, 12, 99, 100, 103–17, 141, 158; as share of national income, 17–19; living wage, 110–11, 115–16, 157, 160; see also Asia Floor Wage

Wal-Mart (USA), 104–5, 185

Wall Street, 139

Washington consensus, 3

West Papua, 192

Western Sahara, 154

WikiLeaks, 89, 95

women, 77, 107, 130–3, 145, 158, 198; women workers, 100–3, 110–12, 145; *see also* feminisation of labour
workers, 18, 43, 101–17, 118, 120, 130, 150, 152, 157, 160; migrant workers, 98, 110; workers' rights, 71, 98–9, 100, 109, 113–15, 145; workers' cooperatives, 153–4, 156; *see also* women workers
World Bank, 2, 15–6, 28–9, 32, 37–8, 46, 47, 76, 83–5, 133, 138, 149, 162; Principles for Responsible Agricultural Investment, 135, 192; *see also* International Centre for Settlement of Investment Disputes; International Finance Corporation
World Business Council for Sustainable Development (WBCSD), *formerly* Business Council for Sustainable Development, 65–6, 69, 78, 176
World Economic Forum (WEF), 30–4, 67, 138; Grow Africa initiative, 126
World Health Assembly, 64
World Health Organisation (WHO), 69
World Social Forum (WSF), 35, 126, 138, 151, 196
World Summit on Sustainable Development (WSSD), 65, 67–9, 70, 97
world system, capitalist, 1–2, 11, 13, 34–5, 153; core economies,

3–4, 11–13, 26, 76; periphery, 26; semiperiphery, 6, 11, 21, 26
world systems theory, 13, 26, 163
World Trade Organisation (WTO), 4, 28, 33, 38–9, 43–4, 56–7, 102, 122, 132, 138; dispute settlement mechanism, 28–9, 40–1, 46, 85; Seattle demonstrations, 41–2, 138; Doha Round, 4, 28, 42, 57, 171; Uruguay Round, 7, 39–40; Singapore issues, 41–3; Agreement on Textiles and Clothing, 102
Worldwide Responsible Accredited Production (WRAP), *formerly* Worldwide Responsible Apparel Production, 105

Xiamen Zijin Tongguan Development (China), 94, 183
Xstrata (UK), 93, 95

Yanzhou Coal Mining (China), 21
Yara (Norway), 124
Yemen, 138

Zain Group (Kuwait), 21
Zambia, 15, 85, 92, 127
Zapatistas, 130, 138, 150
Zara, *see* Inditex
Zelaya, Manuel, 140
Zhejiang Geely (China), 24
Žižek, Slavoj, 174
Zoellick, Robert, 32
ZTE (China), 25